PUBLIC ETHICS:

American Morals and Manners

PUBLIC ETHICS:
American Morals and Manners

JAMES E. SELLERS

HARPER & ROW, PUBLISHERS
New York, Evanston, and London

FIRST EDITION

LIBRARY OF CONGRESS CATALOG CARD NUMBER: 70-85049

CONTENTS

PREFACE

Although this book is from beginning to end a study of the American ethos, it began and ended in France. In 1966 I came here not so much to reflect on contemporary American manners and morals as to get better acquainted with the ideas of an eighteenth-century European thinker—Montesquieu. His pioneering work in social and political thought—especially his fascinating *The Spirit of the Laws*—promised to counterbalance the theological studies on which I had concentrated for a decade, and which now seemed much too narrow for appraising the moral dilemmas of our times.

Montesquieu, I soon found, was not nearly so well remembered in France or anywhere else as he deserved to be—not even in Bordeaux: his own city. To be sure, Bordeaux has its Rue Montesquieu and its Rue *Esprit des Lois*, and good Montesquieu archives at the municipal library (although Paris has the manuscript of *l'Esprit des Lois*). Even the tourist literature at the Syndicat d'Initiative makes a glancing reference to the Montesquieu chateau at nearby La Brède—a stop on the wine road. And there is a little band of competent Montesquieu scholars scattered around the North Atlantic community. But for the most part, Montesquieu is recalled without being remembered. Certainly, that is the attitude of most American social scientists.

Because Montesquieu points us to the study of what is distinctive, humanly speaking, about the search for justice in each community, it turned out that I could not really come to grips with him without first weighing the heritage and promise and crisis of my own community. I simply could not enter into the spirit of *The Spirit of*

9

the Laws without attempting to rethink the dimensions of the struggle for justice in my own country. That is why a project that began in Bordeaux and Strasbourg as an attempt to understand a significant European thinker ends up as a statement about the American experience.

Two broad aims explain the structure and approach of what follows.

First, I have attempted to restore the idea of moral action to the status of a public reality in America, and to point to the need of a new discipline, that of "public ethics." Morality in America is far more than personal conduct, far more than a religious or theological phenomenon. It embraces the political and social realms, and especially the world of actions, including the whole subject of manners, too long the private preserve of writers on "etiquette."

To discuss morality in these more inclusive terms calls for a new principle of coherence. I have tried to get at such a principle by developing the idea of an "American greater community" and its distinctive moral tradition. Seen in this way, morality is inextricably bound up with the human effort to reclaim personal and community space so that external control, whether that of nature or of despots, is to be overthrown. The goal is to enable men to dispose of their own space. It is on these terms, the terms of the existential struggle to free our space for human ends, I believe, that American morality is best understood and studied.

With this approach, we can move to restore unity and integrity to the conception of ethics, a discipline which in the past has been fragmented, partitioned among baronies, as it were, divided up among the domains of philosophy, theology, and social studies. What we now ought to seek is a new recognition of the interdisciplinary character of ethical studies that is inherently demanded both by the moral tradition in America and by the social crises that have shattered domestic tranquility in our days.

There is a second broad aim. Though I intend in this book to set out on the quest of a new discipline of public ethics, I am still a working theologian, concerned not only for the ultimate dimensions of human morality but also for the responsible contribution of contemporary theology to public life. The second part of the book is an attempt to restate the role of theology and of theological ethics for a time when morality is more realistically defined by a public community moral tradition than by conventional ecclesiastical standards.

Unhappily, it seems to me, American theology is a long way from being ready to join in this consortium for public ethics. Among other things, it has attended too slavishly to European theological styles, and not enough to the American ordeal itself. One best appreciates philosophical and theological thought, whatever its origin, not by parsing it or repeating it, saying the same things all over that others have already said better, but by reliving and responding to such thought in one's own terrain, community, and tradition.

There will be those, of course, who will argue that to reflect on the American moral tradition is but a new provincialism, or that our contemporary cultures are all getting to be alike, in any case. I have tried to deal with such objections, some of them weighty indeed, in the book itself. Here I will simply say that we can communicate with others only if we know ourselves, and only if we learn the lesson that we are both like and unlike other men.

I felt the likenesses this spring in Czechoslovakia when I talked to a young worker who told me the Russians should get out of her country, and that we should get out of Southeast Asia. Or when I sat with a rural French hotelkeeper and his wife in their kitchen on the banks of the Garonne one night watching an old movie on television about Chicago gangsters: we laughed at the same silly scenes.

But I felt the differences that still divide us every time I saw European men, sometimes soldiers, walk down the street holding hands. Or every time we sat down in a Strasbourg *débit de vins* with the true Alsatians, who are as different from us as the stones of Florence are from the pavements of Kansas City.

And some of the admittedly growing likenesses are no grounds for comfort. If we are becoming more alike, one reason is that the very walls of Toledo, and the very ruins of Rome, are becoming consumerized and Americanized. Worse, the walls of Carcassonne and the ruins of Athens are surely going to be next. Such cultural "convergence" ought to be repudiated and resisted.

Perhaps it has been my struggles to speak with Europeans, first in 1966 and again in 1969, that have taught me most. On the one hand, an enormous amount of communication can be achieved even between men who share no common language, only their humanity. At the same time, knowing another man's language, more or less, is no guarantee at all of entry into his mind or mood or the subleties of his thought. So we share something fundamental, and yet we remain separate, and the best thing is to face it. To be anything at all, one must be himself—an American, a Frenchman—no matter how far he can reach out by language or travel or common purpose or outgoing spirit. That is true of nations as well as men. We must examine ourselves before we can accept ourselves or, what is the same thing, before we can get outside ourselves.

Much of the research and writing for this book was made possible by grants from The Society for Religion in Higher Education, The American Association of Theological Schools, and The Research Council of Vanderbilt University, to each of which I express my gratitude. For the opportunity to test some of the themes of the book in the form of lectures, I am indebted to Carleton College, Cornell College, Nebraska Wesleyan University, Princeton University, and Trinity University, San Antonio, Texas.

Finally, I wish to thank each of the following friends, who helped me in one way or another with this project: Giles Gunn, William Moore, Roscoe Hill, Dan Howe, Joan Lark Sanders, Richard Rice, Meyer Lunine, James Laney, Annette MacBean, Joel Tibbetts, Theodore Wills, George Williamson, Jr., Nancy Gallup, and Dean Walter Harrelson. My best critic has been my wife, Charlotte, who has stayed with me, as I calculate, through sixty-eight European hotels.

JAMES SELLERS

Bordeaux, 1969

Part One

Toward a Theory of Public Ethics

CHAPTER I.

MORALITY

1. Morality, Politics, and Manners

Morality is no longer the province of philosophers and theologians. Political action can no longer be understood as the special subject matter of political scientists. Manners can no longer be regarded as the practice of etiquette. In contemporary America they are bound up together in a larger reality: the community struggle for survival and salvation. We cannot look at them separately any more.

Let us begin with a concrete illustration out of recent, tragic American history.

Early in June, 1968, Americans were confronted with the third assassination within five years of a young national leader. Now death had come in California to Senator Robert F. Kennedy of New York. As if a crisis plan had already been programmed, the national electronic media began to rehearse what had become a new tradition of penance, adjustment, and compensation. Its primary medium was television and its ritual had evolved out of the earlier murders, also by gunshot, of President John F. Kennedy and of the civil rights leader Dr. Martin Luther King, Jr. Essentially the process consisted of the deliberate repetition of the facts and details of the traumatic event, and of pondering its meaning by a variety of seers, sages, celebrants, and exorcists from the several estates of government, mass communication, and church. (Business, the first estate in this country, furnished comparatively few spokesmen, but that may be because nobility commonly leaves the functions of priesthood to a separate class.)

15

More than a ghoulish electronic wake, the television coverage of this latest tragedy finally assumed all the proportions of a public religious exercise. The Ed Sullivan Show, a long-lived Sunday evening variety entertainment, canceled its regularly scheduled program following Senator Kennedy's death and substituted a memorial—virtually a memorial *service* celebrated in the chin-out, "sock 'em" style of the entertainment business. The program was made up of taped excerpts from previously presented shows: The West Point choir sang "God Bless America." Charlton Heston, an actor who had both played Abraham Lincoln and starred in a famed biblical movie, recited Lincoln's Second Inaugural Address, with its somber tones of divine judgment upon the country. Miss Kate Smith sang "The Lord's Prayer."

When a community is thunderstruck with a deed such as this, the slaying of a prince who might be king, its response is first to take defensive measures against the crisis at an elemental, prerational level. In tribal societies the normative resort is to propitiate the gods who must have sent the calamity, and we can hardly deny that some carry-over element of this kind of reaction was implicit in the national television ritual following this and the earlier assassinations. But a civilized, Western people, equally traumatized, will also be conditioned to adopt, at the same time, a more rational line of response, and this is to search, often with the deepest religious and political sanctions, and amid troubled debate and even angry conflict, for a new pattern of morality and manners that will tend to minimize or overcome the crisis.

The television ritual, culminating in the Ed Sullivan memorial, did make just this appeal to religious and patriotic sanctions against further psychic loss to the crisis. President Johnson appeared on television to insist that the moral fiber of the country had not broken down, that indeed the society was capable of dealing with the tragedy and its threatening moral implications.

But the television-radio response was ritual—symbolic, crypto-theological, preactivist. It was aimed at arrest of damage. It sought to reverse psychic loss, restore resolve, renew condition of being and hoped-for being.

The civilized, Western responses were yet to be fully implemented, the responses of man the aggressive participant in working his own survival and salvation. This response took the form of an acrimonious debate about American manners, or more specifically, about one strand of American manners—the strand that had to do with the propriety of the free, virtually unregulated use of firearms by American citizens.

At once, a chorus of support for stringent gun-control legislation sprang up. This set of responses could be understood as the advocacy of changes in American manners and laws aimed at redirecting the acts of the community so as to reduce further loss of the sort sustained in the assassinations. It is important to see that this movement proceeded in both the spheres of manners and of legislation. There was, on the one hand, a voluntary movement to turn in small arms. Many children turned in toy guns. Within a few days, some toy manufacturers had announced plans to curtail or restrict the production of toy weapons. Some department stores and mail order houses planned to quit selling them. Television and radio networks began to rethink the content of their programs dealing with violence. On the other hand, the Congress soon passed a relatively mild bill restricting the interstate sale of guns, and several much stricter proposals were introduced. The President requested strong legislation that would require the general registration of guns.

But dilemmas about manners always involve conflicting judgments about moral and political values, and thus they are in principle matters of debate and controversy. A predictable counterargument soon set in. A coalition of rifle enthusiasts, hunters, self-conscious patriots, and rightist publishers began to press Congress not to make drastic changes, and its weight was soon felt. "Don't let me hear any of you complain of suffering from a guilt complex," one publisher told a state American Legion Convention. Talk in the wake of the latest assassination about a "national sickness," he added, was "hogwash" and "guff." And as for proposed gun-control legislation: "Tell your congressmen and your senators that American citizens are entitled to protect their persons and property with their own firearms if necessary and that no gun law passed in a period of national hysteria should remove that right, especially in the face of threatened revolution."

Every moral dilemma stems from tension between a present situation—an emergency or crisis, a newly apprehended threat to the life (or the quality of life) of the community—and the previously accepted morals and manners that had been built up in the past to protect us from loss in past situations. The new crisis, argues one group, is not to be surmounted with the old arrangements. The new crisis, argues the other group, is not really a crisis, or, if it is, it can be mastered by the manners, morals, and laws that have always worked in the past. Thus the dispute over gun control brought to confrontation two differing assessments of the sharpest and most poignant tragedy of recent Americna history, the loss of three leaders who were not only political leaders, but in the most forceful sense moral leaders. For some, the violence of the deaths only symbolized the unrest and malaise that marked the times, expressed otherwise in riots, campus demonstrations, and other disturbances. It was well past time, according to those struck with this view of things, to make new arrangements, of which stricter gun controls would be only one rather modest example. For others, the publisher addressing the Legionnaires summed things up well enough: if there is a national sickness in the postassassination days, it can be "quickly cured by hard work, patience, tolerance and charity, coupled with an honest, earnest rigid enforcement of the laws already on the books."

Crisis or no, the winds of change do not blow steadily or always swiftly, for they must overcome the "line of march" that the community has followed in the past in its previous attempts to cut losses, cope with threat, and win through to a new lease on its own existence. In the United States there is a primordial community tenet that says the private citizen has a right to protect himself with a gun. Doubtless a saving axiom in the literal sense on the great frontier, this ancient part of manners was still firmly implanted in the minds of enough congressmen and citizens to defer, for the time being, decisive changes in our approach to firearms.

In sum, the assassination of Senator Kennedy set off a sequence of ritual, anxiety, and debate that epitomizes the contemporary community crisis in America. It is a crisis that reaches coequally into the domains of morality, politics, and manners. It is a crisis that takes the form of an unresolved tension between a new national emergency and older patterns of morality, politics, and manners aimed at overcoming earlier emergencies, but not necessarily efficacious in our new situation.

We could as well have taken our illustration from other foci of the crisis that has beset the American people—Viet Nam, racism, poverty, pollution, the failure of our cities. With each, we could have made the same point: survival itself seems ultimately at stake.

Our first major problem, then, is to redefine American morality, political action, and manners to show how they are parts of the same fabric of community crisis, and how they are much more interrelated than ordinary professional studies in these areas indicate. In this chapter we will undertake our revised definition of *morality,* and also set out certain other organizing concepts. In the following chapter we will reexamine the notion of political action that characterizes an open society or *republic.* And in the third chapter we will attempt to rescue *manners* from the innocuous desuetude of etiquette books.

2. Morality as Defined by Crisis and Existential Space

Conventional definitions of morality do not sufficiently yield to the urgency of our contemporary situation and to the irregular contours of human terrain. Let us begin, nonetheless, with a conventional definition, and then reshape it to suit the predicament of American life.

In the broadest sense morality is a pattern of sanctioned acts, customs, or habits. The sanctioning comes from an establishment of some kind—the spokesmen of the gods or of the king or, in our day, of the "people." Though there is a decisive personal element in all morality, there is no such thing, properly speaking, as a "private" morality, for even the most angular individualist cannot escape deriving part of the sanctions for what he does from some community of reference or legitimation.

Next we may say that this process of sanctioning or authorizing our acts falls into one of two broad types. The sanctions are either drawn from a *terminus a quo* or a *terminus ad quem.* In conventional thought our acts are accounted moral in one of two ways. On the one hand, they may stem out of a sense of obligation (deontological morality), a good motive, source, wellspring, or origin. On the other hand, they may be validated instead by their consequences; they may lead to a good result, end, or goal (teleological morality). Each of these grand ways of morality offers a large number of variant and differing styles. Both a morality that sanctions acts of love and one that sanctions acts of duty, so long as these acts are accounted as good in themselves, are source-oriented moralities. ("Source-oriented" is a better categorial term, I should say, than the usual title of "deontological" that is bestowed on this type, since the latter term implies that the type is restricted to a sense of duty, whereas it is also expressed, e.g., in a sense of outgoing love.) The most hardheaded pragmatism and the most visionary utopian thought can be comprehended under the single category of "teleological" or end-oriented morality. Little exactitude is gained, then, from the conventional habit of typing moralities into these great opposing ways.

A more serious difficulty with this classical way of dividing up moralities is the implication that human beings and their communities, in moral bearing, must be either goal-oriented or else source-oriented. It makes more sense to argue that human morality is both of these things at once. All morality is goal-oriented, for human beings are constituted as historical creatures, and their communities are "going somewhere" in time. Morality would not be "worth" anything if it did not have the goal or end of keeping human beings human and of opening to them a "fuller" humanity. Thus it is always true, without exception, that all morality is consequentialist, programmed for results, goal-oriented.

And yet all morality is also source-oriented, for we cannot gain any perception of where we wish to go unless we have some clues of what we are and where we came from. We cannot move to the question of what we are to become unless we can take hold of some understanding of what is already worthwhile in what we see and know, i.e., of what is "intrinsically" good. Here, in our view, is the real meaning of deontological ethics, which stresses the goodness-in-itself of a good will or of a willing sense of obligation. Here, in our view, is the intrinsic value of love, for it is only by setting aside for the moment any calculation about the future that we can take hold in itself of the meaning of the *presence* of human beings to each other. We can, as it were, yearn for the future, but never experience it. We can experience and know only the present, and the present of the human is the presence of the neighbor in acts of love.

In a sense, then, classical teleologists and deontologists have both been telling half-truths. The teleologist errs in the tendency to define his society's good as being realized only in a dynamic future and in the tendency to disregard the intrinsic worth of presently existing motifs and acts. But the deontologist, to the extent that he rejects a goal-oriented framework for appraising the moral, pretends that society is perfectly static. A rigorously deontological stance would be an accurate description of morality only in the special case of a society at rest, in which present reality were all that could be hoped for or even dreamed of.

The moral category that overrides this dichotomy and in fact redefines the orientation of morality, in our view, is that of the crisis and predicament in which men and their communities perennially find themselves. Morality is sanctioned conduct aimed at rescuing men from the most menacing crises to life, to the quality of life, to the sense of the human—crises that are always there and always appearing no matter how complete the triumph over the last crisis. This centrality of the human predicament is indeed implied in the conventional definitions of morality. A good will is prized because it goes against the grain of quotidian society, pulled down as it always is to the level of a humanity dulled and embittered by bad will. An act of love is a thing good in itself because it is a spark in a night of darkness, a singular presentation of the human in a shuttered street. We aspire to a telos because the present is less than fully human. We aspire to new goals and program for results because in our present situation we are mostly cramped and repressed and denied the freedom to be what we dream of being. In short, both source-oriented morality, by pointing to what is self-evidently good in a tough, insensitive community, and goal-oriented morality, by pointing to what can be hoped for in contrast to the present, offer testimony to crisis, predicament, threat-to-the-human as the basic datum of morality.

But we must immediately push beyond mere allusions to crisis and begin to talk about the form in which these threats impinge on given societies, and especially that one society we have staked out for special attention in this investigation. Our proposition, to be tested and demonstrated in the remaining pages of our study, is that the moral crisis in the Western world, and especially in American society, may be characterized as *extrinsic control of existential space* (*communal and personal*); and that deliverance from this crisis is realized through *gaining the initiative and capacity to dispose of one's own space* (*communal and personal*).

With this model we take a step in the direction of concreteness in specifying what is involved in the moral. Such terms as "humanization," without further specification, are all too ambiguous. We begin to gain clarity when we specify a model that seeks to indicate what increased humanization may mean. For the entire Western world, we claim, but particularly for North Atlantic civilization, and within that community especially for the American experience, the definitive modality of the struggle to realize the human and the moral may be taken as the movement (often founded in revolution) among both communities and persons to gain the capacity to dispose of their own existential space. This modality accounts for the movement from serfdom to entrepreneurship; for the westward migration from seventeenth-century Europe to the American littoral, then to the great frontier; for the secession of Roger Williams from the uptightness of Puritan New England; for the abolitionist and civil rights movements and for the student protests of the 1960's; and in general for the heavy ingredient of "voluntary" action in the makeup of the American ethos.

Our proposed model of space disposition must enter the lists against two competing models in Western thought. One of them is the model of morality based on the right of conscience. The other is the model of morality based on the ownership of property. In the first of these, the freedom of conscience is put forward as the primary locus of the moral; very often what is advocated is the freedom of conscience in *contrast* to the rights of property. The best exemplars of this model are such notable dissenters in the history of American society as Henry David Thoreau and William Lloyd Garrison. At the opposite pole are the more zealous advocates of the right to own property, seen most typically perhaps in the insistence of the middle-class citizen that home ownership is the most convincing sign of moral rectitude, or in the view of the small businessman that the first obligation of law and morality is to confirm and protect him in his economic interests. This struggle over the locus of the moral seems to be proceeding with new fury in our own day with the rise of a new student left more attracted to the claim of conscience than of the sanctity of property, and with the concomitant rise of a new class of suburbanites more dedicated than ever to real estate.

Our own claim, to be argued more fully in Chapters II and III, is that neither of these models—conscience or property—is sufficiently primordial, and that a more fundamental model for American morality is that of the existential struggle to dispose of personal and community space. Under this view conscience is seen as an inchoate and partial cry for justice, but as remaining incomplete and impotent until it has been given resonance and "elbow room" in its own spatial vicinity. Property, on the same view, is a necessary but secondary "furnishing" and organizing of existential space; it is the equipment we use to incarnate our wills and to dispose of the space in which we are set.

Conscience and property, then, are dialectical aspects pointing to the center of moral concern, which is the right of self-disposition. Both conscience and property are necessary fully to give voice and reality to this central motif. Conscience is that insistent message of "selfness" that pushes from the inner awareness outward, the pressure from the will for the self to be not less than a self but, at whatever painful cost, the responder to the cry of the human for vindication. Property is that nailing down of a fraction of outer space to give oneself room in which to act and move and express the will. Perhaps most of the original settlers of New England came to America not to satisfy purely conscientious or religious scruples, nor to yield to the greediness of the acquisitive drive, but to throw off, with the aid of both conscience and property, extrinsic control of the personal and communal lives by insensitive authority. On this view conscience is not especially the mark of a saint, and the urge to acquire real estate is not especially the trait of selfishness. Both, rather, are expressions of the urge to be one's own man. The center of the urge is the drive to dispose of one's own space.

The increased mobility of persons in contemporary society, we may add, far from de-emphasizing the importance of space as the symbol of morality, only further underlines it. For the right to move about is a form of the victory, one expression of the capacity to dispose of one's space. The man who is mobile has found at least part of the answer, in his transcendence over geographical space (which is part of, but less than, existential space).

One may dispose of his own existential space, and a community may exert mastery of its communal space, only if men are aggressive. One must ask for his space if he is to have it, else it will be preempted by extrinsic control. One must take the initiative, consciously will to recover his space from nature, tyrants, or other outside controllers. In short, one must engage in what we ordinarily think of in American idiom as "moral activism." In a space-claiming society we find strong emphasis on "morality" as a mode of making things happen. Even in political affairs, Americans tend to judge their candidates not for sagacity in statecraft or foreign affairs, but for their moral initiative:[1]

> The President must really assume a role in a morality play, a ritual drama in which Americans expect him to slay evil. That idea goes back to the founders' exultant belief that America was truly God's country, the nation charged with the task of proving that a free society could thrive. Consciously or unconsciously, it is shared by the country's harshest critics, including the New Left, whose very anger is based partly on the assumption that the U.S. should be near-perfect, a working utopia.

Here, then, is the basis of the principle of "consent of the governed." It is no passive idea. Consent is originally based on consciousness and activity. One consents to be governed only when he does not "have to." One consents only when he stands on free space. Indeed, once the space has been converted from extrinsic to interior control, consent itself may be allowed to become a reserved power. Consent does not need to continue as a moment-to-moment thought process in which every citizen nervously engages. There is, in fact, very little consent of this sort in most of the things we do. Most of our activities—such as obeying the traffic laws, or voting for a presidential candidate who was by no means our first choice—are constrained upon us by adjacent power. Yet, in a society founded upon the grand, original act of clearing the space of extrinsic control—that is, by revolution—and then upon a second act of constitutional consent, a new political environment is born. Today, in a space-claiming society, it is not the amount of consenting I am able to do that makes me a free person, but it is rather the power of consent that makes all the difference.

So potent is this ingredient of American politics—the moral insistence upon the right and power to dispose of one's existential space—that it can at times outstrip our sense of reality. For, we think, if the ability to *dispose* is at the center of the moral, then the ability to *achieve* must be, too. Thus one of the major American dogmas is the belief that every American should be able to extricate himself from his misery in a relatively nearby future. An American must do something rather than nothing. He must transform his space, and insist that others do so, too. And when he encounters a space that hardheaded analysis shows to be virtually untransformable, at least by conventional self-help methods and anytime soon, he goes ahead anyway. Thus, observes Edward C. Banfield in a biting essay, "Why Government Cannot Solve the Urban Problem," we Americans "do not hesitate to attempt what we do not have the least idea how to do and what may even be impossible in principle."[2]

> That some children simply cannot or will not learn anything in school and that we do not know how to change this are facts that the American mind will not entertain. Our cultural ideal demands that we give everyone a good education whether or not he wants it and whether or not he is capable of receiving it.

Whether for good or ill, morality is part of politics in America. All too often, the moral dimension becomes simply moralism. One of our chief undertakings in this study will be to distinguish between these, and to search for criteria that will allow us to speak of the directions in which our society can and should move if its contemporary predicament is to be overcome.

3. The Concept of a Greater Community

The movement to recover personal and community space from extrinsic control and manage it henceforth through one's own powers is the most spectacular challenge to traditional notions of community in the last three hundred years. It is simply another way of speaking of the "democratic revolution" that has swept over most of the West and much of the rest of the world since the eighteenth century. It overlaps the rise of the sense of personal autonomy, on the one hand, and the rise of nationalism, on the other. It is an upheaval that has ranged so far and wide and penetrated so deeply that we are hard pressed to find ways of talking about it in the vocabularies of the ordinary departments of learning, for it has pushed beyond the boundary lines within which each of the conventional disciplines of learning has been able to maintain a comforting precision. R. R. Palmer describes the phenomenon we are speaking of here as "a crisis of community itself, political, economic, sociological, personal, psychological, and moral at the same time."[3] For this very reason, we will find it difficult to use the concepts of any one of these disciplines as the organizing notions of our study. Our view, rather, is that we must repair to the concept of community itself as it has been reworked in our day as the principle of coherence for our discussion.

Let us restate our assumption. Deliverance from crisis—which in the West takes the form of recovery of existential space from extrinsic control—gives rise to distinctive sets of morals and manners congruent with the boundaries of "greater communities" more or less identifiable as nations. The national community, to put it another way, has become the most salient human "system" for moral and political analysis, understanding a "system," with contemporary cybernetics, as "an organized collection of interrelated elements characterized by a boundary and functional unity."[4] The manners, morals, and political arrangements of a given nation are distinctive, we are maintaining, because it has emerged as a community out of its own crises and its own responses. We do not wish to argue for *absolute* differences between these features of one national community and another, but only for comparative differences which exist precisely in respect of community tradition, history, and predicament. Nor do we argue that within a system there is unrelieved uniformity of manners, morals, or political attitudes. Since all men have minds of their own (and since personal space-claiming is an aspect of national space-claiming), we can never generalize about what *all* Swiss or Germans or Americans may do. Nevertheless, we do argue that national manners and morals, while exhibiting kinships abroad and while manifesting internal varieties, may be understood to be organized into "systems"—as grouped into distinctive sets "characterized by a boundary and functional unity." Manners and morals, we are saying, may be understood to be of the same order of coherence as languages. A given language predominates in France and parts of Belgium and Switzerland, and it is both convenient and accurate to treat this language as a single, complex entity. At the same time, this language is closely related to the languages that are spoken across discernible boundaries, the languages of Italy, Spain, Portugal, and Rumania. Moreover, there are variations within the French-speaking community in the form of regional dialects and many versions of local patois. All the same, there is an identifiable linguistic system, French, that may be distinguished from both more inclusive and less inclusive language systems.

Admittedly, any attempt to set out the notion of a distinctive system of manners and morals congruent with "greater communities" brings us into immediate difficulty. For we are now treating a question not essentially different from the old, vexed question of whether there is really such a thing as "national character." There has been a long controversy among social scientists over the whole issue of national character. As scholars devoted to objectivity and critical method, we are still reacting negatively to some outworn approaches to the subject, such as the ancient appeal to supernatural agency, the argument that "God had designated the given group as a chosen people and had endowed them with the superior qualities that were pleasing to his eyes." Another outmoded explanation assigned determinative force to environmental factors. Most offensive of all, doubtless, were defenses of national identity based on racial factors—such theories as those of Count Gobineau, for example, or of the Nazis in Germany during the period between the two World Wars, or some of the more racialistic forms of the American pretense to superiority.[5]

For these and other reasons, many scholars have rejected the study of "national character" and have been content that the concept be ignored or left under a cloud. Even where the existence of distinctive national character is conceded, social scientists have run into difficulties imposed by their own methodological protocol, since it is not easy to reduce such a complex and elusive idea to conditions amenable to empirical study.

But the inadequacy of older approaches or the inadaptability of empirical methods does not constitute sufficient reason for bypassing the subject. I believe that the concept of the "greater community," properly reconceived, is crucial to the study of modern politics, morality, and manners. Hence I propose now to deal directly with what I take to be the two chief objections to it. These objections may be stated as follows:

Even within the boundaries of a discrete "greater community," particularly a large nation like the United States, the citizens are so different among themselves, both individually and in their groups, that it is quite meaningless to speak of a singular, pervasive "national character."

Because of the growth of worldwide communication, the spread of scientific method, and the common commitment to Western-style technology, today all national differences are being erased, cultural boundary lines are disappearing, and the attitudes and outlook of men in all nations are "converging." We are fast becoming a "world community" in which formerly significant differences owing to ignorance, isolation, and provincialism are fast evaporating.

(a) *The Doctrine of Individual Differences.* Scholars are more and more willing to accept the salience of individual differences in population groups. At the same time they are more and more reluctant to deal in unexamined generalities or outsized motifs as organizing themes for describing and differentiating communities. This resistance to subjective classification shows up not just in the study of national character but in a wide variety of attempts to deal collectively with human phenomena—in the characterization of historical epochs and movements, for example.

At the outset of his lucid study, *The Enlightenment,* the historian Peter Gay confronts just this problem—the complexity of the subject matter, the forbidding variations among the thinkers of the eighteenth century, the disillusionment of some historians that has brought them "to abandon the search for a single Enlightenment." How could one find substantial common ground, this objection runs, between Hume and Condorcet, Holbach and Lessing, Rousseau and Jefferson? "But

I decided," says Gay, "that to yield to the force of these questions would be to fall into a desparing nominalism, to reduce history to biography, and thus to sacrifice unity to variety." It is true that we must respect differences among men. "Yet, mindful that general names are not Platonic ideas but baskets collecting significant similarities, I shall speak throughout of *the* philosophes, and call the totality of their ideas, their strategies, and their careers, *the* Enlightenment, and I shall use these terms to refer to what I shall call a family, a family of intellectuals united by a single style of thinking."[6]

Students in other disciplines, even where more reliance must be placed on field research, such as anthropology, increasingly endorse the same principle. If we rightly should reject crasser schemes for separating men into discrete communities—racial theories, for example—still, Margaret Mead argues, "there is no reason for going to the opposite extreme" and ignoring consistent differences in traits among peoples.[7] Granted, there may be difficulty in finding precise, careful ways to measure and describe these differences. That does not permit us to leave them out of account. Goeffrey Gorer, another anthropologist, sets out the view that a leading trait of the English is preoccupation with their own aggression and its control—as seen in the British concept of sportsmanship, for example. Gorer does not accompany his view with statistical evidence; yet it would seem perverse and arbitrary to reject it, or his perceptive application of this view toward an understanding of contemporary British foreign policy.[8]

Even when we are confronted with a land of such "exasperating diversity" as India, "a source of despair to any sociologist who likes to generalize," we can still talk cautiously, we are told, about national character. To be sure, we must take into account India's multitude of castes, its large number of racial strains, its religious heterogeneity, its linguistic diversity. It is a land with both rural and urban cultures, numerous variances in community life, forms of land tenure, kinship lines, and marriage rites. Surely no excessive or glib extrapolations about Indian national character are justified. And yet, the same scholar in the field of Indian personality who has warned us of this forbidding diversity is convinced that we can gather up certain characteristics that have wide applicability. In India, argues Dhirendra Narain, the child persistently identifies with its mother more than with its father. To foreigners, Indian men seem to exhibit a lack of masculine qualities. "The great feature of present-day Hindu life is passivity." Foreign rule, it appears, established an attitude of dependence on authority, Narain explains, which, "reinforced by the family environment, is contrary to the growth of personal autonomy."[9] To account for the diversity is not then enough. Running cross-grain to the diversity, so to speak, is a set of persistent traits of the national personality, a set of traits that originated in the political past of extrinsic colonial control.

At least two kinds of data are needed, then, to discuss national character and personality—data that express diversity, and data that express the coherence of the community. The need to adduce the first kind is universally recognized. But we cannot avoid the need to adduce data of the second kind. As David M. Potter pointed out some years ago, even those historians and social scientists who reject the "philosophical concept" of national character often continue to utilize such a concept covertly, since there is no way of not doing so.[10]

As we have already observed, however, the importance of the community-coherence concept is now much more widely recognized, and some scholars, especially anthropologists, have recently made creative and bold innovations in the study of national characteristics. One striking example is Edward T. Hall's *The Hidden Dimension,* which treats the differential perception and rationalization of personal space in various cultures. Germans, for example, "sense their own space as an extension of the ego." Since the German ego is highly exposed as a rule, the German "will go to almost any length to preserve his 'private sphere.' " That is one reason, perhaps, that German houses with balconies "are arranged so that there is visual privacy," and that yards tend to be well fenced, and tend to be "sacred," whether fenced or not. In American society, on the other hand, Hall finds wide acceptance of the view that "space should be shared," a concept that proves troublesome for the German.[11]

In offices, Americans keep doors open; Germans keep doors closed. . . . Whenever a German warms up to the subject of American enclosed space, he can be counted on to comment on the noise that is trans-

have in fact had more spectacular effects at other levels, for they have led to the breakdown of the local and the strengthening of the broadly based national community. The latter, encompassing many formerly isolated local entities, finds a new unity in politics, regional tradition, language, and manners, all sinews that are infinitely stronger at the level of greater community than at the global level. Thus the nation or greater community becomes the most significant kind of population system in the present world.

To see how this is so, let us take just one of the factors often cited as leading to the disappearance of local cultures and to the development of a global outlook—the advent of mobility that comes with the availability of fast, cheap transportation. In the evolution of the American greater community, to take an instructive case, it would appear that the growth of mobility did not lead Americans to be primarily "world conscious," but primarily offered an avenue of convergence upward from the purely local to the level of the national. The westward migration along the frontier not only added the knowledge of new terrain and brought new acquaintances; there was an inverse effect that diminished the importance of former locations.[13]

> Every move westward meant an uprooting of attachments; loyalty to a state of birth eroded away as the pioneer adapted to his new locality, yet he lacked the traditions that would create new loyalties of equal intensity. His emotional need for some attachment directed his devotion to the national government, for wherever he moved, this stood ready to provide for his needs.

Even today, new currents of nationalism are stirring in the United States, among the younger nations of Asia, behind the Iron Curtain in eastern Europe, and elsewhere. Some of these new currents are healthy and admirable; others are ugly and dangerous. Negative patriotic animus is found in some of the oldest as well as some of the newest nations. Political loyalties all too often seem based on hate, rather than on love of country. Sober studies suggest that "this negative base of patriotism is becoming more pronounced." Americans strengthen their national lines by vilifying Communism; Russia seems willing to sacrifice Marxist fraternalism when the national interests of the country itself seem at stake, as in the 1968 Soviet occupation of Czechoslovakia. In the new African states, the most elemental tribal loyalties compete with democratic sentiments, often very successfully. With the breakup of several colonial empires after World War II, much ill will has been released, and sent looking for a new vehicle, that was formerly contained within the imperial systems as "intra-system hatreds."[14]

Nor (to take another tenet of the global view) can we rely on the development of extensive communications media to break down these national loyalties, "since it is part of the perverseness of the present human being that the more he knows about others the more he hates them."[15] Fortunately these perversities are not the only aspects of the existence of national communities. For all their faults, these larger groupings have been the means of coaxing lesser groups out of their provincialisms, and they have functioned as a window or outlet to the other population coalitions. What is important to see is that for good or ill, whatever convergence has been in course in modern times has substantially been focused upon the nation or greater community, and that for our time this level of convergence is likely to continue in force. Two hundred years ago, the English and American peoples were very similar in their social character. Now, says Goeffrey Gorer, the differences are fundamental. They are the product of recent, living history. It is not profitable to get into the question of which is the better society, he suggests; there is little reason to engage in invidious comparisons. That would be to miss the factual import of differences in manners, to lose sight of the data in a rush to moralistic judgment. "Only the most limited and provincial people would consider that the Chinese were 'wrong' or 'immoral' to dress in white for mourning because we show our sorrow with black clothes; both devices accomplish effectively the same social ends."[16] While a critique of the foibles and selfish resorts of one's greater community may indeed become a task of the ethical thinker appraising his own society, he must not start with moral absolutes or too quickly dismiss the variations in manners and morals among the world's greater communities.

Convergence on the global level points, in fact, to greater opportunity for seeing the specialness of other cultures, and of taking one's own community under critical judgment thereby. In that sense, the world is not getting smaller at all, but much larger. The more the world's several greater communities are in close contact, the more there is convergence of this culture-comparing sort, the more these communities will be able to see themselves in perspective, and the more each community will be valued as a radiating center of distinctive manners, ideas, and political creativity. What this may imply, among other things, is that we never see our own greater community honestly until outside observation and judgment are brought upon it. National values have to be criticized, seen in juxtaposition and even conflict with competing or collateral communities, in order for them to remain relatively free of deification or self-glorification.[17]

When all is said and done, the vision of a viable world community remains to some extent illusory, this despite the emergence of a few areas in which genuine international cooperation and agreement appear possible—say, in geophysical studies or on the big-power consensus to discourage the development and proliferation of nuclear weapons. Reinhold Niebuhr's somber study, *The Structure of Nations and Empires,* rightly points out that the tight coherence of national communities has replaced both the compact city state and the vast empire of antiquity, and is as yet threatened by no larger-scale competitor. The nation thrives, he thinks, because print and mass communication reinforce those "organic" factors such as language that allow a middle-range community to come into being and to reduce both higher and lower levels of organization to secondary status. It is the national community rather than the international community that commands the authority and dominion and organic ties to enforce community. On this view, convergence theories pitched at the global level simply do not face the facts.[18]

> The rise of the modern nation is a rather ironic refutation of the hope for the establishment of a universal community through pure contrivance because it represents a victory of the moral primal forces of community, particularly the force of ethnic kinship, over the artifacts which the ancient and medieval empires introduced into history.

Convergence ends at the national level even when we seek to compare such similar Western subcommunities as Canada and the United

States, which are bound together by a common language, much common history, a common "New World" futuristic outlook, and other ties. Although these two nations "probably resemble each other more than any other two nations on earth," Seymour Martin Lipset concludes there are "consistent patterns of difference between them."[19] The differentiating effects of what we will later describe as "moral tradition" (Chapter IV) are generally responsible. For no matter how many likening factors are at work—our common dependence, as between Canada and the United States, on industrial resources, a stable political situation, the English language, and so on—the deepest crises that have made each community a nation with its own history have varied enough to set them on, at best, parallel tracks instead of on a single path to destiny. Lipset points to a number of differentiating factors. Their political traditions are not the same, Canada having remained under the British parliamentary system. Their religious traditions have been considerably at odds, Canada having maintained an established church. In Canada, the frontier experience was less individualistic, more governmentally administered. Canada continues to combine democratic and monarchical symbols. Most significant of all seem to be "the value orientations in English-speaking Canada" that stem from "a counter-revolutionary past." Many of the value differences between the United States and Canada may derive from "the revolutionary origins of the United States" as opposed to the counter-revolutionary tradition in Canada; these amount to "two disparate founding ethos."[20]

Canada's historic course was set in part by the influx of Loyalists fleeing the American Revolution, and by the later need of having to define itself sharply as over against its larger neighbor for the very preservation of its identity. This need further emphasized a counter-revolutionary and nominally conservative stance. By contrast, Lipset argues, the "core values" of the United States, expressed in the idealist ideology of the Revolution, were made articles of faith in the Declaration of Independence and elaborated, still in the revolutionist idiom, in succeeding epochs.[21]

Despite the cautionary value of these two dogmas of modern social science—the doctrine of individual differences and the belief in global convergence—the concept of the greater community emerges intact. Indeed, this concept is becoming more viable than ever, for "during the last twenty-odd years national character has been restored to respectability as a legitimate subject for inquiry by the allied forces of the behaviorial sciences."[22] We shall attempt to advance the employment of this concept one step further, by proposing that the deliberate study of the manners and morals of greater communities is the one approach to the subject that goes to the crucial aspects of what is distinctive and special about national groupings.[23]

4. The Problem of Organizing a Study of Manners and Morals

So far we have suggested that every political system is ultimately also a complex moral entity, sanctioning patterns of conduct representing response to crisis; that in the West the crisis has typically to do with the recovery of personal and communal space from extrinsic control; that the study of manners and morals, admittedly a "subjective" undertaking, is of great importance; and that the most significant locus for such study is the national society or, to use our own term, the greater community.

Now we must take up the problem of organizing such a study. One procedure, the "classic" method, is the travel memoir or the collection of letters from a stranger visiting in the land. As we have already observed, the study of manners and morals is often more incisively executed by an outsider than by a member of the community itself. We are not likely to be conscious of the contours of our own conduct, or to perceive what is most interesting about it, or to be aware of its perversity. Thus the first accounts known to us that are critically valuable typically come from the visitor who is taken with the differences between customs of his native land and those of the land he is visiting.

One of the first critical uses of this genre, the travel memoir, was made by Montesquieu with his *Persian Letters,* published at Amsterdam in 1721, a commentary on the manners, morals, and politics of France so bold and irreverent that it was issued without the name of the author. A fictitious account of the travels in Europe of two Persian visitors, Usbek and Rica, the letters not only foreshadow Montesquieu's later political theories, they also constitute one of the first literary productions of the Enlightenment.[24]

Mrs. Frances Trollope's *Domestic Manners of the Americans* (1832) is one of the best-known informal appraisals of American life by a traveler. This sharp-tongued Englishwoman sailed to New Orleans, made her way north along the Mississippi River, and settled for a time in Cincinnati, where she opened a department store. Later she traveled East and returned to England. To say that she was unfavorably impressed with American manners and morals is a great understatement. We get the impression from Mrs. Trollope's pages that the Americans of her day were accomplished at spitting in the streets, wolfing down their meals, drinking to excess, engaging in vulgar displays of patriotism and emotional religion, and little else. Her account is in the style of the "personal raconteur" through what she called her "gossipy pages," and there is a note of the accidental about what is collected in this style of account, owing both to the geographical organization of her account and to the limited stratum of everyday life that she was able to view. *Domestic Manners,* says one of her recent editors, is more the story of Frances Trollope than anything else.[25]

> It neither promises nor affords a rounded view of American society. Because she came to the United States as a threadbare business woman, her tale has a good deal more to do with petty tradesmen and their wives, with trips to market and revival meetings, with cheap travel and cheap boarding-houses, than it has to do with American drawing-rooms.

Montesquieu threw out another valuable clue for organizing a discussion of manners, one that he first employed in his own treatise, *Considerations on the Causes of the Grandeur of the Romans and of their Decadence* (1734). The method here is to elaborate on the principle of government and political genius of a country. The organization of subject matter no longer is tied to a travel schedule but is now based on the priority of political realities. This approach as applied to American institutions is classically seen in the work of Alexis de Tocqueville, whose *Democracy in America* (1835-1840), though based on travels in America, transcends the travelogue and is organized from the very first sentence onward by what seemed to the author the grand political fact of American life, "the general equality of conditions." First, he treats the impact of this new reality on the institutions of law and governance. Then he describes the effects of the equalitarian impulse on opinions, manners, and feelings. Tocqueville's approach is still enormously influential, both as to its form (a logic proceeding from a single, fundamental proposition about national life), and as to its substance (the insistence that this proposition has to do with the equality of conditions).

Max Lerner provides an instructive alternative. First, he rejects all approaches that begin with the primacy of some single organizing notion, such as the primacy of political matters which Tocqueville and, later, Lord Bryce assume in their studies of the American people. Similarly, Lerner rejects all studies that attempt to reduce everything to economic considerations, as with various versions of Marxist analysis; or to psychological or moral factors, as in the work of Arnold J. Toynbee and Reinhold Niebuhr. Lerner thinks that no single "key" can possibly explain or account for the leading aspects of a society as complex as that of America, and that a more fruitful approach is to exhibit the interplay among a plural number of poles or crucial factors in the American experience, such as the tensions between the material and the psychological, or those between revolutionary and traditional motifs in American history.[26] Lerner's reservations about the adequacy of any single-valued method are justified, as is his insistence that there is a strongly *dialectical* aspect in social phenomena.

If we extend the principle of plural explanation much further, however, we end up with a mere catalogue or taxonomy of manners and morals. Too often the commitment to objectivity and dispassionate research, however productive of useful and indispensable data, still leaves us with no way of evaluating, comparing, and ultimately, of understanding human behavior. In other words, a proper study of American manners and morals requires the taxonomical methods of the social scientist but equally the critical method of the moralist or humanist.

Without arguing, then, that there should be a single organizing *theme* for taking in hand the data of manners and morals (Lerner's argument for pluralism is, as I have said, persuasive), I wish to argue for a somewhat related method. There should at least be an organizing *discipline* for the study of manners and morals. And this discipline, I suggest, is that of the professional moralist or ethicist: the discipline proper to the study of national character or *ethos* is ethics.

There are three novel aspects of this proposal. First, in the recent past it has been widely assumed that the social scientist, with his methods of detached observation, was uniquely qualified to study social phenomena, and that if, say, the theologian or philosopher wished to undertake such study, he would do well to take the methods of the social scientist as a model. We are arguing, by contrast, that the ethicist as such is equipped professionally in his own right to engage in the study of manners and morals, though he may continue to be dependent on the social scientist for the reliable marshaling of data. Second, in the recent past the great majority of ethicists—both theological and philosophical—have not been very interested in appraising manners and morals, after all, and have more or less cheerfully abandoned such study to anthropologists, historians, and other social scientists. They themselves, meanwhile, have been much more concerned with the phenomenology of belief and with what German biblical scholars are saying, in the case of American theologians, or with the problems of meaning, signification, and language, in the case of American philosophers. Third, there is as yet not quite an independent discipline of ethics nor an independent professional called an ethicist. As yet the ethicist must win his credentials either as a theologian, a philosopher, or as an out-and-out social scientist. Thus our proposal may take for granted something that it should not, when it assumes that the ethicist is qualified in his own professional right to engage in the study of manners and morals. In response we can only say here that we intend our study to advance the conception of *public ethics* as a discipline and indeed an organizing center of American studies. In the last part of this study we will make some suggestions about how those ethicists who come out of the discipline of theology may rethink their approach in the direction of a public rather than a theological ethics.

Let us assume that we can live with the novel features of this proposal. That brings us to the question: in what way is the moralist or ethicist equipped to engage in a study of manners and morals? We have already stipulated that we understand the study of this domain to embrace, in principle, the contributions from a wide variety of social scientists and humanists, but we have now argued that a special, organizing role is to be played by the professional ethicist. The ethicist, I say, is professionally equipped to take the lead in reflection upon the subjective, normative aspects of national character. As we have seen, one of the problems that most persistently comes forward in any perusal of the literature on national character is the reluctance of many social scientists to take this subject seriously, or in any case to engage in those aspects of it that require the adoption of value systems. Indeed, by intimidation many humanists (whose stock in trade is human values) have also stayed out of the fray. At best it has been thought risky to undertake a selection of values, or to introduce creative schemes for the pursuit of historical inquiry or of contemporary social study. And yet, the search for values that support and enlarge the human is of deep concern to every reflective person, no matter what his profession, given the contemporary crisis in American race relations, militarism, and urban depravity.

There is a mandate—or better yet, a burden. It is to search for the human. We cannot prosecute it by resolutely sticking to an empirical notion of the human. The very word "human," observes Roger L. Shinn, a theological ethicist, at once carries with it an empirical sense and a normative sense, "and the gap between the two is immense." In the empirical sense, "anything people do is human." But in the normative sense, "the word implies some ideal or some recognition of a humanity that is not simply the factual discovery of men's feelings, thoughts, and actions." In this normative sense the word implies a judgment upon many acts which, empirically speaking, are human, but which in a deeper sense are "subhuman or anti-human." To deal with the full phenomenon of the human also requires then some attention to the normative sense, Shinn argues, which in turn "requires an act of the ethical imagination."[27]

Let us not overstate the case for ethics. We are not saying that only the ethicist is aware of this mandate to examine values and ponder a normative sense of the human. We are suggesting only that the ethicist may be distinctively equipped to lead or to organize this sort of reflection, since it is his full-time professional concern rather than an avocation or (as in some other disciplines) slightly suspect undertaking. But the whole enterprise will fail unless there is a consortium at work. It is then important to note that this entire problem is now being actively debated in many of the other disciplines—notably among sociologists and historians. Older scholars in sociology were usually trained to see themselves as detached professionals, uninvolved and even-handed in their approach to the structures of society. But in the last few years, particularly under the impact of what we have been calling the moral crisis in America, many younger scholars have entered the discipline not only manifesting a new willingness to make value judgments and to acknowledge them as part of their scholarship, but intent upon the reform of society as part of their professional obligations.

"The trouble is that everyone makes value judgments," one of these younger sociologists commented on the occasion of a recent controversy between certain elders of the profession and a group of "younger radicals." He believes that the social scientist who does studies for the Pentagon makes "implicit" value judgments, aligning himself with militarists. "You don't escape such judgments by tacitly aligning yourself with the status quo."[28]

Historians too have been moving out of a recent phase of excessive stress upon professional detachment and concentration on specialized monographs and limited subjects. This phase itself, it appears, was an understandable reaction to earlier schools of historians manned by amateurs, literary gentlemen, and if one goes back far enough into the nineteenth century, pious patricians. The response to such early attempts to write American history was for the succeeding generation of scholars to think of themselves as rigorous scientists, committed to banishing all considerations of normative morality from their efforts. "To cleanse scholarship of the subjective coloration of the historian's own personality," says John Higham, "the professionals endeavored to banish the function—so dear to patrician hearts—of passing moral judgments on men and movements." But now, Higham adds, historians of a third generation are much in evidence. The newer, younger historians have dropped the pretense of limiting themselves to a stern objectivity. They tend to see things as participants. They accept the ambiguity of the American experience, and in this attitude they have undoubtedly been influenced by contemporary theology and existentialism, an influence of a very different sort from the example formerly set by physical scientists.[29]

Perhaps we can add that a fourth generation of historians has now appeared on the scene. They are not only open to the moral ambiguity of the American experience and the reality of conflict in national history; they actively make choices, take up a cause, and let that cause illuminate in new ways their inquiries into the past. These historians function in many ways much like the professional moralist or ethicist, especially those who may be included in the ranks of the so-called "new left" and "radical" historians. Staughton Lynd's *Intellectual Origins of American Radicalism* is one such inquiry. The work of a trained historian, and evidencing craftsmanship and competence on the part of its author, this book is nevertheless the writing of a scholar who believes passionately in the American tradition of radical dissent and who presents the ideas and acts of revolutionary radicals and abolitionists as in some sense normative for present-day Americans concerned with criticizing and reform of society. Needless to say, there are obvious dangers for the profession of writing history in this kind of subjectivism; that is one reason we think the professional ethicist is in a better position to lead the search for values.[30]

Such developments in social science helpfully imply that it has never been possible to consider such subjects as social experience or national character without adopting an agenda of value judgments, rarely recognized as such in the past. Once it becomes clear that the study of national character cannot really be confined to "detached" methods, it becomes equally obvious that much of what has passed for objective scholarship in the past was not really that at all and would have benefited from candid declaration of its status.

It seems sensible, then, to call on a wide variety of students to engage in the study of manners and morals. We have been arguing especially for a place in this coalition for those accustomed to dealing with normative concepts—philosophers, literary critics, students of jurisprudence, theologians. We are arguing for the centrality of value judgments in this enterprise—value judgments that must obviously be subject to test, in the public forum, of evidentiary study and of counterjudgment.

But more is involved in this interdisciplinary effort than the pooling of diverse specialties; more is involved than assembling the various levels and facets of scholarship that come from the various disciplines. We must seek a way of organizing these contributions coherently. A far more important aspect of the cooperative study of national character is to be found in what I would call the quest for a "common band-width" of professional concerns. This commonalty is most apparent in the relations among three professions in particular. Lawyers, physicians, and clergymen, possessing disparate skills of practice, yet can converse about a wide range of common concerns because of a common commitment to the welfare of human beings. Similar common interests may be discerned in the communication that exists between certain other professions—between psychiatry and sociology, for example, or between sanitary engineering and nursing. I wish to propose that this band-width of common professional concerns is most easily understood as the area of the moral or the ethical, and that what makes communication among these disciplines possible is the implicitly shared ethical concern for man and society. It is a concern seen anew, and more explicitly, when we confront the moral crisis today in America. It is a concern that outreaches and outruns and in some ways turns back upon and reshapes the interests of our fortresses of specialized professional activities.

In sum, then, I believe that a new discipline of public ethics, or reflection upon moral patterns at large in society, should be the organizing point for study of the American ethos. It is an undertaking needed to fill a serious void in the study of American society, a society unique in its reliance upon moral categories. Few other people, as Margaret Mead observed some years ago, "think of life in as habitually moral terms as do Americans."[31] The goal of striving in America is to overcome predicament and to seek a new future. Morality is the sanctioning of the patterns of action that are to be used in this quest. It is thus somewhat strange that morality has never, in America, been a unified subject of study, approachable as a discipline with critical standards of its own.

5. A Note on the Use of Montesquieu in this Study

What we are seeking is a model for the study of American society that takes the moral quest as the central theme; sees this quest as a public ordeal, a conflict of ideas and an interplay among various cultural and historical options; explicates the concept of the "greater community" as the systemic boundary for the consideration of morals and manners; recognizes the centrality of human initiative in enacting the quest for deliverance. It should be a model that understands the moral dimensions of community life to be a branch of politics, in the broadest sense, rather than as academic branch of theology or philosophy. I believe that a highly suggestive approach to morals and manners offering strength in just these areas can be gained by repairing to the mature thought of Montesquieu, whose early *Persian Letters* we have already cited as a pioneering example of the "travelogue" as a mode of social and political criticism. It is in his massive *The Spirit of the Laws* that are found the ideas that now interest us. But first, let us engage in a short summary of the significance of Montesquieu and his work.

Charles Louis de Secondat, Baron de la Brède et de Montesquieu (1689-1755) was a French jurist, legislator, philosopher and man of letters whose *The Spirit of the Laws* (1748) was one of the first great systematic political treatises of modern times. Its range is perhaps best indicated by the subtitle: "The Connection that the Laws are Supposed to Have with the Constitution of Each Government, Morals, Climate, Religion, Etc." The creativity of Montesquieu's approach to manners and morals has been lost on Americans, partly because of a misplaced emphasis upon a single chapter of *The Spirit of the Laws*. His fame in America is chiefly traceable to his somewhat inaccurate commentary on the British Constitution in Chapter XI, and the major token of his work in America is the principle of the separation of powers in the United States Constitution, a political doctrine of Montesquieu's that has been called "one of the most doubtful" of his contributions (Franz Neumann). Our interest in Montesquieu here does not center in his influence over the generation of the American Revolution or over the framers of the Constitution.[32] Nor do we wish to enter the lists as Montesquieu's advocate in the contemporary debate about where the American idea of liberty came from—whether from moderate Enlightened thinkers like Montesquieu and Locke (the conventional view), or from English radicals and dissenters (so a recent view runs, to the delight of the "New Left"), or from Jonathan Edwards and the orthodox Calvinist revivalists of New England (so Alan Heimert in a very unusual book).[33] We propose rather to sketch and make heuristic use of the fertile ideas of Montesquieu in a quite different project. Though the first of the great modern critical thinkers in the field of political theory, Montesquieu furnishes us a method that unites what much contemporary political and moral thought have separated: he teaches us once again of the "cohésion des idées morales et politiques" (Henri Barckhausen). Though it was Montesquieu, again, "who first laid down the fundamental principles of social science" (Émile Durkheim), yet we cannot make Montesquieu into a modern positivist sociologist concerned only with empirical observation. That is to miss the center of his thought, says Franz Neumann, which was concentrated on "the classic problem of the best government."[34]

Montesquieu invites us to think about the good society. If he is still a conservative about some things, he was ahead of his times in this venture. For the very issues that drew his most daring and imaginative comment have become a major concern, even obsession, today. These are the issues connected with the ideas of justice, humanization, and creative politics. A number of recent studies have celebrated these facets of Montesquieu's thought. His concern "was by no means a mere social and cultural criticism of France. It is far deeper and goes, indeed, to man's basic problem, namely, man's dehumanization" (Werner Stark). Though a man of "intense scientific curiosity and great scientific caution," says Neumann, Montesquieu directed his inquiring spirit toward "an endless discussion about justice within himself." He was "always in doubt, but always in search of justice," and that it could be found was a cardinal belief of his, "deep and passionate." From the early *Persian Letters,* the fictitious travelers' epistles that criticize European institutions for betraying man's destiny, dignity, and freedom, to the mature *The Spirit of the Laws,*

Montesquieu carried on a reflective quest for the spirit and organization of human community that would permit man to rise above the tyranny of nature and the despotism of arbitrary government, and to find himself and to be himself.[35]

To be sure, there is another side of Montesquieu. Though his masterpiece is a landmark in "systematic" political and social thought, the structure of *The Spirit of the Laws* still defies logic in its chaotic meandering. Though the *Persian Letters* played an important role as an early representative of the critical spirit of the Enlightenment, Montesquieu remains enamored of feudalism and even devotes a lengthy (and, I suspect, scarcely heeded) part of *The Spirit of the Laws* to tracing the origins of French feudalism. A critic of injustice and other foibles of society, he remained (like Voltaire but unlike Rousseau), a participant in higher society, which prevented him from moving toward truly radical thought. A proponent of scientific observation in political study, he was a poor reporter himself, as his account of the English constitutional system demonstrates. Ever devoted to the general good of man (he declared himself dedicated more to mankind itself than to Europe, more to Europe than to France), he remained to the end in some ways a provincial European (and even Gascon) thinker, displaying the ignorance and prejudice of a man of his time and place—as seen, for example, in his pejorative remarks about the climate, geography, and peoples of Asia, about which he seems to have known next to nothing. In significant ways a mentor to the American revolutionists and constitution framers, Montesquieu seems to encourage resistance to despotism without ever clearly breaking away from the conservative presuppositions of his own background.

In spite of all these theoretical and human problems with Montesquieu and his work, his bold revision of medieval approaches to thinking about the meaning of community provides us with the rudiments of a framework for the study of American manners and morals. We shall find it convenient to defer, until the next chapter, Montesquieu's theory of government, and until the chapter after that, his view of manners and morals in a republic, and concentrate here on three general aspects of his thought:

(a) *His Theory of Complementarity in Assessing the Sources of National Character*

It would not be amiss to speak of Montesquieu as the first great "systems thinker." For him, the life of the community must be understood as a "mix" of elements that complement each other. Before him, as Durkheim points out, religion, law, morality, commerce, public administration, all seemed discrete subjects, to be treated separately. Most moralists, for example, tended to "deal with morality and rules of conduct as though they existed by themselves," not bothering to consider other factors in society, such as economic circumstances. Montesquieu saw that these elements "form a whole," and that each must be seen in the context of the others if it is to be understood. "He does not separate law from morality, trade, religion, etc., and above all he does not consider it apart from the form of society, which affects all other social phenomena."[36]

Much conventional thought, in Montesquieu's day, was unable to see the interconnections amid this diversity because of the lingering influence of medieval theology, which so emphasized the direct causality of the divine will on events that the workings of natural and social forces could not be appreciated in their own right. Montesquieu indirectly avoids this error by reducing religious phenomena to part of the spectrum of forces that must be dealt with in any accurate observation of society. In a famous and succinct sentence he sets out this more adequate approach:[37]

> Several things govern men: climate, religion, law, the principles of government, the example of past things, morals, manners; out of them emerges a general spirit.

Here is the best place, incidentally, fully to see what the word "law" means in Montesquieu's treatise. *The Spirit of the Laws* is not a discussion of law *per se,* but rather an attempt to describe the "general spirit" or distinctiveness of various greater communities. In his insistence upon the central character of law in expressing the relationships between things, Montesquieu has been widely misunderstood. For the notion of law has two widely different meanings for him. There is the broader meaning of law: a statement of the connections between things. When Montesquieu wants to think of the community as a whole, seeing the complementarity among its various elements, he is using the idea of law in the broader sense. Then there is the conception of law as what is on the statute books. Law in this sense is one of the items that assists in organizing communities. It stands on a par with the forces of religion, morality, economics, and so on. Law is in this sense one way—the legislator's—of affecting human conduct. The society as a whole has an ensemble of means, each of which has its complementary function.[38]

As we move from greater community to greater community, Montesquieu hypothesizes, we will be able to observe a different combination of these contributory elements. Savage communities are more dominated by elemental forces of nature and by the ravages of climate. Life in ancient China was shaped by manners, but in republican Rome, by governmental institutions. Each great community has some potential distinctiveness, and the observer's business is to let each nation's specialness show itself.[39] So far we have been describing what sounds like a theory of pluralism rather than of true complementarity as a rationale of the relation among the various constituent elements of community. But there is a more profound tension that polarizes these forces, and this is the tension between the grip of nature and the sense of the human. Montesquieu often uses code words for these opposing forces: "climate" and "morals." But the point is to picture the community as engaged in a struggle to overcome baser impulses and influences, through law, justice, and other means, and to give the human spirit in its moral dimensions more latitude. But this leads us to our next point.

(b) His Dialectical and Realistic View of Man

Within this galaxy of community forces, a struggle is going on, a struggle that is really characteristic of the human predicament and is thus indicative of the nature of man-in-community. One set of forces consists of the "moral" factors in the will and at large in the community. The other set consists of what Montesquieu chooses to describe (in an unfortunate figure, we concede) as the influence of "climate." The moral forces include laws, customs, manners, religious phenomena, educative activities, and in general what we would think of today as cultural evolution. The forces of climate include all that is elemental, both in nature and in human nature, and also that aspect of causation that whole cadres of modern historians and natural scientists have thought of as "environmental." This tension between forces bespeaks in short a dialectical view of man, a picture of man that has him constantly engaged in a struggle to overcome the influence of baser nature and of the cruder environmental causes, for these forces submerge him as it were, keeping him from being himself. It is when the moral forces, including a carefully elaborated legal structure of the community triumphs, that man rises out of submission, whether to nature or to human despots, becomes himself, and finds himself at home in a community that by its structures of law, justice, and manners permits freedom.

Montesquieu agrees, then, with neither Hobbes nor Rousseau about the natural condition of man. For man is neither *homo ferox* nor *homo angelicus*. Rather, he is always poised between the possibilities of his human makeup—the natural or animalistic, and the social or moral.[40] The fable about the "Troglodytes" in the *Persian Letters* already captures this idea. In this story, man is pictured as not fated to exist in the grip of a bellicose, warlike nature. In fact, Montesquieu suggests here, even man in his "natural" state has a preexistent aptitude for justice, and it is indeed on the very basis of this capacity that he is able to ask for and establish a government based on willing consent and citizen participation. On the other hand, this capacity is not so firmly developed that it is certain men will infallibly develop just governments. And even when they do, the temptation is also always there to relax and relinquish autonomy and permit a new despotism to arise. This is seen at the conclusion of the Troglodyte story, when the inhabitants tire of virtuous participation in the burdens of governance and seek out one of their wiser number and ask him to be king.[41]

There is no determinism here, then. When Montesquieu speaks, as he often does, about the various effects the climate is said to have on men, he is to be understood as describing the predicament that the human community encounters in becoming itself. Physical causes do hold men in thrall until by political initiative they begin to assert themselves. As he puts it in one of his lesser-known essays:

> Moral causes play a larger role in the formation of the general character of a nation and decide more about its quality than physical causes.[42]

Such environmental forces as climate, oppressive here, beneficent there, operate directly only at the lower stage of human community, where nature controls man instead of submitting to human dominion. But in the more advanced forms of community—communities that are structured by law and motivated with the human will to freedom —man begins to emancipate himself from nature and to dominate the environment. Tocqueville significantly refers to Montesquieu to make just this point when he observes that the productivity of the land often has less to do with the sterility of the soil than with the desire for liberty among the inhabitants.[43]

On the other hand, this moral struggle does not imply that man emerges above nature. Neither physical nor spiritual forces can wholly take over man, for he is a kinsman of both. In complementarity and even in conflict, the two elements form the context in which man acts and reacts. Indeed, the struggle between the moral forces and the suppressing forces continues even in the realm of ideas. Just as physical forces threaten to dominate man at lower levels of community organization, so mental forces even in higher forms of community may continue to oppress. Thus a moral struggle must continue in this higher domain against such threatening forces as superstition and ignorance. It is this kind of ordeal, in fact, that more properly characterizes the human predicament. Richter suggests that Montesquieu was so realistic in his estimate of the corruption of French society that he doubted if it could be righted by mere legal reform: "His view of human nature put great stress on the passions, and he believed that jealousy and the desire for domination are among the mainsprings of despotism."[44]

Hence Montesquieu's anthropology tallies with his view of the diversity of forces in community. In both realms, the nature of man and the makeup of community, he sets out a characteristically modern view that stresses tension and ambivalence. "He upheld the value of conflict in politics—the importance of pluralism in systems characterized by conciliation, compromise, and bargaining between intermediate groups and the central authority."[45]

Although our aim has not been to adduce parallels between the thought of Montesquieu and the tenor of contemporary existentialism and theology, we think it is still important, when we are considering the nature of man, to underline a basic similarity. Montesquieu's insistence that the human predicament may be viewed as a struggle between "climate" and "morals" is restated in our own time in, say, the anthropology of Reinhold Niebuhr (we imply no genetic connection between the thought of the former and that of the latter). Niebuhr, too, sees man as living in the intersection of two dimensions of being. He is "a child of nature, subject to its vicissitudes, compelled by its necessities, driven by its impulses." But he is at the same time "a spirit who stands outside nature" and who can sense the transcendence over nature of the mandate to justice and the yearning for love. He is under the sway of nature and at the same time able to transcend this constraint. Man, as a creature, is at once both finite and free. This tension in his makeup extends into the very highest reaches of his existence. As Niebuhr sums it up in a recent statement.[46]

> He is able to break the tight social harmonies of nature, to project ends beyond the limit of natural impulse. He is able to transmute the natural impulse for survival, which he shares with all creatures, into different forms of self-realization, embodying the pride, vanity, and will-to-power of the human ego. This freedom over natural impulse makes man, who is undoubtedly a creature of nature, into a creator of, and agent in, history.

On this view, and on that of Montesquieu, moral patterns may be seen as weapons employed for the invasion of terrain formerly occupied by natural forces, including those forces of baser human nature. At the same time, every newly minted moral pattern may itself be recaptured by resurgent forces of selfishness or pride. Thus the careful redefinition of death that is brought on today by organ-transplant capability represents a new step in the struggle against the ground-zero of death that is always tugging on us, the newer techniques becoming part of a "moral pattern" to the degree that they offer further transcendence over gross natural forces leading to death. But they must be carefully and painstakingly defined for another reason: another retrogressive pull that is always exerted on us is that of our own human nature that tempts us to corrupt every technique and distort every moral pattern for partial ends. So we must carefully hedge about the transplant teams with a definition of death that will at once extend to the potential recipient of organs the chance to live, unhampered by a past epoch's definition of death that no longer serves, and yet guards the donor against being made into an organ bank for those with greater chances of living. Thus, in one scheme, life or death can be based on five physical indications—heartbeat, pulse, brain activity, breathing, and status of reflexes. When these functions cease, the attending physician may now consider it proper to stop supporting life artificially in that patient and think of the effort to keep his life going as immoral.[47]

The human community is thus forged out of a struggle between morality and environment. But there is one further ingredient, according to Montesquieu. The values of humanity are not abstract and uniform. Rather they are expressed distinctively in each greater community:

(c) *His Understanding of the Integrity of Greater Communities*

Before Montesquieu, historians tended to attribute events to final causes, thus obscuring the role of human initiative and activity. The medieval approach had also tended to stress universals, and to comprehend the great political and moral problems under large archetypes that stressed pure ideas rather than concrete manifestations. Montesquieu ends this way of approaching human affairs. Men are now seen as agents in the pageant of history. Whereas such historians as Bossuet continued to stress final causes, Montesquieu finds a way to depict history as happening through "the acts and the choices of men in the conduct of the affairs of their nation."[48] Such questions as the conflict between political power and the yearning for liberty, he

believes, can no longer be helpfully discussed in terms of ideal archetypes. "There is, he believes," Neumann comments, "no universally
applicable solution." Instead there are only types of solutions, peculiar
to various cultures and countries.[49] "The solution depends upon the
configuration of space, time and tradition in each specific country.
It is thus neither arbitrary nor accidental. . . . Even then the solution
is not an ideal one. It is at best an approximation."

The quest for justice, admittedly, is universal among men, and
Montesquieu, like other men dedicated to the enlightened ideas of his
time, recognizes it as such. "If I knew of something which might be of
value to my family and which might not be so to my country," he
declared, "I would seek to forget it. If I knew something of value to
my country which might be prejudiceable to Europe and to the
human race, I would regard it as a crime."[50] Montesquieu upholds
this goal, but insists that it may be pursued and realized only in a
concrete embodiment. Solutions themselves are never universal. They
are representations in time and space that depend on culture and
other relative factors.

This relativism in approach to solutions marks Montesquieu off
from most of the other great seekers-of-justice of the Enlightenment.[51] Voltaire, too, concedes the relativity of laws, customs, forms
of government. Still there is a difference. Unlike the author of *The
Spirit of the Laws,* Voltaire is less ready to use these relative laws and
communities as agencies of development in the struggle against injustice. No nation actually lives under good laws, says Voltaire. All of
these laws have been dictated by the selfish interests of legislators.
They are based on ignorance and superstition. What the variety reveals to Voltaire, then, is the bad state of the existing laws of mankind.

Voltaire thinks of the contradictory and bad laws that now exist as
offering a kind of negative contrast to what men should aim for. We
may not be able to reach certainty about all sorts of things: we
should not waste our time with metaphysics, first causes, or world
systems. We should take natural scientists as our model and concentrate on that which we can know. The natural scientist, for example,
can take hold of the problem of gravitation and rightly concentrates
here rather than concerning himself with the cause of things. Just so,

those of us concerned with good laws do know one thing: we know of our obligation to do good rather than evil. On that, he suggests, with classic Enlightenment simplicity, all are in accord. Our duty is plain, and that is to sweep aside bad laws and establish just ones. Only that will suffice.

Thus Voltaire aims at a universal moral law, whereas Montesquieu, agreeing that we are universally faced with the predicament of injustice, and universally on the quest for justice, aimed at a solution by realistic reforms of the laws of greater communities. For Voltaire, there is a knowable idea of right or wrong that is independent of present laws, dogmas, and religions. Just as there is only one geometry, so there is only one morality, planted in every man by the Eternal. If men will only use their reason, Voltaire suggests, they will arrive at the same conception of justice everywhere. Montesquieu argues only for the capacity to reason, not insisting that it take the same course everywhere. Where men reason, whether perfectly or not, Montesquieu thinks, despotism will fail.

Now that we see the contrast between Montesquieu's realism and relativism, on the one hand, and the more conventional universalism of the Enlightenment, on the other, let us see how Montesquieu develops his position. He postulates that the communities of mankind are differentiated by geography or space, so that their customs, manners, and laws vary significantly. He chooses a most unfortunate concept to serve as the symbol of this differentiation—"climate."

Montesquieu often manages to sound as if he thinks of climate as a deterministic force suppressing choice and will. Again, he entertains, seemingly, no principle of logical consistency in his explanations of how climate operates. He can put his proposition flatly at times, blandly declaring that "the character of the spirit and the passions of the heart vary decidedly according to climate."[52] When he attempts to illustrate this proposition by pointing to the habits and ethos of various peoples, he often sounds arbitrary and even silly. A nation that exists in a cold climate will tend to have the attributes of forcefulness, self-confidence, and insistence upon one's superiority. Such peoples at the same time are less likely to go all-out for vengeance, less likely to be suspicious, less capable of ruse. Sorel, in a witty ridicule of the climate theory taken this way, allows that he can indeed recognize some of these features in the cold-climed peoples, such as Germans and Anglo-Saxons, especially the tendency to resort to force, and the insistence upon their superiority. But there is also, contrary to Montesquieu's schema, the well-known "perfidy of Albion," and "the quarrelsomeness of the German," neither of which is provided for in the climate theory. Indeed, Sorel goes on, in this usage of the theory, Montesquieu has it that "a hot climate produces, among the Asiatic peoples, the same effects that it is necessary to attribute in the Russians to the cold." But maybe such an arbitrary theory has a cause all its own. "We are tempted to suspect the influence of the fantastic climate of Gascony," he concludes.[53]

But the climate theory is capable of a more reasonable interpretation and usage. At one point Montesquieu restates the theory in the form of a political ecology, and declares:[54]

> Laws are closely connected with the fashion in which various peoples provide for themselves. A more extended code of laws is required for a people who attach themselves to commerce and to the sea, than for a people who content themselves with cultivating their lands. And a more extended code is necessary for the latter, however, than for a people who keep herds. And a more extended code is necessary for these than for a people who hunt.

The value of Montesquieu's theory lies not in any predictive values that may be associated with the effects of climate. Its value is rather to illustrate that laws, manners, and customs may be likened to "works of art" that grow out of the society they express, that they serve to organize these societies in a nonarbitrary fashion, and that they provide appropriate tools for conserving and developing the special promise of these societies.[55] Man is a shaper of nature, and since nature is complex in its challenge, man does not everywhere reshape nature and construct community in the same fashion. Political man is thus an artist, giving form to the life of communities. Societies are more than simple "givens," but are something to be constructed.[56]

In this sense, the climate theory is still very much alive in contemporary scholarship. The famed "frontier theory" of Frederick Jackson Turner, now enjoying a renewed reputation among historians, points to the influence of environmental conditions in the West in reshaping American society so that it becomes a much modified development of European forms. Or again, anthropologists cannot dismiss the influence of climate itself as a differentiating factor in communities and cultures. According to Carleton S. Coon, for example,[57]

Fair skin, blue eyes, and blond hair are concentrated in northwestern Europe and decrease in frequency quite regularly as one moves southward and eastward. A pigment map of Europe closely resembles a weather map showing the number of cloud days each year.

Climatic changes played a significant role in the history of Europe, Coon goes on, by varying the options of migrating peoples. At times when the continental climate changed decisively, such as with the onset of the great ice sheets, life became hazardous. "Entire tribes and nations, which had become populous in the meantime, moved southward, invading France, Spain, Portugal, Italy, Greece." In the settlement of the United States, national groups tended to settle in places where climates and work opportunities were familiar to them.[58]

In any case, Montesquieu's view of the specialness of greater communities does not rest purely on climatic variations. The influence of climate is posed by him as a symbol of geographic or spatial variation. The other pluralistic forces in the community—laws, morals, manners, principles of governance, religion—also contribute to the organic unity that characterizes greater communities and sets each off as a discernible society with its own history, defects, and promise. And in the final analysis, as we have seen, the whole point of the climate theory is to describe the physical constraints upon humanity that the moral quest is challenged to overcome.

We shall postpone further consideration of Montesquieu's views of the nature and structure of governments until the next chapter. Here we simply reiterate that his approach to politics and society has the advantage of picturing the tensions and conflicts that form the background of community. And it is in his linkage of politics and morality that we see his greatest value to our study. "If we admit that Montesquieu . . . interests us in the first place," a recent study argues, "we will be obliged to recognize that his true glory is found much more in his moral judgments than in his technical contributions to constitutional theory."[59] In truth, the conditions that Montesquieu thought were minimally necessary to good government were what we would describe today as a public ethics. The value of government itself is based on the human values it can express and permit. Montesquieu's thought thus helps us to approach modern societies, appreciating that each community is a distinctive mix of cultural attributes and a unity that has perhaps been best of all described by Margaret Mead in a single sentence: "The way in which people behave is all of a piece, their virtues and their sins, the way they slap the baby, handle their court cases, and bury their dead."[60]

CHAPTER II.

REPUBLICS

"I could not but ask myself if virtue were a plant," Mrs. Trollope reflected after seeing some of the nineteenth-century American West, "thriving under one form in one country, and flourishing under a different one in another." If the Americans of the West— meaning places like Cincinnati—were right, then how "dreadfully wrong" the English must be in their manners and morals. Americans, she concluded "are so strangely like, and so strangely unlike us; the connection with us is so close, yet the disunion so entire; speaking the same language, yet having hardly a feeling in common."[1]

We have already proposed, in Chapter I, that it may be possible to understand the distinctiveness of greater communities by inquiring into their existential predicaments and the moral patterns they produce to overcome them. Now we must advance one step further by moving beyond the conception of greater communities in general and taking up the specific case of the American greater community. We must now ask concretely what the continuing characteristics are of the moral struggle in the American ethos. Our aim is thus to seek out a set of categories or concepts that will afford a workable key to interpreting the moral quest in America, and so to move toward that "public ethics" we have already anticipated as one of the goals of our study. We do not seek to "prove" this or that about American morality or the American experience, but rather to put forward for test certain abiding presuppositions or historic "lines of march" as offering a satisfactory thematic key for interpreting present-day America and its moral crisis.

1. Organizing Themes for the American Ethos

In a key study of 1941, Lee Coleman was struck by the great diversity of themes, and the frequent mutual contradictions among them, that showed up in writings on "Americanism" and "the American Way." What does "American" really mean? It seemed that it could mean almost anything. Is the trait of "obedience to law," for example, a significant ingredient of "Americanism"? Some observers, Coleman found, insisted that it was. One group of authors consistently pictured America as "a government of law, not of men." But another group asserted what is seemingly just the opposite about the country. American laws are frequently incomplete, they held, and Americans are often lax about enforcing the laws that are already on the books. Thus a distinctive American trait is a preference for direct, sometimes violent action, either outside the law or in contravention of it. Ostensibly, the two claims about Americans nullified each other.

Contradiction between themes was not the only difficulty. Another was the sheer multiplicity of the traits that were nominated as descriptive of "what is American." Coleman reports that more than fifty traits of "Americanism" were frequently mentioned in the books and authors he studied. The most frequently cited included the tendency to join (associational activity), belief in democracy, equality, and individual freedom; disregard for law ("direct action"), preference for local government, stress on religion (especially in a nationalist context), and biases toward prosperity, puritanism, uniformity, and conformity.[2] Quite apart, then, from the disagreement between certain pairs of asserted traits, we are simply overwhelmed by the sheer length of the list of themes that we may be able to assemble by pursuing the "literature" assiduously. Worse, not even the largest list we might assemble would satisfy the nominalists who believe we can never stress adequately the diversity of any large, modern society. This objection was classically expressed a few years ago in a critical review of David M. Potter's *People of Plenty*, a book that begins with a persuasive argument for the usefulness of the concept of American character. "I can envision 162,000,000 American characters," says

the critic, alluding to what was the population of the United States at
the time. Perhaps, he goes on, we might even assimilate the idea of
grouping these diverse characters into, say, "327 categories with wide
divergencies in each." But even when that is done, the hostile re-
viewer insists, "I still cannot see an American national character."[3]

There will continue to be an important role for the patient cata-
loguer of many and diverse traits and characteristics of the ethos, not
least of all the industrious researcher who compiles a longish list and
then points to the discrepancies among the items on the list. There
will certainly be a place for the skeptic who doubts that we can ever
reduce the diversity of a culture to an intelligible (and not misleading) set of categories. Yet I believe there is a better approach to
cultural study than either the art of cataloguing or the art of cynicism.
Today more and more scholars, not overlooking the diversity of
American culture, believe that the burden is on the student of cultural
phenomena to reflect upon and organize, rather than simply to list,
his data. Several approaches to meeting this obligation are identifiable. The most common is probably to attempt to discern broad patterns of unity in culture or history that hold together the erstwhile
diverse facts and traits that can admittedly be assembled. Another
approach gaining ground today is to focus on human personality and
to attempt to see the ways it is shaped and molded by its surrounding
culture. Still another "focuses attention on some central problem or
antinomy within a culture or segment of culture, such as a literary or
religious tradition."[4]

We have already declared our intention of adopting a version of
this latter approach, by viewing the American greater community as
unified by existential predicament and by its moral and political responses. Now we must justify this approach in the light of the diversity of the American experience. We must be on guard against the
dangers of "monocausationism," the attempt to explain a complex
and many-sided set of developments by a single cause (such as "environment," "slavery," "the frontier," "economic self-interst," to
name a few that have been employed in past studies). All too often
American history itself has been turned upside down, rewritten by
our needs to understand ourselves and our own social problems
anew.[5] Another danger with the single organizing theme is that we

will choose as our point of focus a theme that is not truly at the center of the American experience, or one that is not really distinctive for it in comparison with other national cultures. The frequent claim that America is a "materialistic" society is, for Jacques Maritain, just such an ill-advised choice for elucidating what is distinctive about America. The usual run of claims for the materialistic bent in America is unconvincing, he says, although not because they aren't true:[6]

> I don't deny these things; I do say that to invoke them as a proof of so-called American materialism is to talk nonsense. For, in the first place, they are in no way specifically American; exactly the same symptoms, in relation to similar sociological or psychological areas, leap to the eye everywhere (especially in Europe) where the industrial regime and its congenial ideological fumes are prevalent; only the vocal expression seems perhaps to be a little cruder and more naïve here.

Taking these cautionary notes duly in account, we are still free to conclude that much of the proliferation on a lengthy list of American character traits may be owing to underorganized data; many of the items ostensibly given original standing on the list may be reasonably understood as secondary, as examples or facets of a much smaller number of controlling themes. The law of parsimony applies to this as to any other area of reflection and inquiry, and where a set of traits may be understood as manifesting diverse expressions of one or more much larger themes, one then becomes responsible for elaborating that smaller number of more comprehensive rubrics. We need not insist on reducing everything to a single theme or claiming that a few key themes will explain all there is to explain about the American ethos. All we wish to do, in fact, is to propose the existential predicament and the resultant moral and political patterns as one useful prism for viewing the American experience, and to propose that our method of inquiry be that of the professional ethicist. We are confident that the moral dilemma is of considerable moment and centrality —not to say dominance—for understanding the American greater community on its own terms. We do not care to or need to claim more.

Many students of the American ethos have produced illuminating studies by dealing creatively and imaginatively with only one larger theme, provided it is a flexible enough theme to take the realities of pluralism and diversity into account. One of the most familiar examples is David Riesman's employment of the notion of "directedness" as a central item in the American character—with its deployment into the subsidiary aspects of tradition-direction, inner-direction, and other-direction. Or again, the idea of movement or change itself, understood in its full range of effects, can be a useful organizing principle, as in the employment of a singular but complex concept of motion—the "M-factor"—by George W. Pierson. "What made and kept us different," he argues, "was not just the wilderness of the North American continent, nor its vast empty spaces, nor even its wealth of resources, powerful as must have been those influences. No. It was, first of all, the M-factor: the factor of movement, migration, mobility."[7]

The most famous organizing notion of all, beyond doubt, was supplied by the historian Frederick Jackson Turner in his interpretation of the frontier experience as central in differentiating American life from that of Europe. Never discounting the continuing influence of European beginnings on American institutions, Turner laid new emphasis on the impact of the West in reshaping the face of American civilization. Turner was always open to the possibility of multiple influencing factors, but at the same time he put forward the frontier experience as a more promising key for interpreting the distinctiveness of the American greater community than the thematic keys that had often been employed by previous historians—such keys as political liberty, English tyranny, and the effects of slavery. Because of the novelty of his proposals, Turner was attacked by colleagues who opposed both the supposed monolithicity of the frontier thesis and its importance even in a multiple-influence theory. But the tides of scholarship have shifted again, and Turner's view has recently enjoyed a revival and refinement among his successors. Ray Allen Billington is one of these later historians who has reaffirmed the centrality of the frontier experience in shaping American character, although he is careful to avoid exclusive claims for this factor. The central elements in the American character that may have been considerably influenced by the frontier life, Billington suggests, are these:

(1) the drive toward success, commonly seen in terms of upward mobility and of a concern with conformity; (2) the shift in American character that David Riesman has recounted in *The Lonely Crowd,* from reliance on guidance by extrinsic tradition successively to inner-direction and other-direction; (3) a spirit of intense competition and rivalry which "in turn fosters a sense of failure that stimulates a craving for love and recognition"; (4) preoccupation with the individual.[8]

That these traits must have been forged at least in part on the great frontier seems to be attested in the picture foreigners often gained (and still do) of Americans, who came through as "an inventive, self-reliant people, who placed little trust in tradition but were inclined to experimentation and innovation even when time-tested practices were suitable." Adept at many skills, Americans tended not to be specialists or craftsmen but jacks of all trades, generalists. Moreover, they were always on the move, showing little attachment to precedent, place, ancestral ways, or sites left behind. Americans seemed scandalously wasteful, "throwing away objects that would be used happily by a European and sacrificing nearly new houses to make way for the next 'development.'" Lawlessness continued to seem a consistent attitude, and it seemed to be a country in which people took "malicious pleasure" in defying authority.[9]

We have laid out Billington's findings not especially because the frontier experience itself seems so central to us, but to exhibit the fertility of results that is possible when a single theme or prism is imaginatively employed by the historian. The selection of a prominent problem or molding force does not by any means limit us to a thin, poverty-stricken, or one-sided interpretation of the American character. Rather, the thematic key, if it is appropriately chosen with the diversity of American life in mind, may be able to expose precisely the range and plurality in the culture, while offering clues about what holds the greater community together.

Once we have selected a starting point or organizing discipline that promises to include and give expression to the important subthemes, the way is open to solving another problem we have noticed: that of the apparent contradiction between some of the subthemes or traits. For it may be that the American experience, even when organized from the point of view of some singular theme or discipline, may still turn out to be highly antinomous or dialectical, exhibiting not a simple, linear, one-sided set of traits, but manifesting on the contrary an ambiguous, conflicting response to crisis. It is not in the identification of a set of unambiguous, uncomplicated characteristics that we can hope to find the distinctiveness of the American greater community. That lies rather in the way the tensions are expressed, and in the way conflicting values compete, given a common crisis and hope for resolution. Thus there is a dialectical reaction to "tyranny" among the patriots of the late colonial period, a tension that still characterizes American ideology. One reaction is that revolution is undertaken for the sake of restoring lawful government—hence the American "trait" that this is a government of "laws, not men." But another reaction was the assumption that all authority is dangerous—hence the American "trait" that least government is the best government. So the observers of American society were right, after all, in seeing both a "law and order" and a "direct action, outside the law" aspect of the American character. These are not simple contradictions, indicating the impossibility of getting at the national character. They are dialectical reactions to a distinctive historical and ideological problem in American life, the problem of extrinsic colonial control of the original American community by rulers in England. Actually these two attitudes are very close to each other. Both are antiauthoritarian and as such highly distinctive: one of them, however, sees law and the office of the duly elected magistrate as the safeguard against tyranny, whereas the other sees magistrature itself as the possibility of tyranny.

Margaret Mead's summary of the conflicts in the American character evokes this dialectical aspect so well that it is worth quoting in full:[10]

We have a certain kind of character, the American character, which has developed in the New World and taken a shape all its own; a character that is geared to success and to movement, invigorated by obstacles and difficulties, but plunged into guilt and despair by catastrophic failure or a wholesale alteration in the upward and onward pace; a character in which aggressiveness is uncertain and undefined, to which readiness to fight anyone who starts a fight and unreadiness to engage in violence have both been held up as virtues; a character which measures its successes and failures only against near contemporaries and engages in various quantitative devices for reducing every contemporary to its own stature; a character which sees success as the reward of virtue and failure as the stigma for not being good enough; a character which is uninterested in the past, except when ancestry can be used to make points against other people in the success game; a character oriented towards an unknown future, ambivalent towards other cultures, which are regarded with a sense of inferiority as more coherent than our own and with a sense of superiority because newcomers in America display the strongest mark of other cultural membership in the form of foreignness.

Finally, we must pursue one more uncertainty: does the American character change in time? Undoubtedly it does, but does it change substantially in time, so that what we may describe as the significant traits at one moment are out of date and nondescriptive at a later time? Is there, in other words, a historical identity for the American ethos?

Our view is that although decisive change does occur in the American character over the passage of time, it is not destructive of the American identity. The moral struggle for disposing of one's own space, we believe, has consistently shaped American character in the past and continues to do so out of a persistent "line of march." The details, issues, and arena of this predicament evolve and even undergo various discontinuities and mutations. But the form of the predicament remains, as is evidenced by the continuing concern in this country, the nagging question whether equality is for all members of the society, or whether certain elements of the community shall continue to be denied the promise of the Declaration of Independence. In the decades since that Declaration was adopted, the argument and debate and, at times, violent struggles, have involved numerous issues, but there has been a discernible continuity in them—as the history of the ordeal of the black man in this country, for example, illustrates. In mild disagreement with Riesman, then, and in agreement with such social scientists as Seymour Martin Lipset, we understand certain ideological values to persist across American history and to influence the form in which we receive technology, so that these values may be assumed to shape technology as much as, and perhaps more than, technology reshapes our values.[11]

We are not arguing for a soporific identity between yesterday's America and today's or even for a smooth evolution, for one of the central themes in American history, as we will shortly be arguing, is the "revolutionary impulse," as the definitive occasion for organizing and reorganizing community in America on the basis of recovering one's own space. Yet the original revolution burned a deep concern for equality into the American community, so that the upheavals and breaks and discontinuities in American history will usually be found to involve conflict and innovation aimed at the challenge of implementing this revolutionary promise. Even such a departure from convention as the student protests of the late 1960's, despite their radicality, show a strong connection with the American revolutionary tradition. The very anger of the black man and the student today is based on the assumption that the United States can do better, can be more morally responsible in distributing the benefits of democracy— an assumption that has provoked conflict from the birth of the nation on.[12]

The persistence of the quest for one's own space, we argue, and for such related goods as equality, outweighs the transitions and upheavals of American history, including the transition from a "rural" to an "industrial" and now a "cybernetic" economy, a transition which has in the telling sometimes been based on knocking down the straw man of a rural economy. (American society began to take its industrial destiny seriously much earlier than conventional accounts suggest of this transition.) In short, the American character is to be understood as distinctively constituted both in time and in space by its moral struggle, its ideological aspirations. That is why we have entitled this chapter "Republics." For it is in the political organization of republican society that these persistent moral concerns come to be embodied. As Bernard Bailyn puts the situation, a republic was the inevitable form of realization for the American greater community, once it secured its freedom from England. "What would an independent American nation be? A republic, necessarily—and properly, considering the character and circumstances of the people."[13]

2. Montesquieu's Model of the Structure of a Republic

We have already pointed to the thought of Montesquieu (Chapter I) as offering a framework for seeking out the moral dimensions of the political order. Montesquieu, we saw there, took account of the ambiguous, dialectical nature of man (a feature we have immediately had to contend with in assessing the American character). He believed that the good society comes from a combination of constitutional-legal arrangements, on the one hand, and the forces of manners and morals, animated by community spirit, on the other. He understood that the resultant solution of political problems is shaped by "the configuration of space, time and tradition in each specific community" (Franz Neumann). Now we propose to view the specific political implications of this approach to human community by examining Montesquieu's delineation of the structure of republics.

We begin with Montesquieu because he gives us a promising model, a new horizon of political community as viewed from the Europe that was just awakening to the vision of Enlightenment, justice, *bonheur*, political integrity for the citizen. This model, which was to find fresh, concrete embodiment in America, consists of two poles. At one point of focus is the pole of republican initiative, by which men may realize themselves in common political activity; at the opposite point of focus is the pole of extrinsic control—the despotism or tyranny so cordially despised in both the pages of Montesquieu and in the agitation of the colonial rebels of America: for in governments under this system, men are deprived of self-determination. Here, then, are the ranges of possibility for reorganizing the human community, just as a new country, America, was about to undertake such a venture. Montesquieu himself laid out these two poles not as a handbook for colonial Americans, but rather as a way of "straddling" the French monarchy with alternatives. His own chief object, when all is said and done, was to subject the monarchical form of government in France to deserved criticism and to move it away from the arrogance of unrestrained power toward the countervailing pole of moderate, republican forms in which more standing room is given to the individual citizen. And so the republic, which

Montesquieu would not have advocated as such, still becomes a horizon by which Europe's monarchical governments, so often sunk in despotism, might be measured and judged.

The first thing we need to see is the importance, in Montesquieu's model, of the notion that human community is possible only through a structured government. On his view, it is the shaping and restraining and rechanneling forces of law, morals, and manners that allow men and their communities to find their liberty and humanity, to be their best selves. These structures not only mobilize the community for the struggle against and upward out of nature; they also protect the community from the lower impulses of human nature, especially the will of the powerful to confiscate human space. But the function of the structures is more than conservative: when the laws and customs are properly developed, according to the ecology of the country, they evoke from the men and women of the community the best in them. Without such structures, men do not command their own space, they cannot be themselves, and justice is impossible. The question to be relentlessly pursued, therefore, is that of the form of government for given greater communities—according to their own time, place, and circumstances—that can best elaborate these liberating structures so that justice will triumph, and mankind will realize a moral victory over the constraints of elemental nature.

Given this goal of seeking an appropriate structure, Montesquieu then asks about the various possible forms of government. He holds that a greater community may be organized in any of three basic forms: as a monarchy, as a republic, or as a despotism.[14] These are not really comparable forms. The monarchy is the state of government that actually obtains in Montesquieu's own greater community of France, and it is the dominant option prevalent in Europe. It is thus implicitly in a class by itself as the form that must be accepted, at least by him and other Frenchmen and Europeans of his day, and criticized, with a view toward modifying it in the direction of a better government. The model of despotism is symbolic, representing the nether pole of possibility, the worst thing that could happen to a monarchy. The republic, properly safeguarded against mere popular rule, represents the zenith of possibilities, especially when we remember that for Montesquieu the best republics include the provision for aristocracy. He is in the final analysis a monarchist. Though he has long been interested in the city-states of antiquity, the Italic city-states of medieval times, and the European republican governments of his own day, nowhere does he indicate his belief that France could or should be transformed into a republic. What he envisions for France, rather (and by extension, for Europe), is a development of monarchy away from the potentiality of despotism toward a structured form of government that reassigns power, not only to an aristocracy, but to other elements in the citizenry, and which, in any case, provides for dignity, if not autonomy, for the ordinary citizen.

Not only are these three forms of government—monarchy, republic, despotism—thus incommensurable, strictly speaking; really they are normative statements about the structure of authority and responsibility, or formal categories for speaking to the question of the disposition of power.[15] In the last analysis they are not so much side-by-side descriptions of alternative types of government as ranked, subjective, descriptions of the various types of wielders of organizing power, and of the modalities by which this power is manifested in the community.

In a monarchy one man governs, but through a structure of reliable and established laws, and with the cooperation of subordinate agencies that Montesquieu calls the "tempering" or "moderating" forces —such as the aristocracy or the local *parlements*. Though the power of the monarch is absolute, it is not arbitrary, since it is distributed, tempered, and moderated through the intermediate agencies and through the meditating structure of laws. Thus in a "tempered" monarchy the moral ends of dignity and justice are served.

In a despotism, on the other hand, one man governs, but without a distributing network of laws and without delegated responsibility. The despot governs through his own will alone, through whim and caprice.

What is the structure of government in republics? Let us consider this form of state in more detail.

(a) *The Republic: Willed Initiative*

The republic as one of the principal forms of government is subject to variations, depending on whether the people act directly and as a body to engage in lawmaking, statecraft, and governance, or whether they confer these functions on a part of the people. When the people rule as a whole, the republic may be styled a democracy (a variation of the republic for which Montesquieu has little use). To all intents and purposes, when he speaks of the alternative, a republic in which a part of the people rules, he is thinking of an aristocracy, and it is this form about which he speaks most favorably. Above all, the key to the soundness of the republic is its respect for the institutions of law and for those selected to administer and execute the laws.[16] In another connection, Montesquieu adds what amounts to still another variation on the idea of a republic, the federation of relatively small states that have chosen a republican form of government. Federation is the only fashion by which a large country, he seems to think, can successfully manage the republican experiment. Otherwise, republican government at large in a country of great size would tempt the people to relinquish even representative government. If a small republic runs the risk of being taken over by a powerful foreign state, a large one can be destroyed by its internal weaknesses. The country of great size naturally beckons for a despot. But a federation of republics, "a society of societies," would be able to resist external force like a monarchy, while at the same time maintaining its greatness without internal corruption. For the potential usurper would not be able to appeal at large to the whole vast populace. He would have to take over one constituent republic at a time, but the first case would alarm all the others, who could then take proper measures.[17]

So far we have alluded only to the types or forms of government, the structures by which power to rule is organized and distributed. Now we must take up another and equally important aspect of Montesquieu's theory of governments, his conception of the spirit or motive that may be seen to exist as the special expression of the possibilities of each type. The account of structure—whether monarchial, republican, or despotic—does little more than give us a static picture of the channels of government, a "still life" of the government form. Montesquieu has a more dynamic analysis. He asks: what drives flow through the channels of government? We must go on with him to ask how each of these model structures actually performs, moves forward, gets its society organized—how its genius is manifested, what it looks like in motion. For each model we must ask, in the colloquial phrase, what makes it tick. As Montesquieu himself distinguishes between these two aspects of his theory, the first—the description of form—designates for a government "its special structure." The second—the account of the forces that move within the form—takes us into the realm of the "human passions" that are at work within the structures of governance.[18]

First, the despotism. The passion that is invoked in a despotism is obvious: it is fear. Since the only agency of government is the arbitrary power of the prince, it is necessary that he keep the mailed fist raised over the populace at every moment.[19] Let us leave it at that for the moment, pausing only to remember that the despotism for Montesquieu is something of a symbol of evil rather than a veridical description of extant governments. It is a political translation of the Christian view of the depravity of man; Montesquieu's interest is in criticizing the despotic strands, tendencies, and possibilities in monarchical government.

We are less certain, on first glance, what Montesquieu means when he turns to monarchies and tells us that they operate by the principle of "honor." Similarly, we feel we have been handed a vague term when he says that democracies operate by "virtue."

First, there is a translation problem. Montesquieu states the motivating principle of a democracy to be la vertu. The easiest, but not the best, translation is the direct English cognate, virtue. Let us refuse to translate it so quickly for the moment and attend to Montesquieu's concept itself. In a democracy there is no prince furnished with an army to maintain the laws by force. And since the people are established on a basis of parity, there is no pride of rank to exploit. If there is any will or motivation to see that the laws are obeyed and that justice is done, it must come out of the hearts of the citizenry, from the will and ability of the people to act on behalf of the greater community. It is this quality, rather than fear or ambition, that makes things work in a democracy. This quality is la vertu.

This quality involves, we may now notice, not a single talent or gift, but two. In the first place, a right heart is required, a willing spirit, a motivation toward the good of the country, or in the words of a recent biographer of Montesquieu, "general affection for the human race."[20] In the second place, activity is required. A right spirit is not enough. The good will must be translated into the acts of citizenship. *La vertu* calls for "l'action féconde," and in *Persian Letters,* Usbek says we cannot give this name to a sentiment if nothing results from it.[21] Thus double gift or capacity, taken rather as a double-sided unit than as two separate qualities, is what Montesquieu means by *la vertu.*

Our whole point in this discussion is to catch sight of Montesquieu's notion of the animating principle of a republic. But if we turn around and simply translate *la vertu* by the simple English opposite, virtue, we will have minimized our chances of preserving this glimpse. We will have to row against the stream to remember what Montesquieu has in mind. For the word "virtue" in English brings in a connotation of the moralistic, puritanical idea of "niceness" that it has acquired in Anglo-Saxon manners. We must find an alternative word or phrase. One possibility would be a longish circumlocution, such as "commitment to one's greater community expressed in acts of citizenship." But that is far too cumbersome. A shorter substitute is "willed initiative," and it is this phrase that we will ordinarily use to translate Montesquieu's term *la vertu.* It conveys the idea that the citizen of a republic finds the beginning of his participation in governance in his own inner spirit, but that this spirit takes the form of action, and especially that kind of action that expresses willingness: initiative. Another closely corresponding term, which we will also use on occasion to translate *la vertu* is "voluntaryism," a word much beloved of contemporary American church historians to express the general spirit of much of the community life in America. This term indicates that the motive of public action is voluntary, and that in a republic that operates by voluntary structuring, there will be a large number of freely chosen associations, religious freedom, and stress upon willingness to obey the law.[22]

There are further nuances to the meaning of *la vertu.* It involves renouncing self, says Montesquieu, "always a very hard thing to do," and he goes on to include in the positive attitude and effort of "love of the law and of country" a continual preference of the public interest to one's private interest. So central is willed initiative to the citizen of a republic, we can say, that not only the maintenance of the government rests on it, but ultimately one's own personal integrity does, too. The republic introduces a new human environment. Henceforth one can be his best self, no matter what his concern—public or private, political or social, religious or personal—only if his attitude in *all* undertakings shares in the spirit of willed, outgoing initiative.

Only when this spirit remains both passional and active, only when it keeps alive both foci, inclination and performance, does the republic escape ruin. If we are speaking of a democracy, not even settled forms of organization, law, and delegated agencies are enough: they are indispensable, but not enough. In order to preserve a democratic government, it is necessary that the people love it. "Everything depends, then, on establishing this love in the republic."[23] And this love cannot be displayed either in a purely sentimental emotion, or in a blind activism. Perhaps one of the reasons Montesquieu favors aristocracy, as among republics, and monarchy, as among all the forms of government, is that the odds are not so high against them. To anticipate our analysis of the American ethos in Part Two, we can already foresee that one element of crisis perennially present in the American republic is the difficulty of maintaining willed initiative.

The story is quite different with monarchies, where politics moves forward by other means, and depends on *la vertu,* or general willed initiative, as little as possible. If the structure of law and of supporting agencies to the crown is properly elaborated, the state will go on whether there is love of country or not, whether there is self-renunciation or not, whether there is sacrifice of one's own interests or not. Such a monarchy can thrive without exhibiting all of "the virtues that we find in the ancients," and indeed we may not ever have seen these virtues of antique republics practiced in monarchies as we know them today.[24] If a monarchy need not depend on the willed initiative of its citizenry, that is because it has another avenue of governance, another motivating principle. This is the principle of *honor,* or as we might better put it, the employment of rules of status, distinction, and preference as a basis of recruiting supporters of the monarchy. The motivation is the aspiration to standing (or "status seeking," as we might put it in colloquial English). In a monarchy, of course, some ranks are born with status and are brought up to conserve it, as in the case of a hereditary nobility. But Montesquieu also allows a place for the attainment of standing on the basis of quality or merit, quite apart from hereditary honor. In any case, the principle of honor contemplates that one will serve his country—or more precisely, his monarch—not out of self-renunciation, but out of pride or ambition, the wish to be honored for one's standing, station, or lineage. Thus honor stands in direct contrast with what is called for in a pure democracy, where everything depends, as we have seen, on the act of unselfish willing, on voluntary agency on behalf of the commonwealth. We can then descry, if we hold willed initiative and honor side by side as alternate motifs of governance, a complementary set of themes. In fact, we can go on to say that these two modalities of action are not exclusively to be found only in the forms of government with which Montesquieu theoretically links them—willed initiative with republican government, and honor with monarchy. Taken together, they represent the acceptable extremes of all moderate, structured government, and each form of action offers a solution to the problem of governance that overcomes a defect in the other.

Although human beings are capable of governing themselves, on Montesquieu's view, human nature is for all that still frail, and a government that is constituted on the lines of pure and simple love of country alone risks failure at any moment. Thus the alternate equipment of government by status and rank is not to be rejected. Indeed, most of the time Montesquieu seems to think it is to be preferred. For in a monarchy, too, Montesquieu is clear, the wish for justice and integrity can have its place. And even when governance is structured in hierarchical form, beginning with the monarch, and descending through successive strata of rank and station, there is still room for the introduction of some elements of willed initiative among those who are capable of it.

There is indeed a strong resemblance between willed initiative and honor, especially as these two principles stand together, over against fear, the motivating principle of government in a despotism. They are both possible enabling forces for structured, temperate government. True, honor, unlike willed initiative, does not require that everyone know what the general interest is, or that all will it and act responsibly in seeing that it is executed. In a monarchy, one serves rather by filling his role, and one derives his pride and his satisfaction from his status. Yet, as Althusser argues, honor "is the economy of virtue."[25] Honor, that is, performs the same things as virtue at less psychic price, for it does not require the day-to-day or even minute-by-minute exertion of personal, existential will that is demanded in a republic. If Montesquieu prefers the atmosphere of monarchy and chooses honor as the best means of governance, it is in part because honor in its distinctive style can perform elliptically what willed initiative has to do by existential sweat and tears and by the expenditure of prodigious energies. Honor proceeds to organize and move the country by arousing those passions that are born through admiration for station, rank, condition, rather than through the self-renunciation of patriotism, the ascetic, evangelical condition of love of greater community. Willed initiative veritably depends on a conversion of the populace and the perpetual testifying of one's faith, expressed in acts of love to the commonwealth. The likeness in achievement and the contrast in motivation, in fact, makes us wonder if these two spirits, honor and willed initiative, are not far more bound together ontologically than Montesquieu recognizes. They seem to be related in much the same way as such Puritan thinkers as Jonathan Edwards linked inward and outer approaches to morality. He spoke of "two kinds of beauty"— the inner beauty of willing consent to being, leading to "cordial union," and the external, secondary beauty of doing the law conscientiously, following the objective course of justice—which may get the same things done, but without the inner appreciation of being that stemmed from the former kind of beauty.[26]

We have postponed a look at the driving principle behind aristocracies—a form of republic—until we understood what Montesquieu means by both *la vertu* and by honor. For the aristocracy partakes of both principles. In a pure democracy, as we saw, what is crucial is that all the fortunes of the greater community are bound up with the single modality of "love of country." Such willed initiative for the commonwealth is also important in an aristocracy, but it is not the only mode of action that keeps government going, nor does the country's fate depend on the loving, active citizenship of the populace as a whole. This effort may fall only upon the chosen leaders, the aristocracy. In an aristocracy, the body of the people will depend on the nobles for prizing and guarding the rule of law. This means there is still a place for willed initiative, for love of country, for active performance to express one's commitment; but it is the nobility upon whom this burden primarily rests. There is, of course, a subtle problem here, one that always arises when a limited group of the people asserts itself in leadership. This is the problem of the political integrity of these leaders. If it is true that certain advantages over pure democracy flow, in an aristocracy, from the people's entrusting the rule of law to a body of nobles, there is still always the problem of how these leaders will be properly checked upon. It is the old, old question: who will be the custodian of the custodians? And Montesquieu is well aware of the risks: "Such is the nature of this form of government, that it seems to put the same men both under the law and exempt them from it."[27] Such leaders, he suggests, can responsibly govern in one of two manners. Either they can proceed through the display of the most heroic form of *la vertu,* placing themselves on the same footing of equality with their people (if this could actually be done, says a skeptical Montesquieu, the result would be a very great republic indeed!); or else, they can settle for a modified version of *la vertu.* Under the latter, they can at least declare as operative the rule of equality and shared initiative among themselves. In other words, they can rule through restraint or moderation, curbing ambition, leaving some influence to the people, balancing the power of magistrates with shortness of their terms, and relying on the all-important institution of law to render justice.[28]

Each of the governments we have viewed closely so far—democracy, monarchy, aristocracy—are governments of law, depending on organized and structured distribution of power, utilizing an appropriate combination of law, morality, and manners. (Admittedly, Montesquieu is more nervous about pure democracy than either of the other two.) Radically opposed to all of these governments, with their motivations of willed initiative, pride in status, and moderation, is the great symbolic opposite of "the spirit of the law" itself—despotism, to which we have already paid glancing attention. Despotism is a threat on the horizon and in the memory. More than that, it is ontologically real in human nature. In potency there is such a thing as complete despotism. Viewed as threat, it can invade the form of any government, given the possibility of corruption of political bodies.

Despotism has actually appeared in the monarchy of France in times past. The only salvation against despotism is structured government in accordance with the spirit and nature of the community. The passion that drives in a despotism, as we have seen, is fear. For in such a system willed initiative is quite unnecessary, and a sense of honor would be dangerous. Thus instead of structure animated by these drives, the despotism operates through the arbitrary dispensing of power. "The immense power of the prince is transmitted entirely to those whom he chooses." Men who are capable of thinking for themselves—either in the self-sacrificing rationale of the democrat, or in the ambitious rationale of pride—would be all too likely to think in terms of revolution. It is thus necessary that fear be evoked to control those outbreaks of courage and of humanity of which men are always capable, and to quell the sentiments of ambition. Whenever the despot cannot instantly destroy those to whom he has handed power, all is lost.[29]

(b) The Republic: Equality in Reorganizing Space

Now let us look at the same data, this time not so much from the viewpoint of the proper spirit and mode of action as of the configuration of community space that is implied in the various forms of government.

Just as there are, broadly speaking, three forms of government, we can discern three configurations of community space in Montesquieu's political theory.

The easiest case, again, is the despotism, which consists quite simply of unorganized community space. In Althusser's succinct characterization, "Despotism is indeed a political idea, the idea of absolute evil, the idea of the very limit of politics as such. The first characteristic of despotism is its being a political regime which has, so to speak, no structure."[30]

In truth the despotism not only consists of blank space, it also consists in the temporal dimension of nontime. A despotism has no time dimension, no past of institutions or tradition to make use of in the present hour, no future of human institutions that it anticipates serving. It is a "regime of the instant." But if it has no time, that means it takes up its being wholly in space, albeit empty, unorganized space. This space is the vast empire, the natural habitat of the despot. One of its characteristics is excess (excessive space, which requires excessive power to keep in subjugation, all of which contrasts with the structures, restraints, and moderation of the other forms of government, which retain jurisdiction over moderate spatial limits). But for all this excessive spatial spread, the despotism consists of structureless terrain, desert space only. Despotism, says Althusser, is for Montesquieu "temps sans durée," but also "espace sans lieu."[31]

Next we may consider the government of a true monarchy, as distinguished from a despotism. The power of the monarch, too, is absolute—but not arbitrary. When a prince reigns, the power of governance flows from him, but unlike the case of the despot, the true monarch does not distribute his power arbitrarily or capriciously, or from moment to moment. In the monarchical government, the space of the community is organized into perduring subordinate agencies that wield power. This power, to be sure, must derive from the monarch. But when the power is distributed according to law, it acquires a relative transcendence from its source, and the subordinate receptacles of power are accordingly enhanced and given endurance in the commonwealth by this partial acquired power. For the monarchy, then, the space of the community is not held as a blank fief by the prince. This space rather is organized by what Montesquieu calls the tempering or mediating institutions, usually well warranted in community tradition, that serve as liaison between monarch and the well-being of the people.

At this point, as at others, Montesquieu's preference for aristocratic (not to say feudal) forms is apparent. Let us grant that he addresses a crucial issue, the necessity of securing strictures, restraints, and counterweights upon monarchy. At times, indeed, he seems to think this is a more important item than the question whether government is monarchical or aristocratic. But there is a left-handed motive discernible here. This concern for structure, under the circumstances, not only serves the ends of governance, it offers a continuing role in modern statecraft to the nobility.

He contemplates a wider variety of restraining agencies, we must add, than the nobility, though this body comes first in honor. The "intermediary corps" consists in addition of the local *parlements,* court officers, ecclesiastics, intendants (regional administrative officers), and provincial and municipal authorities. Each of these agencies may be liable in itself, of course, to corruption and the temptations of acquired power. But each one, despite that danger, has its special function of contributing in its own best way to "tempering" the monarchy. [32] The intermediate institutions are thus both susceptible of evil and yet necessary, since power arrests power. Every man who has acquired power is sorely tempted to abuse it. He will wish to use it to the very utmost limits—hence the appropriateness of "moderation" as the animating principle of the optimum tempering body, the aristocracy.[33]

When he thinks historically of the need for tempering agencies in France, the reign of Louis XIV naturally comes to mind, and Montesquieu manages to suggest, on the basis of this example, that without tempering institutions, even the monarchy of France may evince more or less the character of a despot. Louis XIV had moved some distance in that direction by destroying resistance to the excesses of his authority. Thus, after all, Montesquieu's interest in nobility is by no means purely a reactionary conservatism. It has the same function, in this historical context, that Magna Carta had four hundred years earlier in England.

We have to imagine the community's space as hierarchically or vertically organized in a monarchy, for the "vertical" notion of pride in station and in role explains, let us recall, all of the passion of the subordinate agencies, with the single exception of the aristocracy, which operates both through honor and willed initiative. We must also think of this vertical organization of community space as symmetrical, since Montesquieu fears unrestrained popular rule as well as the unrestrained rule of a despot. Thus another function of the intermediary corps is to mediate and provide a structural outlet for the popular will as well as for the power of the king.[34]

On the whole, then, in Montesquieu's view, the properly organized monarchical community, with its various agencies of transmission and communication between prince and people, makes for the most stable and productive of governments, saves both princes and subjects from their peculiar temptations to excess, and ultimately encourages humanization. It is a system that, through a vertical organization, eventually confers part of the community's space on the subjects themselves although not in the same way as happens in a republic:[35]

> It is in monarchies that we will see the subjects gathered around the prince to receive the transmitted glory of the sovereign. Each person thus occupies a larger space, as it were, and can exercise those gifts that give the soul not independence but dignity.

In a monarchy, then, we enter the domain of those forms of government in which the people begin to find themselves enjoying the space of the community, and in a sense, having a share in this communal space. Speaking in the spatial metaphor, monarchy is a midway point between despotism and republican government. In a despotism no one can claim any space of his own. In a republic the people, as we shall see, participate originally in the organizing (or reorganizing) of community space. In a monarchy, the space is distributed from the top down, but the subjects do enjoy a limited occupancy of the community space in the sense of conferred dignity if not of independence and self-governance.

At this point, logically, we should take account of a defect or hiatus in Montesquieu's understanding of the organization of community space. Though committed to the principle of tempering agencies, he has none of the modern sense of improvisation. He normally thinks of traditional institutions as the only viable agencies of moderation and restraint. The adoption of old institutions to new functions, the replacement of a dilapidated structure by a more suitable contemporary innovation, are possibilities that seem not to have occurred to him. But this difficulty with his approach to governmental structure is best considered when we take up the question of the "time dimension" of political institutions. Here, we are principally discussing the "space" of politics.

At last we are ready to examine the configuration of the space of republics. The space of a pure democracy is simply visualized: it is uniform and completely filled. In pure form, it is precisely the opposite of the space of a despotism which, we recall, was desert empty, devoid of structure. The space of a monarchy was partially, irregularly, and vertically elaborated by historic moderating and mediating agencies. But the space of a democracy is uniformly filled with participants in the governmental process. In other words, the spatial principle of a pure democracy is *equality*, which corresponds in democratic polity to the *caprice* of a despot, and to the *radiated dignity* which characterizes personal space in a monarchy.

We are not surprised to find that Montesquieu views with some distaste the uniformity of the organization of space in a democracy. He prefers, as ever, a preorganized space for the people to come into and enjoy. And yet, he gives us a convincing argument—not against equality as such, but in favor of a creative form of equality, and against the dead-level monotony of the pure democracy, which Montesquieu regards as destructive to the human project. This latter form of equality he refers to, with some illogic, as "extreme" equality, and he gives us a carefully wrought critique to differentiate it from another form of equality that is found in moderate governments.

What is the difference between excessive equality and the more moderate form of it? True equality, first, lies somewhere between outright inequality and a mindless obsession with uniformity. The first of these extremes, to be sure, leads in a direction that Montesquieu might applaud, for inequality can be compatible with monarchy or even with an aristocracy and still afford some scope to human dignity. But the other extreme, that of fixation upon equality at the price of other values, is to be rejected out of hand. Why? In a word, because excessive passion for equality may lead to denial of the form of government itself.

But let us amplify a bit Montesquieu's argument against the spirit of excess equality. This deleterious state of affairs does not result from just *too much* equality; in fact, it is not a quantitative notion at all. It is a qualitatively different structure of community space, as far removed from the proper spirit of equality, he says, as earth is from heaven.[36]

What is proper equality? It is certainly not the sort of arrangement by which anyone at all, willy-nilly, may expect to assert himself to be a leader. Nor does true equality mean that anyone may, at his own option, ask to be exempt from the burdens of leadership. Proper equality is rather the willingness of the citizen to place himself under the leadership *of his equals;* and it is also the willingness to lead, to function in authority *over one's equals*. The point is that these functions are arranged among equals, who continue to be acknowledged as such, even though the functions are not equal. In this kind of community, one does not seek to be a master or have a master, but to have one's equal as his master, and to exert mastery only as the equal of other men.

He is committed elsewhere to monarchy and aristocracy, but Montesquieu enters for the moment the spirit of this sort of state. He is entirely convincing, even passionately persuasive, in his advocacy of temperate equality. Men are naturally able to participate in this kind of equality, he asserts, although they are unable to maintain and sustain it without elaborated legal structures. Society, alas, has by and large taken this natural, moderate form of equality away from men, and that is why we need communities organized by constitutions and law, to set up once again the conditions for the emergence of true equality.

"Such is the difference," he concludes, "between a democracy that is ruled by law and one that is not. In the first, men are equal as citizens, and in the second, they are all equally magistrates, senators, judges, fathers, husbands, and masters."[37] In other words, equality properly puts all men on an equal basis of being responsible for willing the good of the country. Proper equality means that every man is obligated to act through "willed initiative." But the channels into which this love of country flows must vary, must follow the contours of law, manners, personal gifts. In an extreme democracy, the people do not merely share the responsibility for supporting the country. They all assert a claim, equally, to rule, and to be exempt from rule. In an extreme democracy, when all are able to imagine themselves installed in the office of rulership, jealousy of those actually in authority soon sets in. And jealousy of the particular magistrate in power leads on inevitably to resentment of the very office of magistracy, and of the very fact of power. The man who sets himself up as an adversary of those who govern soon becomes enemy not just of the parties in charge of the government, but of the foundations of government itself.

Even in a democracy, then, the principle of equality cannot properly be understood as purely uniform self-assertion. A republic that is filled with equals who are not able to tolerate a provisional and functional "vertical" reorganization of community space is just as subversive of the good society as is despotism.

And yet, the note of participation remains strong here, perhaps stronger than Montesquieu himself allowed. One "gets into" the society by commitment to it. Thereafter this participation, which stamps the citizen once and for all as the equal of other citizens, enters him also into the pool or reservoir of contenders or possible choices for leadership. At the very least, he is to be asked to give his consent to the schemes and programs of leadership, since that is what is implied in being led, in a democracy founded on equality. Thus even in a moderate democracy the citizen does not find himself without space to stand on, as in a despotism, nor living on borrowed space, as in a monarchy, but offering the space that is indisputably his to the community. The point is, he is able to dispose of his space.[38]

(c) *The Republic: The Revolutionary Time Dimension*

Though we have been concentrating on the symbol of space, we have already encountered the significance of time for governance in two connections. In our discussion of despotism, we found that it could be characterized as a state with no time dimension at all, as a regime of the instant depending upon the contingent will of the ruler. In our discussion of the true monarchy, we were led to conceive it as a state that depends essentially on time-binding institutions to limit, restrain, and moderate the power of the ruler.

Because the despot does not commit himself to the reliable distribution of power through law, he has no need of precedents, on which lawful administration depends. Nor does he require time-binding institutions that conserve the best in community tradition, or sanctions from history, to give the community its identity. His own supreme person is the identity of the community.

The true monarch, on the other hand, relies essentially on time-tempered institutions and on a reliable structure of law, which means the government finds itself dependent on the traditions and precedents thrown up on the shore of the present by history. In fact, we may conceivably discuss Montesquieu's whole notion of the moderating agencies as a species of time filter proposing the tests of history as means of checking power and assigning dignity to the people.

What, then, of the time dimension in a republic?

Before we embark on this discussion, let us take up a prior problem, the more general issue of Montesquieu's understanding of the past. So far we have established only one point, and this is that Montesquieu has a high regard for antiquity, the lessons of history, and the institutions of governance forged by precedent and tradition. There is a strongly beneficent side of this conservatism. By recovering ancient institutions—Montesquieu was thinking above all of the historical situation in his own country—the monarchy could be tempered with mediating structures, the threat of despotism could be surmounted, and contemporary France could become a commonwealth offering justice and dignity. As Dedieu puts this side of the case, in such a state, aware of its own tradition, the prince can be "all powerful for good, and powerless to do evil, because he has around him the privileged corps that interposes itself between his rights and those of his subjects; because there is a safeguarding of the laws, an independent justice, and powers that counterbalance the exorbitant power of one man alone and rebuff despotism."[39]

One can readily see here already why Montesquieu, certainly no conscious revolutionary himself, was yet so celebrated in revolutionary America. This kind of political theory calls up the gravest sanctions of history against irresponsible monarchy, and seemed to be a prescription for the very plight the American colonists thought they must overcome before they could be themselves: it was all a question of recovering, from the despot, their own ancient rights as Englishmen. (The fact that George III was more to be characterized as an inept ruler than a tyrant, or that the real oppressor was Parliament, need not put us off at the moment. The colonists did suffer from extrinsic control of their space, and thus they were visited with the deleterious effects of despotism. It is unfortunate that George became its symbol.)

There is another side of this interest in the past on the part of our author, of course. Montesquieu was a feudalist as well as a noble. In some ways his feudalist affinities come through more strongly than his affiliation with the nobility. Indeed, his criticisms of the unrestrained monarch may be the best sign. For the feudal system, unlike the nobility, stood on historic foundations independent of the crown, whereas nobles owed their standing to the royal act of conferral.

Montesquieu thinks in concert with those forces before the Revolution that favored a decentralized monarchy checked in its powers by the Estates General and by provincial aristocrats. He is not in sympathy with the coalition of royalist and bourgeois forces led by the Abbé Debos, Abbé de Mably, Argenson, and others, including the Encyclopedists and Voltaire, all of whom condemn feudalism and are more or less willing to countenance an enlightened despotism as the way to promote *le bonheur.* If Montesquieu, like Thomas Jefferson, must be accounted as one of the most enlightened men of his time, he must also, again like Jefferson, be seen to manifest some formidable conservative sentiments. If the *Persian Letters* are to be accounted a pioneer document of the Enlightenment, the defense of the feudal laws in *The Spirit of the Laws* can be read as a frank accolade to the past, and the whole of his masterpiece has been termed by Méthivier, admittedly an acerb critic, a "monument to aristocratic thought." One too easily forgets, adds Méthivier, that Baron Montesquieu, the parliamentarian, *philosophe,* cultural critic, irreligionist, and admirer of merit in government, is also "a pure feudalist, defender of all the feudal rights and privileges." He justifies the seigneurial laws, discounts the fiscal responsibility of the nobility, and makes too much over the pretended blue blood of the noble race.[40] Indeed, such self-interest might take the form of defense of privilege all the more in the case of a latecomer to the nobility. "Let us recall," says Kassem, also a frequent critic of the Gascon baron, "that the Montesquieus were not introduced naturally in their nobility; it is only toward the end of the sixteenth century that the Montesquieu land upon the left bank of the Garonne, bought by John II of Secondat, was made into a barony."[41]

Still and all, it would be cruel and unusual to read no more than vanity (though it may indeed be present) into Montesquieu's defense of nobility. When he is discussing the structure of a monarchy, he gives an altogether plausible argument for a hereditary nobility. The noble should be confirmed in his office not as a barrier between prince and people but as a connecting link between them. But if the noble is to stand up against the prince as a separate entity, he should be confirmed in his space in a fashion analogous to security of the prince in his realm. Thus "the lands of the nobles, as well as their persons, should be privileged." Just as one "cannot separate the glory of the prince from that of his realm," so one cannot separate the dignity of the noble from that of his domain. These are no doubt inconveniences, "but they disappear when compared with the general usefulness of the nobility."[42]

This will sound like unwarranted and outrageous privilege to any decent American democrat, of course. But that is just the point. If we are to have a monarchy, it is necessary to deal with the monarch in kind. In another chapter, where Montesquieu is discussing the character of an aristocratic *republic,* he pictures the dangers of precisely this form of nobility. In this sort of state, with its basic standing as a republic, the "extreme of corruption" is threatened when the nobles become hereditary, for their security makes it difficult for them to evince moderation.[43]

An aristocracy can maintain its own peculiar strengths only if the laws are such that they make the nobility feel more the risks and a fatigue of authority than its delights; and if the government always has something to dread. . . . Fear of the Persians induced among the Greeks respect for their laws. Carthage and Rome, by menacing each other, also strengthened each other. Strangely, the more these states enjoy security, the more they are liable to become corrupted, like stagnant water.

Barckhausen thinks this is one of "the most obscure" passages in *The Spirit of the Laws.* And indeed, when it is compared with Montesquieu's defense of the privileges of nobility elsewhere, we do seem plunged deeper into confusion. Yet we have only to recall that when he defends the hereditary aristocracy he is actually considering how the laws should develop the principle of *honor* in a monarchy ("Comment les lois sont relatives à leur principe dans la monarchie"). Honor is both "parent and child" to the nobility, and can be sustained only as the nobility itself is nourished and perpetuated.[44] But in republics, honor is no longer the operative principle. It is still present, but it is subordinated to restraint and a form of willed initiative that the leaders practice among themselves. What must happen to the governing structures in a republic? They must be nourished too, but nourished not by protection and privilege; they must be nourished by criticism and reform.

We are now ready to make our chief point, and that is the status of the time dimension in the constitution and development of republics. The despotism is, so to speak, punctiform; it has no time dimension. The tempered monarchy has been shaped out of a past that nourishes it and makes it a creature allied with time. What of the republic? Logically, if we can show that republican sentiments arise out of the protest against despotism, then we can argue that republics *found* and *inaugurate* a time for their peoples.

But this hypothesis involves a strong element of discontinuity in time, an approach to time that we do not customarily associate with Montesquieu. For the most part, Montesquieu understands states as "natural" outgrowths of ecological conditions ("climate") when confronted with the shaping effects of moral forces (law, manners, religion, and so on). Democratic government may have been suitable for the small city-states of antiquity, but monarchy, properly moderated and tempered, was the natural form of state for France. But what of a new greater community, such as was building among the colonies of the New World?

Montesquieu does not develop the special case of American polity. Nevertheless, his elaboration in some degree of the theory of the federated republic of republics shows that he was at least open to new configurations of statehood. And yet he did not draw out his logic sufficiently to make his case. I wish to contend that there is one special case in which government, on Montesquieu's own principles, is reorganized in sharp discontinuity with its own past. This reorganization, I contend, is not sufficiently described as a simple reform (a possibility which Montesquieu clearly allows for), but must be understood to occur by a phenomenon that he does not explicitly provide for—revolution.

This is the case of a colony in an overextended empire, where the benefits of moderate government may obtain at the center, but where the lines of governance are stretched so tautly that extrinsic control, or despotism, has to be resorted to at the periphery. Such, for example, was eventually the case with imperial Rome and its provinces:[45]

Liberty existed at the center, but tyranny was felt in the outlying parts.
. . . When Rome . . . extended her conquests, the senate was no longer
able to keep direct watch on the provinces, and the magistrates at
Rome could no longer govern the empire. It was necessary to send out
praetors and proconsuls . . . who had powers combining those of all
the magistrates in Rome, and even those of the senate and people.
They were despotic magistrates, well suited to the distance of the
places to which they were sent.

Now, if we imagine this kind of extrinsic control to be visited upon
a transplanted colonial people who come from a tradition that
stresses moderate, tempered government, we may justifiably conclude
that a hue and cry may be set up by the colonists calling for restoration of the older forms. On Montesquieu's own terms, let us recall,
men are always able to appreciate the blessings of a just order, no
matter what their present condition. If, in addition, they have the
historic memory of a lost justice, they are all the more capable of
calling for an overturn. Let us suppose just one more thing: that the
ecology of the new space occupied by the colonists conduces more to
a republic, or a federation of republics, than it does for a reduplication of the tempered monarchy. All of the ingredients are present for
revolution.

Let us be clear, however. We are not attempting to make Montesquieu over into a revolutionary theorist of the contemporary sort.
He was, without doubt, as Hugh Trevor-Roper suggests, in some
ways "at heart, a republican and deist," and a *reformer*—but "how
could anyone think of the Président de Montesquieu as a revolutionary?"[46] Let us remember, on the other hand, that a revolution in the
earliest modern sense meant precisely an overthrow of a corrupt or
usurping government in order to restore a more ancient order. Given
Montesquieu's view that there is a certain natural form of government
for every greater community—a certain natural form that can confer
dignity and justice—the overthrow of a corrupt government can be
seen as a consistent development.

One simply cannot put together the despot and the willed initiative
of the republican citizen without getting a revolution. And the best
evidence that revolution is constructively implied in Montesquieu's
republican theories is seen in his own subsequent standing as ideo-

logue to the American Revolution. Despite his erstwhile monarchist, aristocratic affinities, Montesquieu became, for the American patriots, "a veritable oracle in the struggle for political liberty."[47] His celebrated chapter on the British Constitution was, in this sense, not so much a primer in political science, as a goad to resistance.

It is true that Montesquieu does not envision justice as an abstract right that can come apart from the development of the historical possibilities of a greater community. But it is also true that when the form of government is despotic, and justice is out of the question, and when there are men of self-esteem in a community, revolution is to be feared. Montesquieu says so directly: "As virtue is necessary in a republic, and honor in a monarchy, fear is necessary in a despotic government: for virtue is not at all necessary, and honor would be dangerous. . . . Men capable of much self-esteem would be men who would make revolutions."[48] Modern, enlightened men, Montesquieu is fully aware, would no longer accept the lot of misery. Social assistance is needed not only to prevent suffering, but is simply a wise precaution to fend off revolution that would otherwise be likely.[49]

To predict a revolution is not the same as to advocate one. It is true that we have to extract the whole category of revolution from a reluctant author. In his formal statements, we find little or nothing about the formal category of revolution. Montesquieu is cautious, indeed, when he is thinking directly about change in the form of government.[50] But our point is that there is, in effect, a lacuna here in Montesquieu's views about the time dimension of republics. If he had forced himself to develop his theory of republics all the way, we believe, he would have provided a place for revolution. Indeed, we see something of this process underway in miscellaneous fragments of his political thought, especially in the *Pensées*. He declares that liberty is obtained only through bold *coups d'éclat* but "it is lost through insensible force." Again, in a short discussion of the government of England, he asks whether "it is permissible to resist tyranny"? He decides that it does not make good sense to insist that the authority of the prince be more sacred than that of the law that the prince refuses to follow. Civil war may be understood not only as the resistance of the subjects to the prince, but also as a conflict produced "when the prince does violence to his subjects."[51]

Princes are mortal; the Republic is eternal. The empire of the prince is transient; obedience to the Republic does not end. There is then no greater evil, none with more deadly consequences, than the toleration of tyranny that perpetuates it into the future.

Considering the same question in another section—"Is there a case in which it may be permitted to a subject to disobey his prince? —Montesquieu answers: "It is very dangerous to a prince to have subjects who obey him blindly." If the emperor of the Incas had not had subjects who followed him as dumb beasts, they could have prevented a handful of Spaniards from conquering them.[52]

A free people, Montesquieu argues elsewhere in the Pensées, is not to be identified with this or that form of government. A free people is rather one that has a form of government established and safeguarded by law—i.e., tempered monarchies and republics. Nor can oppression be limited by the form of government. One cannot doubt, he says, that the subject peoples of Indonesia regard it as "cruel servitude" to be governed by the Holland Company[53]—another example of the special kind of despotism that may be found in remote colonial outposts.

Because Montesquieu's intention is to criticize monarchy, and not to plumb the depths of the republican experiment (at times he seems to think republics are a thing of the past), he has simply not worked out the time dimension of republics. We have suggested by extrapolation, however, that the outcome of self-esteem and willed initiative in situations of colonial subjection to despotism may well be overthrow of the prince—or revolution. A revolution of this sort, let us remember, is not total or even radical in the contemporary sense. It is not committed to novelty. The object of such a revolution is to recover liberty, to secure once again the freedom from fear and the right to be governed by law and by a moderate government. Revolution in this sense may be a greater community's way of recovering its own essence.

Thus a republic may be founded in revolution. It takes up a new time, or reenters time, but it is a special kind of time. It is a time that is shaped by the revolutionary impulse. For republics may have to depend not only on the day-to-day application of willed initiative by the citizenry, they may have to be reconstituted from time to time by new revolutionary impulses, especially when the spirit of willed initiative fails, a new despotism succeeds, and it is time once again for forceful, swift blows for liberty. The time dimension of republican government may and certainly does involve the usage of such historical institutions as can be shaped to the ecology and spirit of the new community. But it also involves the periodic freeing of these institutions from extrinsic control. And we cannot limit these tides of liberty and relapse to governmental affairs. In the republic, the whole of common life may be understood under the same conception of time. The revolutionary impulse comes in education, race relations, women's role in society, and in the whole of manners. For becoming a human being in a republic means clearing existential and community space of extrinsic control. In a republic this clearing-out process goes on in every domain of life, and across time. Life in a republic depends on periodic reform, and in some areas and epochs, on perennial revolution.[54]

(d) *The Dimensions of Republican Government: Summary*

We have arrived, then, at three dimensions of republican government, based on our examination of the political thought of Montesquieu. These dimensions—now rearranged from the order in which it was convenient first to consider them—are the time, space, and quality of human action that may be associated with the manners and morals of a republican greater community.

Temporally, the occasion for the foundation of a republican community is the impulse to recover personal and common space from extrinsic control. We have inferred that revolution—at least in the "conservative" sense—may be the normative occasion for the establishment of a republic. By extension, the revolutionary impulse may be applied not only to governmental predicament, but to all precincts in which human life is threatened, compressed, or strangled by extrinsic control.

Spatially, the generic form of moral predicament in a republic is the confiscation of personal and communal space by a "despot" or extrinsic controller, who forbids participation in reorganizing the space. The outcome of reform or revolution may be visualized as the reappropriation of one's own space. The empty desert of outside control is to be succeeded by the furnishing of space with the institutions of community participation. There is thus a principle of equality at work in this spatial reorganization, although it must be an equality that seeks to reorganize, rather than disorganize, the community.

Juxtaposing, for a moment, the time and space dimensions, we may say that the quest for equality is never complete at a given moment, but that it goes on, entering new areas of community life, as the republic forms itself in history.

Qualitatively, the form of action in a republic is willed initiative— a voluntary preference for the commonwealth embodied in concrete action. The most difficult aspect of republican life is maintaining this spirit, which may fade at any time, or relapse in the false security of thinking only of past gains. Willed initiative must be brought to the task not only of preserving, but of widening equality, while at the same time consenting to a division of functions in which equals are allowed to govern, and in which equals agree to lead.

3. Distinctive Elements of the American Experience

After a more careful definition of "manners" in the following chapter, we will be ready to apply our categories toward organizing the American experience. We will try to see in what ways life in America stems from a revolutionary impulse, from the motif of participation in controlling existential and community space, and from willed initiative. We will seek to examine these three dimensions not just in political arrangements, but in the full spectrum of manners and morals. By way of anticipation, however, we can say now that we will not be able to conclude that these dimensions of life have been implemented fully, heroically, or even admirably in America. Each of the three dimensions, while a permanent influence on the American experience, is embodied defectively.

Human beings are ambivalent in their makeup, always pulled between their allegiance to nature and their allegiance to moral challenges. Without both elements, they would not be human beings. That is why we will not find, for example, that all Americans are "revolutionaries," but that an impressive number of them are, in fact, quite antirevolutionary in their sentiments. Our point is that the revolutionary impulse has *set the bias* for the understanding of time and history in America, but that responses to this bias are ambivalent. "America, therefore, becomes a realm of paradox: a nation born of a revolt that was moderate, yet genuinely revolutionary; a society that is liberal in its ideals, yet conservative in its behavior; united in its divisions, and divided in its unity."[55]

The theme of revolution, we shall find, has been understood in two contrasting ways. On one side are those who stress the finality of the original American Revolution and so are no longer imbued with the continuing spirit of revolution. On the other side are those who stress the incompleteness and partiality of past revolutions and so have become historically cut loose in the interest of new assertions of the revolutionary promise.

We shall find this dialectical tendency displayed in each of our three dimensions of the American ethos. There are contrasting versions of equality and disposition of space, and contrasting versions of "willed initiative," which among them will include both some of the most serious aberrations and some of the most admirable traits in the American character. But even these conflicts point to a set of issues that has been decisive and that will undoubtedly continue to shape the American experience. These conflicts further point to the future, to the unfolding of the human pageant.

In the final analysis, America still at best *hopes* to become a republic. There continue to be strong elements of "monarchy" (status-seeking, pride, intermediate agencies) and "despotism" (fear, repressive penal codes, intimidation of minority groups) at work in every historical society, including the American greater community. One of the leading purposes of a study of manners and morals is of course to clarify both these defects and our hopes.

CHAPTER III.

MANNERS

The South African surgeon who performed the world's first heart transplant, the "intellectual roughnecks" who have protested on one university campus after another in our days, and John Humphrey Noyes, who founded the Oneida Community in 1848 on the basis of perfectionism, "Bible Communism," and complex marriage, all have something in common. Each moved beyond accepted etiquette or practice in some significant community to propose a new arrangement, and each drew the criticism of a community used to old arrangements.

At this writing the new surgical procedure has been widely tested by other surgeons and seems to represent a significant innovation in the practice of the medical profession, causing in turn grave reconsiderations in the field of medical ethics. The campus protesters have been widely condemned for creating disorder and property damage and for disrupting university life, even though there is also widespread recognition that the protests point to genuine and serious failures in American education. Noyes and his community were finally rejected by their fellow Americans, who did not believe the cause represented by these irregulars justified such wide departure from conventional moral patterns.

The acts of the surgeon, the students, and the Oneida perfectionists were, to begin with, unsanctioned and untested in their communities and had the status only of bold strokes put forward to relieve a pressing human situation, or to protest a failure in the community to realize the human, or to reconstruct a new community.

Such acts may be directly contrasted with acts that we find com-

95

mended in etiquette books, which are acts that have won sanction in the appropriate community and are now put forward as illustrative of functional performance that either serve the community's purposes or, at the very least, do not interfere with them. But not only the acts endorsed in etiquette books fit this class. A student may properly complain about the insensitivity of the administration at his college by writing a letter to the student newspaper, or by speaking up in a discussion group, or even by making an appointment and having a talk with the dean or president.

Finally, there is a third class of acts that must receive a still different classification. Let us consider for a moment the status of beards on the faces of Americans. The beard on the face of a sandaled, tieless student stamps him as an agent given to unsanctioned performances of the first class of acts we have discussed. But the beard on the face of a neatly dressed man in his forties or fifties in midtown Manhattan identifies him as a possible professional of some sort—a medical man, a psychiatrist, an architect, an advertising executive. The beard is sanctioned. Finally, let us picture a man of the same age in the same part of Manhattan, but clad in brogans, overalls, and a broad-brimmed black felt hat. This man's beard identifies him with an obsolescent rural environment, given his farmer's dress, and if it is sanctioned at all it is not the sanction of currency that stands behind it, but only the fading extension of some sanction from the past.

Acts of the first class, after much testing and controversy, often pass the filter of community acceptance and move into the second class, where they serve some function for a certain time, then pass into the pantry or lumber room of the third class.

Strictly speaking, it is with acts of the second class that we are concerned in this chapter. It is with acts that have achieved the status of *manners,* or acts that have won legitimation as current practice, acts that are either eufunctional to community purpose, or at the very least not dysfunctional.

Still, we cannot limit our discussion to acts of the second class. For the acts of the first class that may seem unaccepted or even uncivilized are the most common source of new sets of manners. Acts that may seem rash or boorish today may be tomorrow's accepted manners.

Nor can we ignore acts of the third class, acts that have lost their currency. For these acts can contribute to the furnishing of new sets of manners, also, as when the Black Muslim leader Malcolm X was able to reach into the nineteenth-century pool of puritanical manners, rejected as obsolete by much of the American community, and fashion from its ingredients a new morality that played its role in the black man's new struggle. "Although many could not share his Muslim religious beliefs," says M. S. Handler, "they found in Malcolm's puritanism a standing reproach to their own lives. Malcolm had purged himself of all the ills that afflict the depressed Negro mass: drugs, alcohol, tobacco, not to speak of criminal pursuits. . . . Human redemption—Malcolm had achieved it in his own lifetime, and this was known to the Negro community."[1]

Now we can be reasonably clear, we trust, on what this chapter is about. Manners, quite literally, are the handiest means of getting along. (The word, with its French cognate, les manières, is derived from the Latin *manus,* hand.). Manners take in a class of actions, gestures, and rhetoric that are currently at hand, sanctioned by an appropriate community, to be used, as the contemporary idiom has it, for "coping."

We can distinguish manners from morals by saying, for the moment, that manners have to do generally with acts, whereas morality has to do with attitudes that shape acts. No absolute distinction can be made, but in this chapter we aim to concentrate on the performative side of the spectrum. We should also distinguish manners from customs, for the two terms are sometimes used interchangeably. We understand manners as *current customs,* and reserve the category of custom for those acts of the third class that we have discussed above —acts that have faded from currency, yet still bear some authoritative community legitimation.

1. The Topical and Profound Senses of Manners

We can see at once why manners have acquired the trivial connotation of "politeness" or civilized conduct having to do with nothing very important. For they do take in everyday social conventions. They do so in principle, as we have seen, since manners are the ready-to-wear clothing of the world of action. But it is a serious error to suppose that this shallow meaning of manners takes in the major referent of the term. Ultimately manners are the everyday, quotidian, surface manifestations of the struggle for existence and deliverance that characterizes organized human life. Contrary to the received impression, manners have most properly to do not with "social etiquette," but rather with community predicament and with moral crisis.

Unfortunately, not only in casual usage, but also in the ostensibly more precise usage of theologians, ethicists, and social scientists as well, manners continue to be thought of almost altogether in the surface modality. This is all the more strange in view of the recent tendency among these disciplines to excavate the deeper meaning that lies latent in such related terms as "culture" and "society." When we speak of "culture" in any serious way, we can think of at least two levels of meaning. There is a refined and somewhat superficial sense that we use in such phrases as "the cultured members of the community." This is a way of speaking of the exemplary learning, art, and opinion of an elite group in the community. On this view, the symphony orchestra is a part of the "culture" of my community, but the Grand Ole Opry is not. This definition seems increasingly offset, thanks to the quest for depth in contemporary studies of the human phenomenon, by a more profound conception that understands culture as the transmitted experience of an entire community, or of the human community itself; or as all of man's symbol-using, communication, and shared activity.[2]

The related term "society" may also be understood both in a profound sense and also in a topical or superficial sense. In the case of this term, the profounder meaning has made great headway in all literate circles during the past generation or so. We do not need to assume, with the editor of the " 'society' page," that the term refers primarily to the weddings, parties, travels, and benefactions of the rich, the influential, and the celebrated. In any serious conversation the term means, at par, that fragile bond of union that gathers men into groups and communities. And the word is increasingly reserved for some of our gravest reflections upon ourselves, as when we contemplate the "moral breakdown," as we are fond of putting it, that confronts "society" today.

Unlike the recent history of these two terms—"culture" and "society"—the notion of manners presents a different sort of case. Why has the profounder meaning of manners not been able to flourish competitively alongside the topical meaning?

Much light is thrown on this question in a study made some years ago by the historian A. M. Schlesinger, which sought to explore the successive understandings of conventional, polite behavior in American society as reflected in books of etiquette. In early modern times, before the nineteenth century, the profound and topical meanings of manners were bound together. Politeness and morality were so closely identified as to be "scarcely distinguishable." Manners and morals were correlative ideas (a concept, as we shall see presently, that is to be found in both Montesquieu and Tocqueville). Schlesinger takes the writings of Lord Chesterfield (1694-1773) as the turning point, after which the two aspects of manners began to be separated.[3] The rise of the middle class brought to the arena of polite, learned conduct a group that had no previously acquired cultural equipment for getting on in its new social environment, so that these classes began consciously to imitate the ways of those "they had formerly deemed to be of finer clay." What had been a natural, easily formed style of social acts to the elite now became a set of conventions to be studied and memorized by the newcomers. At this point, the conception of etiquette arose as a compendious summary of rules covering the most common needs on the new terrain. In short, "etiquette now managed to disentangle itself from ethics, taking on its modern meaning of a generalized pattern of behavior designed to lubricate social intercourse."[4] Perhaps we can liken the emergency that brought forth the etiquette book to the American tourist's trip to Europe, and his need for a language guide, which will by no means teach him French or Italian, but which will give him in phonetic English the foreign phrases that will be most useful to him.

Schlesinger concedes that the study of this new, isolated set of practices is worthwhile in itself, since "etiquette" has now become "a functional trait of civilization." But he rightly wishes to see more significance accorded the concept of manners than that implied in "the rise and progress of courtesy." Manners should be understood not as idle practices apart from life's meaning but as conduct pointing to the very center of it, "revealing men's hopes, standards and strivings." In this sense, the history of "learning how to behave" serves as a barometer of changing attitudes toward more profound matters, and, as he adds, "this is particularly true of the United States."[5]

Tocqueville, for his part, takes care to say in his study of the Americans and their democracy, that he understands manners in the older sense, "for I apply it not only to manners, in their proper sense of which constitutes the character of social intercourse, but I extend it to the various notions and opinions current among men, and to the mass of those ideas which constitute their character of mind." For Tocqueville, then, the term includes "the whole moral and intellectual condition" of the people.[6] Taken in this profounder sense—essentially the same, original meaning that we have insisted on above, with Schlesinger—manners then become, for Tocqueville, the most important artifact or medium of observation—more significant, for example, than acts of legislation—in seeing through to what is distinctive about the American people.[7] "The importance of manners is a common truth to which study and experience incessantly direct our attention. It may be regarded as a central point in the range of human observation, and the common termination of all inquiry."

If the democratic and political fact of equality, then, is the theme that Tocqueville takes to be most distinctive for understanding the Americans, it is their manners that are taken to be the most reliable media for viewing this theme as it is actually embodied in the life of the community. We agree on this central role of manners. Said in another way, one of our principal claims in this study is that the moral dimensions of a greater community may not be understood apart from an appropriate study of its manners, taken as the ensemble of acts, gestures, and rhetoric at hand, currently sanctioned, employed to cope with predicament, with threats to personal and community life. We cannot understand the ways of a society simply by attending to its laws or its political forms or its complex organizations. We must also form some rationale for viewing its manners and asking for their moral significance. We must ask for the implicit ontological connection between our acts, laws, and rhetoric, at the surface, and the inner yearnings of men, at the core. There is a hidden, latent urge toward fullness of being, toward deliverance, lying at the nerve of all our manners. It is the task of the student of manners (especially the professional ethicist) to get at this inward premonition of the promise of being. Just as the metaphysician has the task of seeking out the latent metaphysical *Ureinsicht* within humanity that has to be "thematized and made explicit" by philosophy, so the ethicist has the task of viewing this urge toward deliverance hidden (and revealed) by our manners, and to bring the inwardmost sense of crisis "out into the open in accurately defined concepts and certain judgments." This is not necessarily the task of revealing or proving something new and unknown, but it seeks to give careful expression "to what already is implicitly acknowledged without being explicitly recognized."[8] Our task, in brief, is to flesh out our study of the distinctive themes of the American ethos by viewing the distinctive American ordeal of lostness and striving as it is reflected in our manners, good and bad.[9]

2. Manners in a Republic: Complementarity with Law

Once again we will find a helpful framework for our discussion supplied by Montesquieu. As we have already seen, he approaches the human commonwealth with the view that political activity and moral activity may not be artificially separated, for they are one in being directed toward the general welfare.[10] Especially in a republic, the sentiments and activities of the citizen take on significance far beyond that of private or personal meaning, for it is the citizen's willed initiative, with its foci of commitment and action, that provide the empowerment, the quality, of the society itself.

Laws in the statutory sense, says Montesquieu, are the "special, precise institutions of the legislator," while "morals and manners" are "institutions of the nation in general." Thus morals and manners are part of the "spirit of the laws." They express usages that the laws have not formally established. In some domains, morals and manners govern us in ways that the laws are unable to, and should not be used for. There is a major difference between the purpose, or reach, of laws, and that of morals: "laws govern more the actions of the citizen, morals more the actions of the man." The same distinction separates law from manners, since manners, for Montesquieu, are an expression of morality: "There is this difference between morals and manners: the former have to do more with interior conduct, the latter more with exterior conduct."[11]

Thus the institutions of law are correlative with those of manners and morals. They both express the spirit of the nation, but each in its own way. It is a positive, mutually contributory relation, rather than a division of the kingdom of human conduct into compartments. Indeed, Montesquieu assumes that there is a dynamic interchange between these modalities. However important it is to recognize a division of function between them, they do not cease having significant interrelations.[12] Doubtless Montesquieu oversimplifies the relation when he takes up particular cases. He argues that a people with a strong moral tradition will need only simple laws. There is a grain of truth here, although he misleadingly states it. As we shall see, manners can serve as a surrogate for law in a society that depends upon the willed initiative of the citizenry. This does not imply, however, that the need of legislation is notably slackened, or that the laws can be simple in any modern society. Indeed, it may be the society with the most robust moral tradition that finds itself in need not of simple laws, but of a similarly robust and ample legal structure, so that the forces of morality and manners are not left without alternative and countercheck. Montesquieu himself points to a society in which manners and morals have all but swallowed up the other institutions, including that of law. Though in some ways, he thinks, the Chinese are well governed, in other ways this land shows rigidity, inability to change, and runs the risk, if ever the moral sense should be lost, of anarchy.[13]

Still, Montesquieu's basic point stands. There is a close and sensitive relationship between the morality of a people and its laws, and more profoundly, between the manners of a people and its model of humanity: "The customs of a slave people are a part of servitude; those of a free people are part of their liberty."[14] It is not too strong to assert, then, that "love of country conduces to sound morality [la bonté des moeurs] and sound morality leads to love of country."[15]

There is a special aspect of this problem that must be dealt with in any consideration of American manners and morals. This is the constitutional concept (which has long since also existed as a strong political and theological tradition) of "separation of church and state." From our present point of view, a more accurate phraseology would be "separation of law and manners." For the church in America, with its heterogeneous divisions, beliefs, and practices, is only one sector of a larger area covered by the principle of voluntary association and activity apart from the state. In America, the whole field of voluntary activity, including that of the churches and their adherents, constitutes the referent of "manners."

In our view, then, the primary relationship to be investigated is that prior functional division between law and manners. It is *this* complementarity that gives primordial sanction to the constitutional separation of church and state, which is only a special case of the more elemental dialectic. One of the reasons the study of manners in America has been neglected by ethicists is the prominence this secondary dialectic of church and state has assumed, blotting from vision the more profound relationship.[16] Another reason the manners-law dialectic has been ignored is the widespread assumption that there is no difference in principle between manners and law. Durkheim's view, which departs from Montesquieu's and has had wide following in America, is that "laws do not differ in nature from customs but on the contrary derive from them. They are simply customs more sharply defined."[17] We must disagree, at least for the American ethos. Laws and manners both serve people and constitution, but in correlation, and in analogy to the familiar doctrine of separation of church and state—which, indeed, as we have said, is but a partial expression of the underlying principle.

Law and manners are united in the Constitution, or rather in the making of it. For in this foundation document, the people have set out a governmental form that will permit them to dispose of their own existential and communal space. The Constitution, by an act of willed initiative, proposes a foundation for willed initiative—for the construction of meaningful life through voluntary association. In providing for this kind of community, the Constitution provides for a government of laws that will keep our living space at our disposal for voluntary association and activities. Thus manners—the ensemble of voluntary activities—and law stand together in ordaining the Constitution, and in turn, being "provided for" in the Constitution as the recognized ways of free men's lives.

In the life of the republic since the founding act of the Constitution, laws and manners then enter separate but interrelated missions.

The laws in America serve the people as the political means of organizing the space of communities. We are thinking here chiefly of the body of positive law, which has a larger purpose than keeping at bay those who would disorganize community space or establish hegemony or extrinsic control over it. In America, law also begins to furnish, equip, and arrange the living space, to make it bear fruit, and to take on the conformations of justice. Everywhere, the law pushes against those who would disorganize community space, and encourages those who would reorganize community space for greater justice and equality.

And yet by its own nature, law cannot complete the movement to realized promise in a republic that depends on willed initiative, on voluntary association, as the quality of action that makes community space new and livable. In a republic that defines willing support of community and willing cooperation with neighbor as the highest goods, law can only provide the outer form within which the inner realities of justice and equality must be built up. Faced with challenges to renew urban life, overcome poverty, and head off youngsters from careers of crime, American lawyers are becoming intensely aware of this partial character of the laws in America. At a recent meeting of the American Bar Association, one speaker—past president of the New Jersey State Bar Association—called for a new role for the legal profession. "There are some social problems which will not yield to an adjudicative solution," he insisted. The implication was that traditional legal institutions must be reshaped.[18]

Part of the solution, of course, does lie in reshaping and broadening the legal institutions. Lawyers must perhaps become better urbanologists and poverty experts—maybe even moralists of a sort. The legislative branches of Federal and state governments must be overhauled to permit more flexible responses to community and national predicament in America.

Even so, at the maximum contribution from the side of law, the problem will not be solved. There is no democratic community without an articulated legal system—true freedom, Montesquieu thought, is not simply being cut loose, but is rather being at liberty within a community in which law prevails. But law alone does not realize the promise of such a community. To travel this additional distance to its promise, the community depends on manners—that domain of conduct where willed initiative in personal and group activities is expressed.

We cannot really speak of the primacy or even the significance of either of these entities—law or manners—in a singular fashion, as an isolated phenomenon. For the very existence of a moderate government—a government that rejects extrinsic control of community space—depends on the correlation between law and manners. The two entities must be kept "separate" in the sense that neither is to be allowed to dominate or submerge the other. But the relation is one of constant mutual influence rather than of divorce.

When a community relies wholly or predominantly on law at the expense of manners to accomplish its promise, form is substituted for substance, structure for commitment. Overreliance on law minimizes the importance of willed initiative, of citizen interest in government, of voluntary association and activity. Barzini's comments on the tradition of relying heavily on legislation in Italy gives us a good example of the evils that set in from this side of unbalance. The laws themselves, if they are made the sole vehicle of justice, can become the enemy of justice:[19]

> There are too many laws in Italy. A topical tangle of statutes, rules, norms, regulations, customs, some hundreds of years old, some voted last week by Parliament and signed this very morning by the President, could paralyze every activity in the land, stop trains, planes, cars, and ships, shut every shop, industrial plant, hospital, school, and office, if they were suddenly applied.

In such a land, not only is there less premium placed on personal initiative; the alternative that is supposed to be relied on in its place, the law, itself becomes trivialized. On the one hand, there is a curious Italian superstition that when things go wrong, problems seem to get out of hand, nothing seems to work, "a new law is usually passed, often too difficult and complicated to be applied properly, in the hope that it will have thaumaturgic effects." But that leads to a proliferation of law, with inevitable contradictions and impossible statutes. In the end the whole affair may be treated with contempt. Finally, the force of the law becomes subjective, changing according to the influence or standing of the person who is involved. For the rich and for those who know the right people, taxes tend to be milder. In short, everything in the end turns out to be "not a balancing of legal rights but a confrontation of pure power."[20]

The opposite case of misplaced emphasis is just as evil. When a people relies on manners at the expense of law to accomplish its ends, kinship and propinquity are substituted for equality and form, bloodlines are substituted for structure. Manners grown hardened and inflexible without the countervailing pressure and prodding of law become fully as tyrannical as Montesquieu's monstrous Oriental despots. In the American South, it was manners hardened into the customs of a closed system that effectively created a despotism over the black man until the tempering force of legislation, plus the fresh air of new, prophetic manners (seen in the nonviolent demonstrations) began to reinforce justice.

The insidious domination of reified manners even in the courtrooms of the South is illustrated in this little exchange among a police chief, a black attorney defending demonstrators, and a judge, in Albany, Georgia.[21]

> "Now, C. B.," drawls the Chief.
> "Yes, Laurie," says C. B. [the black attorney] quietly.
> The judge raps sharply with his gavel, and the Chief turns to him:
> "I don't want him to address me by that name."
> C. B.: "I am no more appreciative of his addressing me as C. B."
> The judge: "We're going to proceed in an orderly manner. His official title is Chief Pritchett."
> C. B.: "I say respectfully that my official title is Attorney King."
> The judge: "We're going to proceed."

The proper end of both law and manners in a republic is to secure and provide for the disposition of personal and community space. Because every human act, legal or voluntary, may be placed in the service of a limited perspective, these two modalities of action must be kept joined in confrontation. In that direction lies the means to avoid the bloodlessness of legalism and the bloodiness of local custom.

3. The Special Role of Manners in This Complementarity

Despite this symmetry, the province of manners deserves special attention—if only because in previous epochs and nonrepublican polities, no such symmetry existed. In the American experiment, the realm of manners had to receive augmentation in order for the law-manners dialectic to become a reality. Thus as compared to the monarchical heritage of Europe, the American ethos provides a correspondingly larger role for manners.

It is precisely in the institution of manners, and in the changing face of manners, that we are afforded the clearest glimpse of the struggle for the good society. That is why Santayana, although undertaking a moral inquiry about America, invites his reader "to forget himself and, in so far as such a thing may be possible for him or for me, to transport himself ideally with me into the outer circumstances of American life, the better to feel its inner temper."[22] Since the good society has not yet arrived, since the struggle is going on at every stage to rise above the constraints of nature and the baser side of human nature, we cannot therefore expect to encounter nothing but admirable manners. Part of what comes into our sights will surely strike us as unworthy or only partly promising behavior, at best. Yet we must take the good with the bad if we are to move by imagination to the profounder meaning of what is said and done.

Manners as the overt expression of morality are especially important for appreciating moderate governments, Montesquieu suggests, for the very reason that the governance of such society depends more or less on wide participation of the citizenry. It was the persistent force of morality expressed in action rather than specific laws that tempered the absolute power of the monarchy in France, and in much of the rest of eighteenth-century Europe.[23] Among moderate governments, a republic depends most of all on the force of manners, since it depends more essentially on personal and voluntary group initiative.

It is important that we understand manners in a republic not in the sense of unchanging customs, however, but as expressions of the current predicament and response (or at least as expressing a *recent* predicament and response). Thus we are not to confuse manners with mere politeness, or the forms of courtesy, or see them as a vehicle of honor. When they are pressed into these uses, manners become rigid and indestructible, as in ancient China, "where they teach manners in the schools as laws."[24] In a republic, men are required to act and express themselves as a means of moving the country forward. Manners thus function not as the constraints of hierarchy or antiquity but rather as the agency of development. Thus we can expect manners to change relatively faster in a republic, and to have less the character of law (affording, by contrast, the complementarity with law that we have already spoken of). The more communication there is among the people, says Montesquieu, "the more easily they change manners, because each man is more a model for the next man; one sees better the uniqueness of individuals."[25]

This phenomenon of turnover in manners is especially visible to us in the form of the changing manners of youth, a subject to which we shall have to return. The generation gap is evidence that there are an indefinite number of ways of reorganizing community space. Much the same thing happens as when a younger couple takes over a house, moves in, rearranges the furniture (or replaces it), and sets about "redoing" the interior of the house. It is still the same house. When the younger generation, by its protests and other unorthodox manners, seeks to rearrange the space of the national community, the test must be this: does the rearranging further what has already gotten underway in the moral tradition of the greater community? It is not so much a case of the tradition's rightness in its achievements as of its definitiveness in its promise: when the goal of rearranging community space to permit more equality is abrogated, then the greater community as we have known it has come to an end, and a new greater community, for better or worse, is launched. In the meantime, the widest variety of changes in tactics can be contemplated and tested.

In addition, the moral tradition that has set the terms of the struggle for space so far has a sheer inertial force that cannot be turned off or even turned away by anything less than a cataclysmic upheaval or crisis. "Only a profound social revolution, one that destroys the mainstays of the preceding order—habitual social relations, socializing agencies, and ideas of right and wrong—can produce sudden major changes in values and character."[26] In other words, whether drastic change in the values or character of a greater community is desired, on the one hand, or feared, on the other, persistent biases are likely to continue. Even the new world of technology, despite the drastic breaks in manners and history it is advertised to bring, has to be accommodated to the ethos of a vigorous greater community. It is instructive to ask, for example, how much the "Americanization" of Japan since World War II has modified the distinctive biases of the Japanese greater community. These new forces have come in such forms as military constraints, massive industrialization, and the advent of democratic forms in various arenas of social and political life. Whatever the benefits accruing to a mature people by the introduction of such political forms, for Japan the democratic process itself is accompanied by disturbing threats to the previously acquired and recognized notions of self-identity. So a set of manners must be found that will accept the new reality, yet meet the existential demands of tradition. One aspect of this new set of manners, evolved to meet the threat that is bound up with the new situation, is the "ubiquitous calling card." Japanese people, it seems, continue to be embarrassed by the democratic American custom of "introducing people without first informing both parties of the other's status." Though democratic folkways are indeed taking root and evolving, they do so as grafts on the trunk of a previously formed set of distinctive biases about the nature of selfhood. Despite the reality of the new situation, "Nevertheless status anxiety persists; the average Japanese needs to know the status of everyone with whom he deals before he can act with confidence."[27]

In our own situation, we cannot accept in any simple form the easy dictum that the technological revolution has become the primary radiating center for a new set of moral values and manners. Our expectation, rather, is that we shall find, mirrored in the manners of contemporary Americans (even the premanners of the rebellious sectors) a confrontation between the demands of the new cybernetics world and the buried radiating center (within us and within our history) of a set of persistent, enduring assumptions about the goal of personal and communal activity. Thus the incoming manners will be new and different and shaped to a highly visible extent by the new situation, including the constraints and liberty served up by the technological order; but these new manners will express, in latent ontological substance, the continuing dilemma of time understood as a revolutionary challenge to extrinsic authority; of space understood as a mandate to organize personal and community space for new accessions of justice and equality; and of quality of action understood as personal, voluntary, and common initiative. And in every one of these dimensions we shall find the "goodness" of the manners corrupted by the ambiguity of human motives.

4. The Place of Language in the Study of Manners

In the study of human actions, it is a grave mistake to focus upon deeds, or things done, if in doing so we overlook words, which can "do things" too. We put our mark upon the world not only by deeds but also by speech. Words are a form of acting; they carve up and reassemble the natural world long before our tractors and bulldozers leave the contractor's yard; they destroy and reconstruct existential space with criticism, candor, succor, and support. Deeds, on the other hand, are a form of speech. They give out, in the currency of achievement, what was only a fancy in our inner minds; they prod and push, rip apart and clap together, turn sand and grass into rows of houses, and rows of houses into stinking tenements, clouds of smoke, and asphalt parking lots.

Deeds and words are both actions, performances. They are subspecies of a larger phenomenon, manners. Both find their role, for the human agent, pressed to cope with his predicament, needs every modality of performance at his disposal. Manners, as that constellation of current performances at hand to be used in coping—and ultimately to be used in seeking blessedness—inevitably consist of a complex expression, part word and part deed. Admittedly, up to now, we have laid the greater stress by implication on the deed, on the muscular side of manners. Lest that tendency get out of hand, we must now pause, briefly, to reflect on the special role played by speech as a component of manners.

For our purposes, we can settle for three distinctive roles played by speech in the formation of manners. Better yet, we might think of these roles as distinctive *levels of engagement* of speech in manners.

(a) *The Level of Simple Agency*

At the level of simple agency, words—especially words put together to constitute rhetoric—serve on a par with overt deeds. They can replace deeds, they can supplement deeds, and they can perform acts too complex for mere deeds. Activity may derive much of its meaning from the rhetoric that accompanies it rather than the proceeding itself. That is often true of the enjoyment of sex, for example. One of the darker uses of manners is to conceal one's existential space, not just in the ordinary rituals of privacy and solitude, which are mature forms of disposing of one's own space, but in the dysfunctional forms of withdrawing from one's community or misrepresenting one's identity.[28] Deeds can be used to conceal what one is doing, but the lie built with strands of rhetoric is much more effective, especially the lie in modernized form, such as the chatter of press agentry. Our deeds lie more on the surface, our speech has deeper roots into our selves. Thus words employed as manners serve more faithfully to project our inner predicament upon the world.

(b) *The Level of Pattern*

At the level of pattern in manners, words, rather than being hurled at the men around us as weapons, are used for organizing and regulating our weaponry. Speech at this level creates patterns of simple agency, configurations of the performances that have been alluded to at the first level. Here we find elementary codes of behavior, rules of etiquette, "unwritten codes" of gang conduct (which though unwritten are nevertheless precise and verbalizable). At this level, nonverbal activities clearly have a place, in policing or enforcing the patterns or codes, as when a teen-age gang punishes an errant member. But speech is the dominant partner in its creative function, and in its powers to organize and enforce patterns of conduct.

(c) *The Level of Metamanners*

Finally, there is the level of metamanners, at which patterns of action, far from being sanctioned with a view to unremitting continued practice of them, come under some form of critical inspection, review, and revision. At this level, speech as a destructuring and restructuring power is altogether hegemonous. Among the functions of speech at this level are to mediate conflicts between patterns or codes of manners at level two. At this level, the authority that informs the mediation is not that of still another pattern of manners believed superior to either of the two in conflict, but is a direct extension of the moral sense of the greater community, as tempered by its past, and as newly alerted by current predicament. In other words, the community's perennial, primordial values are the final court of resort. And when two codes of conduct—say, the code of the teen-age gang, and that of an overmuscular police force—come into conflict, those who mediate at the level of metamanners will enforce the deeply latent value set of the greater community itself. That is why the work of presidential riot commissions, for example, frequently seems to be as antiestablishment as antiagitationist. That is why much of the work of humanists and sociological thinkers seems visionary and devoid of practical programs.

We do not mean to imply that presidential commissions, humanists, and sociologists are the natural or anointed spokesmen for the deeply latent value set of the greater community, of course. Our point is that these spokesmen, whatever their credentials or lack of them, aim in principle to engage in the language of metamanners whenever they set out to review, criticize, and compare extant patterns of manners. Whether they succeed or not is another question. In the American greater community, it is doubtless in the welter of attempts at metamanners that safety from the *Diktat* in manners lies.

Now, for clarification we might say that this book is a venture in metamanners. It is an attempt to take in view, criticize, and perhaps even suggest reform, with certain norms in mind, of American manners and morals. And that aim discloses one more question that we must ask while we are discussing the relation between speech and manners. From our normative stance, we must ask *which kind of language* is most suitable to the ethos of a republic. What we are looking for, at level one, is that form of speech that answers to the moral action termed *la vertu* by Montesquieu and understood by us in this study as *willed initiative*. It is our view that the proper form of speech in a republic is *debate aimed at persuasion,* for this is the form of verbal act proper to a community that is organized by equal participation and voluntary commitment. Just as willed initiative contemplates actions that aim at organizing the commonwealth in the mode of equality, so the free institutions of a republic encourage free and unlimited discussion in the search for this end, and each participant is entitled to hope for the adoption of his program, not on the basis of fiat, but on the basis of the merits of his ideas for the community, as demonstrated and talked about.

We can also say something about the ingredients of the debate. The revolutionary impulse that founds republican government leaves its mark, which means that debate will perennially continue about what has been accomplished in the past, and what is still demanded in the present and future. Thus there will be a permanent argument in America about the worthwhileness of past precedents and the validity of yet unfulfilled dreams. Similarly, there will be continual conflict between the advocates of equality in space organization who begin with liberty for the individual, and those who think first of participation in a group. There will always be debate between activists, who want to change things for the sake of change, and sentimental standpatters, who view America as already the greatest nation on earth.

5. A Typology of Bad Manners

Manners are ready-to-hand ways of dealing with what is felt to be threatening on our existential horizon. Ultimately they are action and speech units pressed into a communal quest for salvation. They express, at the surface of our lives, our inner, often unarticulated yearning toward being. This seemingly grave and solemn way of describing manners and their function does not at all preclude their being enjoyed, or regarded as "fun," or practiced as trivialities. Today's fourteen-year-old generation, for example, is addicted to the telephone, and suburban nights are filled with the chatter, briefings, and some-times lunatic shrieks of boys and girls shirking their homework. But to write off this ritual, this strange new saturation use of the instru-ment, as simple fun-talk, is to miss what is transacted. For the new-teens, the wire is the survival link, the conduit that brings existential nourishment. Beneath the fun is the restless pursuit of those distinc-tive human attributes, association and speech.

While we may judge ultimate human purposes, it is much more difficult to decide about the "propriety" of manners. To oldsters, who emerged into adolescence in a day when the telephone was a com-munications device of some sanctity, to be used only for conveying information, today's teen-ager, who can easily keep two telephones busy in relays during prime evening time, seems to have unshapen and uncouth manners. Must we wax wroth, however, with the new telephone manner? Must we not reflect, at least briefly, on the differ-ential salvation quest that drives the teen-ager to his mosaic of eve-ning talk? In short, it is no longer so easy to pronounce some man-ners good and other manners bad.

A more workable division, then, may be that between conventional manners and dissenting manners (or between manners as indicative of currently accepted practices and acts that have not yet won such sanction, as outlined in the introduction to this chapter). Conven-tional manners are those styles of manners that reflect the satisfaction of dominant groups with the increments of being already obtained in the community. Dissenting manners are the styles of manners (or acts corresponding to premanners) that reflect dissatisfaction by groups of various stances. Both kinds of manners, on inspection, will be found ultimately to penetrate to ultimate questions about the human condi-tion. This heavily freighted latent meaning will be found underlying even the "best" practices of "good social form," each of which is likely in itself to have represented at one time a break with earlier, more traditional manners, for it is at the disjunctures between styles of manners that we see reflected upheavals in our conceptions of what it is to be a human being in "saving" association with other human beings. Not so long ago, for example, arranged marriages were con-sidered proper for the sons and daughters of genteel families. But a later conception of human dignity that stresses the existential specialness of persons could not tolerate this expression of propriety. While there are still numerous hoped-for and semi-planned matches between the offspring of "good" families (or simply families in parity), a new style of marriage-partner selection has emerged and has made the former good manners of arranged marriage not only obsolete as a standard but also unjust by the later standards of personality. Probably the accepted etiquette for marital choice today does require consultation of parents by the children, but even that standard is weakening. We see more and more examples of outright bypassing of the parents, and more than a few cases of calculated defiance, and here we see even a more novel conception of youthful integrity, still inchoate, crossing the boundary into accepted practice.

Our interest is neither in the conventional distinctions between good and bad manners, nor in the interesting contrasts that we might pursue between conventional and dissenting manners. Rather we wish to define good manners as those current practices that reflect the distinctive dimensions of the republican ethos, as we have already outlined these dimensions. And we wish to define bad manners as practices that dishonor, distort, or abuse the dimensions of republican community. To tell the truth, our assumptions about the human condition lead us to expect that we shall more easily discover bad manners, in this sense, abroad in the land, than good ones. Nevertheless, even in their very departure from the norms of republican activity, the everyday, received bad manners of factical American life point to what is yearned for and ought to be striven for.

These everyday bad manners, as we might expect, can be organized about the three dimensions of American experience:

1. One class of manners is structured by the revolutionary impulse that biases the conception of time and history in American life. Good manners should show some appreciation of the historic line of march toward equal conditions that was set off in the explosive birth of the American republic; but these manners will also be future-oriented, out of the realization that the struggle to free personal and communal space of extrinsic control is a perennial imperative. The bad manners that we find currently practiced are distorted and partial efforts to grope after this pilgrimage. There are bad manners that simply embalm the American past, on the wrong supposition that the revolu-

tion is all over, and that further movement toward space disposition is simply "agitation"; and there are bad manners that simply look to the future, discounting the meaning of the past.

2. A second class of manners is structured by our commitments to the challenge of organizing our space for personal and communal participation. Either our manners are skewed toward the singular importance of the individual (leading to what we shall call the bad manners of the "self-appointment" syndrome in American life), or they are oriented toward the dominance of the team, system, or mass. A variation is found in our understanding of what it is within our space that is to be organized, and how. Are people to be organized as if they were natural material? Or are people so spirit prone that they cannot and should not be organized at all?

3. Finally, there is a class of manners that, under distortion, reflects our divided mind on what constitutes the essence of willed initiative or voluntary action. One side of the dialectic produces a subclass of bad manners that stresses purely outward activity (or "activism") rendered without inward thought as to the promise that should inform and control the actions of members of the greater community. On the other hand, there is an equal distortion that stresses pure sentiment, or excessive confidence that what one knows in his heart is sufficient, or that "love" is a solution to all problems.

Our aim has been to set out a theory of public ethics that would provide a means of taking into view and appraising American manners. To enter into any exhaustive examination of American manners at this point would be to exceed our purpose, or our competence. (Ideally, a theologian and a social scientist should team up to undertake so vast a project.) Nevertheless, we do not propose to leave the theory we have outlined unconnected to the realm of everyday life. We shall conclude, rather, by examining, with no pretense to completeness, some of the manners of deeds and speech that are most significant in the American ethos.

6. Manners Oriented by the Revolutionary Sense of Time

Every student of folklore knows that a large class of manners is regulated by the conception of time inherent in the community. In some societies, there are customs and rites connected with definite days and with seasons of the solar year. There are rites observed on indelibly meaningful occasions, such as dates of birth and death. There are rites and ceremonials connected with the ordeal and pilgrimage of the community at large, as in the memory of the Hebrews of their captivity in Egypt and their Exodus.[29] A decisive time in the history of a people, as when it is born *ex nihilo* out of despotism (or reborn out of it), will leave its mark on future generations, and even restructure the view of time entertained by that people. Down into recent times, for example, the sense of identity among various Polynesian peoples was structured by the memory of a time of prodigious sea travels from some dimly remembered homeland. Thus the Maoris of New Zealand developed a cultural identity based on the arrival of the "great fleet" from Tahiti in the mid-fourteenth century, and the Maori traditions, customs, and genealogies stem from the age of the great canoe voyages.

For the American greater community, the decisive time of times was at least prefigured by the settlement of the land by seafarers from Europe. The symbols of Plymouth Rock and Jamestown have proved to be potent, indeed, and to possess an extraordinary half-life. But the decisive occasion, the moment when a distinctive "American time" began to be coined, was the later overthrow of extrinsic control and the restoration of the right of self-government—the American Revolution. This seminal event has left its indelible mark on the very notion of time in America and has ordained a set of options for the handling of the problem of change. Out of its reaction against the real and imagined despotism of British rule came the outlook of vigilance that feeds the flame of future zeal against all sorts of extrinsic control, public and personal. But out of the solid new political and commercial foundation that was won in this upheaval came the outlook of complacency that may accept many kinds of change, but not further revolution: "I know of nothing more opposite to revolutionary manners than commercial manners," says Tocqueville. Americans "love change, but they dread revolutions."[30]

(a) *Embalmers of a Revolutionary Past*

If the revolutionary impulse were solidly and healthily implanted in the American character, our sense of the past would propel us toward the future, and remind us that large segments of contemporary community space are still shadowed by one form or another of extrinsic control. But under the fragile eye of republican virtue, this corridor of history takes on a far different aspect. All too often, the revolutionary impulse, under the conditions of reality, becomes a monumental past to be revered, worshiped, and embalmed.

The embalming process is varied. Classically, the ritualized Fourth of July celebration has been a favored modality, especially when accompanied by stylized descants on patriotism. The difference between a "good-mannered" and a "bad-mannered" Fourth of July celebration lies in what purpose it serves. If it is used as a remembrance of things yet undone, it corresponds to manners in the service of republican governance. If it is used as a way of forgetting the storm and strife of the present crisis, it corresponds to manners directed against the greater community.

But Fourth of July celebrations have lost much of their former hold. Now the principal means of embalming the past, no doubt, are television employed as a time machine, and everyday moralizing about former virtues (cant). In terms of sheer visibility, the most popular route to a frozen past is in the realm of food-purveying, from the franchised operations that recall farms of yore, old-time cattle roundups, and plantation fare, to the country food store in the metropolitan airport, to the reproductions of old-time "mason jars" on the supermarket shelves, these filled with the reproductions of old-time chowchow, hot pepper relish, farm-type jelly, and other rustic victuals. Grocery-store advertising takes advantage of our thirst for losing ourselves in a past that never was by reminding us that "hog killing time is just around the corner." All in all, food persuasion probably serves up more flash-frozen American archaism than any other branch of commerce, and has probably already surpassed museums and reduplicated colonial and frontier cities (Dearborn Village, e.g.) in overall impact.

If one listens long enough to talk-back radio programs during an election year, one tends to lose sight of America's dynamic futurism entirely and to think of the republic as modeled on the lines of certain quiescent antique societies, where a studied archaism was an ongoing way of life, as in Egyptian culture in the middle and late stretches of that civilization. In such societies, the later heirs tend to think it impossible to better the earliest models of conduct offered by their ancestors.

An interesting variation on this approach is the use of one stretch of the past to blot out not only the present crisis but also the memory of a more creative, more disturbing other stretch of past, as when patriots remember the McKinley era but know nothing of the Lincoln-Douglas debates. The most common form of this selection process perhaps occurs in American church life, as when the pious recall with some little passion the revival hymns and gospel songs of the nineteenth century, greatly preferring them to the music of Bach and Handel. Thus at the level of manners, forgetfulness need not be on the grand scale of that of France's *Ancien Régime*, by which an entire society is held to the customs and restraints of two or three centuries ago. Indeed, we need not be dealing with events very far back in the past. One insidious form of forgetfulness, and a highly effective one, is to freeze the forms not of a past century but of the last decade or so. This still happens among provincial city councilmen, who derived security and community substance from bearing arms in the Cold War of the 1950's, and who attempt to perpetuate this age of heroism by shouting through ordinances forbidding the sale of Polish hams in grocery stores.

Of late in America the boundary line between the golden past and the unpleasant present has leaped forward, and our sanctioned, middle-class, middle-aged ideology now takes as its watershed not the division between the last century and this,[31] but between the recent age of heroic struggle (War War II, the Cold War), and the soft, degenerate, permissive era since then.

Television, to be sure, has fought a mighty rearguard action, continuing to offer a variety of nineteenth-century scenarios of forgetfulness, especially in its processed versions of the cowboy life, the struggle against the Indians, the settlement of the frontier, and the total saga of the West. The use of television as a time machine does not help us to appreciate our heritage so much as it offers an assist to our ever-present efforts to get rid of the living past. One can hide in a glorified segment of the past—and television can glorify it as no other medium can—not merely to avoid the present, but to set aside the burden of one's tradition. Television viewers seem to come into being, as it were, out of a blank past, bringing a *tabula rasa* to the screen, bearing nothing consciously of what made them, betraying nothing knowingly of what they were promised, or what they are obligated to promise those yet to come. Given the context of frontier and western escape shows, not to mention a later accretion of World War II adventure programs, one wonders what will actually be made of such laudable attempts to take the past seriously as various programs on the ordeal of the black man in America. If television has become a time machine, it may not be easy to convert it instantly into a teaching machine.

Every display of bad manners, we recall, is accompanied by a characteristic form of speech. The speech form that accompanies embalmment of the past we think of as a certain form of *cant* about the assured state of blessedness of the American commonwealth.

Why is this talking up the past so necessary? The American Revolution, let us remember, may be viewed as an ideological upheaval, a revolution in ideas put to practice. "Modern America is perhaps more than any other country actually built on words," says Goeffrey Gorer, "on the words of the Constitution and the Declaration of Independence, and, behind them the Word of God."[32] The foundation was laid in the quasi-sacred words of the Constitution. The past-embalmer, faced with attempts by the Supreme Court and other present-regarding institutions to extract relevance from these hallowed sentences, resorts to wordsmithery of his own—the cant of the patriotic businessman. But we can extend the subject matter and speak of cant generally as exemplifying the manners of a wide spectrum of Americans.

Cant is a form of speech—or, more literally, "singing"—that insists on the efficacy of past credos regardless of contrary evidence. It is implicitly aimed at the illusion of handing on the wisdom of the past. Hangers-on at denominational conferences, I have observed, tend to talk in terms of precedents, even though these are quite often precedents that in no way touch decisions that must be made. Letter writers to the afternoon newspaper will greet the appearance of a Black Muslim in town with garrulous comments on the American system of job opportunity and the historic Christian virtue of industriousness, as if the credo itself were the reality that must be attended to instead of the predicament. Cant freezes in words of amber the morality that was efficacious in some past predicament

Cant has nothing to do with history or with remembering, and much less to do with coping in the present on the basis of remembered wisdom. This is illustrated in the helplessness of the cant deliverers in any demanding social situation, even in the situations of table courtesy. Here all Americans are truly delivered into a new, leveled-off equality, all equally distant from the refinements of past elites. At a motel on the edge of a boom-town in the Midwest I watched cant-prone businessmen stand around in the strangeness of dark suits and the terrifying awkwardness of a formal meeting. Women have abandoned their former role as the beneficiaries of male chivalry, even in the circles of those whose cant commends the past to us. One has only to notice their conduct in the public sector.

Cant, in short, is a restraining wall against much of our heritage. It is not surprising that cant, as such, is often found in company with insecurity and guilt. Indeed, guilt becomes an alternate, sinister conduit of the pressures of the past into our present. There is an entire spectrum of manners that is formed and fashioned by this route of ingress—repression by the dyke of cant, filtering into our world through the subterranean channel of guilt. Guilt, unattended by any viable notion of promise, holds any deviation from the *embalmed* past a transgression against the community's primordial holiness. This mood then becomes the means of determining what is transmitted from the past and what is forgotten. Many women continue to feel that they must teach Sunday School, for example, because they are vaguely bothered by guilt feelings if they don't. Yet intellectually they realize that nothing is accomplished in Sunday Schools, nothing to be compared with the outfitting for life, practical and moral, that issues out of the public schools. Guilt transmits the past, then, quixotically and irregularly. Some of us can make the transition from Victorianism to the present in drinking habits or even civil rights, but have extreme difficulty in seeing the implications of revolutionary promise for, say, our stance toward indigenous peoples in Southeast Asia, or toward the sexual revolution among younger members of our society. In past-embalming manners, guilt must be consulted *de facto* and at times even knowingly honored in adjudicating which strands of our history are to be grasped and clung to.

In the absence of an open reading of our revolutionary promise, superstition also functions to filter elements of the past into the present. Numerous credulous beliefs continue to guide middle-class folk in the suburbs as much as if they were peasants in fifteenth-century Poland. Lemon juice will cause you to lose weight. Honey and vinegar will cure arthritis. Fruit juice and vitamins are miraculous. Physicians can heal psyche as well as soma. The Supreme Court has abandoned the Constitution. The colored people don't want to work.

At a more appropriate point we will have to take up the refractive effect of our business civilization on manners and on the uses of the past. When we get to that subject we will also be covering to some degree the special manners associated with manhood. Here we do need to observe that women, too, purvey a distinctive set of manners. Some think that women are the chief transmitters of moral concepts in our society. Perhaps so. Certainly they are the chief transmitters of innocuous manners unconnected with revolutionary promise. With women, society pages have replaced history as the source of moral legitimation. If one inspects the titles of books reviewed at women's literary clubs, one realizes that only a shadow of the wisdom sought by literary clubs in the past is any more honored. What is honored is standing, social position. If it is true that a certain kind of moral uprightness is encouraged by women in American society, it is only because the home is productive of safeguards against revolution that approach a high moral intensity.

(b) *Deifiers of a Revolutionary Future*

Another set of manners—exemplified stunningly by the civil rights and student protests of the late 1960's—seeks to isolate the revolutionary impulse, discount much of the past as not having yet realized it, and live out a kind of conduct that understands the status quo as despotic, not even moderately latent with revolutionary promise.

These protests have taken a wide variety of forms, of which guerrilla operations on university campuses, leading to the capture of buildings and the closing down of classes, have been the most notorious. Next to the takeover of campuses, perhaps the most striking protests have been the clamorous demonstrations against militarism that have occurred in Washington, D.C., and elsewhere. Indeed, at one of the latter demonstrations, a crowd of no less than 30,000 gathered noisily in late 1967 at the Pentagon. There were several hundred arrests (240 according to one newsmagazine, 684 according to another). After the demonstrators had gone, sixteen tons of litter had to be removed including, according to one worker: "Nothing but bras and panties. You never saw so many." Another residuum was the spread of painted slogans left behind on the walls of the Pentagon: "Love," "Peace," several obscenities, and one thought for the day: "Old Soldiers Never Die—Young Ones Do." Workers used steam to erase the graffiti, although some were done in unerasable black plastic paint. Total clean-up bill was $12,000, but this figure did not include $149,000 for airlifting military police and paratroops to the spot, nor $176,000 paid out in overtime wages to Washington, D.C., police. The whole affair, according to one marcher, "was degraded into a messy love-in. . . . It was disorganized, disorderly and ineffective."[33]

At this writing, student agitation and near-insurrection continues on many campuses, and it is by no means certain that education can continue for some of them in the accustomed way, or at all. It is certain that protest, and often protest that will not brook compromise, has become a style of life for at least a portion of the younger, nonestablishment sector, with corresponding effects on life styles and manners.

The immediate effect of this revolutionary style is to repel or outrage the elders. Indeed, that seems to be one of the aims, for the apologists of the protesters say it is the repellent aspect of the style that permits this generation to be itself and thus maintain its integrity. That is why, as T. Walter Herbert, Jr., observes, the movement seems to go out of its way *not* to be understood, not to compromise. To be understood and accepted is "to be fitted into someone else's categories, to become part of someone else's value system." If one is to belong to one's self and not be controlled, then one may have to seek a style that will keep the would-be controllers at arm's length.[34]

It is a mistake, however, to focus our attention too exclusively on the repulsive style of the protests. What is of chief interest to us is the conception of "political time" that is implicit here. First of all, the protesters are acutely aware of the reaction *against* a revolutionary time frame among their adversaries in power. The time orientation of university bureaucrats as described by Mario Savio, former philosophy student at Berkeley and a leader of the late "Free Speech" movement there, may typify the antirevolutionary trough into which many (or most) Americans have fallen. "The conception the bureaucrats have," says Savio, "is that history has in fact come to an end. No events can occur now that the Second World War is over which can change American society substantially. . . . the bureaucrats hold history has ended."[35] Savio's analysis, we might add, corresponds to our own characterization of some Americans as "embalmers of the revolutionary past."

Reacting to this stopped-clock appearance given by the powerful, the protesters have moved to the opposite extreme: they have insisted on a revolutionary outlook totally dissevered from the past. The society has quit generating options that would offer relief from extrinsic control over persons and communities. The choice that is left, on this view, is to reject the entire system and to propose one's own options, despite the odds involved in taking on police, university authorities, the political parties, and the armed forces.

A related protest movement, that of the black power or black nationalist forces, shows a similar cynicism and doubt that change within the system is any longer possible. Unlike the student protests, the black man has been more concerned with the right to space as the end of the revolutionary impulse. "Essentially what we are fighting for," says a Newark, N.J., black leader, "is the power to define our lives. Newark is a city where black people are in the majority, and we mean to be masters of our own space."[36] In that respect, the civil rights movement and its sequel, the black power movement, have demonstrated an "authentic" revolutionary goal, since the historic time frame does not end with upheaval, but rather begins there, with the end in view of regaining the right to dispose of one's space, and of the insistence on participation in reorganizing that space to further equality of opportunity. And yet, to the extent that the black protests proceed with no gains credited to the past, they display a distorted version of the revolutionary impulse. Indeed, it is the failure to connect revolt with the revolutionary past, rather than the resort to violence, that is more alarming about any of these movements.

All of these modalities of upheaval fall short of genuine revolution because they rely upon manners that are almost blindly futuristic, knowing no precedents, acknowledging no bonds with the impulse toward managing one's own space that has constituted the republic itself. At best, perhaps, this impatience with the past is genuine, especially when establishmentarian forces have literally taken over the "time" of the republic and have viewed revolutionary history as at an end. One can understand the impatience of a Malcolm X toward the conventional Christian face of the black community, or worse, the tendency of the blacks in Boston's Roxbury to imitate the very suburban manners that freeze out the revolutionary spirit. Malcolm coldly rejected even those among his own if they were "like the sleep-in maid for Beacon Hill white folks who used to come in with her 'ooh, my deah' manners and order corn plasters in the Jew's drugstore for black folks. Or the hospital cafeteria-line serving woman sitting there on her day off with a cat fur around her neck, telling the proprietor she was a 'dietitian'—both of them knowing she was lying."[37]

We can observe, in any case, that the dissenting manners of revolutionary protest are just as susceptible of becoming despotic themselves as the conventional manners that do no more than embalm the past. The genuinely prophetic manners of the dissenter can become rigid, unproductive, and stifling if they are isolated from the living travail of the greater community. Here the revolutionaries (or would-be revolutionaries) should be able to learn from an early American dissenting movement—one that could have leavened the manners of the republic if it had had its say within the context of the greater community. Unfortunately, this group, the Quakers, resisted the opportunity to influence the spirit of governance in Pennsylvania and contented themselves with withdrawing. This will to separation from the rest of the community finally carried the Quakers away into a dreary set of dead manners of their own. "The very ways which earlier Quakers had used to show contempt for rank and custom gradually became themselves customs as rigid as those they were meant to displace," Boorstin comments. The Quaker made a point of refusing to remove his hat, but this ostensibly critical manner, when it became insisted on blindly, "became as arrogant and purposeless as the non-Quaker's insistence on hat honor." The plain dress of the Quaker was meant at first to show contempt for fancy fashions and extravagant display of finery. In the end it became "a uniform to which the Quaker attached more importance than his neighbors did to their gayer garments."[38] To withdraw from the community's historic line of march toward equality in reorganizing community space is to engage in an equivalent withdrawal, with the same promise of rigor mortis for the dissenting movements.

Let us now briefly ponder the style of language that is appropriate to this side of our dialectic. With the past-embalmers, we found a certain predilection for "cant" or a singsong, rote celebration of past deeds and virtues as a way of obscuring the challenges of the crisis-ridden present. Conversely, with the deifiers of futurism, we shall find a reluctance to chant about what has been done and said before. The definitive modality of speaking for the dissenters is "free speech," a way of talking that pushes aside convention and constraints from the past and makes a fetish of speaking without limits, inhibitions, or proprieties.

First, there are the highly visible nonverbal gestures and stances, all designed to get free of previously laid down conventions of social communication—the long, unruly hair, sandals, dirty clothes, and serapes of the students; the dashikis, beads, and African hairstyles of the blacks. Herbert, it seems to me, grants far too much idealism to these styles when he argues that "The uncleanness of dress and grooming which excites so much pious dismay is actually a conscious badge of moral purity. . . . The uncleanness is intended as a reproach to the conformist who is neat externally but dirty inside; it aims to shock the decent with what is true about themselves."[39] Like any other symbol-interpreters, neither Herbert nor I really knows what meanings the symbol-bearers may be consciously commending, or whether they are consciously commending any symbols at the level of specificity usually insisted on by determined interpreters. In the case of the unkempt, ill-dressed students, I am willing to give the symbol-bearers the benefit of the doubt in some cases and to concede the intent of prophesying to a depraved society. In other cases, I am reasonably certain, the students are unwashed and carelessly dressed because they are boors. They have written off the good with the bad and consigned the whole of accepted manners to the dustbin. Their dress simply denotes getting free of a burden without signifying any new program for the health of the community. Their habits speak more of the freedom to be at random than of the freedom to reorganize community.

Similarly, the speech itself of the protest movement expresses "independence" in the literal sense, cutting oneself away from dependence on past conventions and constraints. It is not structuring speech, much less restructuring speech; it is destructuring speech. It is speech used only for the preliminary part of the proper work of speech, for it is the return to words that seek structures and cooperation that characterizes the human community. One can see this failure to mount the proper task of speech in the fixation on "empty" words among the protesters—words that assault convention and strike down the past (sex obscenities, for example) but that say nothing in themselves. Obscenity and profanity can shock and gain attention, but speech built on these elements has no substantive outcome, no creative dimension. Besides, such language rapidly wears off its edge and loses its shock value. Vigorous four-letter words, long the stockblock-busters-in-trade of the campus free speech forces, have now become semidomesticated in the college patois and are not felt to be much more than mild vulgarisms. Moreover, by that kind of reverse taste-making by which the settled classes imitate the restless and younger people, these words are now becoming common coin in certain sophisticated dinner-party circles. In New York Society, reports Tom Wolfe, various "pariah" styles are coming up fast. "Dinner-table expletives . . .; also clinical commentary at dinner about various exotic feminine diseases and sexual hysterias; also homosexual movies, camp jesters, this and that—it is all part of the new *chic* of Society in New York. Such a marvelous book of etiquette one must now write!"[40] When free speech, meant precisely to mark off the freedom of the speaker from what went on before him, becomes the borrowed style of the Society dinner, it has ceased in any case to serve its function.

But the free-speech movement may find new modalities of expression. When its poets and essayists turn from the empty celebration of cutting away, and turn to the new, footloose communities they dream of—then they may find a free speech that has substance. It could even be that the movement will make contact with Walt Whitman and the great storytellers of the American frontier, its true historical antecedents. When they will have made such overtures to the tradition, however, their movement will cease to be a distortion of the revolutionary heritage and become a part of it.

(c) *The Future of the Time Dimension*

Granted that America had a full-fledged revolution once, it is a difficult assignment to argue that it is still represented in the dialectically distorted versions of manners we have just examined, or that revolution is to be regarded as the manners-shaping temporal form in which the American greater community develops. That is our contention, however. Despite the losses we have sustained from the first ideology of revolution, still the impulse toward equality in disposing of space continues to be felt; revolution (at times acknowledged chiefly in reaction against it and departures from it) continues as the definitive time frame of the American experience. Both past and future have their special normativity as a result. Looking past and, so to speak, deeply within the distorted manners we have just sketched, we can discern three "healthy" functions that the past serves, and three "healthy" functions that the future should serve in a republic founded on revolution.

It will be easier to summarize these functions by considering the proper value of past time most carefully, then by contrasting these values with those we see for the sense of futurity.

The past is far more normative in America than our indifference to history would indicate. Both the past-embalmers and the deifiers of the future have overlooked America's living past. We tend to think of America "as having no history or having a short history." And yet, in the field of political order, America "has the longest effectively continuous political history in the world, marked by only one great breakdown, the Civil War—and that ended in the triumph of the Union."[41] As a greater community with a new solution to the problem of organizing space, America is *effectively* as old as the city states of Greece or Rome. And yet, in the psychological sense, its people have been unable or unwilling to bear the burden: we have not governed as well as our Constitution allows, and we have not renewed our chances at the good society by nourishing a revolutionary tradition that would keep opening the doors of equality. Most of all, we have failed to make the most of this unprecedented history.

What are the positive functions of history?

First, *remembrance of the human promise*. For the American republic, history should serve at least in part a frankly moral purpose. The past is laden with reminders of the sense of promise that men established when they threw off extrinsic control and founded a new nation. The original promise, with its successive implementations, models, and supporting values, is never finished, official, or definitive. It must constantly be revised, expanded, repaired, transformed in the light of new crises. Yet it forms the basis, the reminder, the impulse to clear community space anew of extrinsic control.

Second, *encouragement that the human promise is really unfolding*. A functioning greater community will register outrage at injustice precisely because it remembers out of its past that injustice has been met and exorcised before for earlier and different groups. It knows that extrinsic control was overthrown on earlier occasions, and it wants to know now, why not again? The same conditions of despair that now prevail among minority groups in Watts, Harlem, and New York's Puerto Rican enclaves once were present among the "Okies" and "Arkies," the migrants of the 1930's from the nation's central "dust bowl" into the large Northern and Western cities. Today's sense of desperation and unmanageability was there, too, for by 1940 it seemed that these minorities, far from participating in the national recovery of the day, were falling further and further behind. But the full story wasn't yet in. By the spring of 1960, when a new census was taken, "a remarkable thing could be noticed: the Okie and the Arky had statistically vanished." They had become, say, normal Californians, especially their sons and daughters and grandchildren, living everywhere, holding normal positions. Thus, "the malady we call American poverty is a curable disease . . . but it is not always a rapid or pleasant cure."[42]

To be sure, the black man's plight today is not the same as that of the dust-bowl migrants. The moral significance of newness is to show us that the present is not a mere rerun of the past. But the present may be related, for all that, to the past: the plight of the ghetto people is not absolutely removed from that of the people of the dust bowl.

Third, *briefing in tactics*. History furnishes not only symbols of promise, and fragmentary evidence that the promise unfolds, but also models of strategy for participating in the pilgrimage. The nonviolent methods of the civil rights movement of the 1950's and 1960's were based on tactics both of Mahatma Gandhi and of the American labor movement of the 1930's. Today's radical dissenters, disaffected with government structures, military conscription, and insensitive leaders, are increasingly turning to the tradition of dissent in this country— Thoreau, the abolitionists, some of the sect groups—for counsel and strategy.

History is not a solid given, however, waiting there to be discovered. The past, in great part, has to be defined according to the moral crisis that has to be dealt with by the greater community in its present and as it enters its future. Thus the challenge of our times forces a retrospective reappraisal of the past: it is not that the past keeps changing, but that our crisis keeps changing, and that we must recur to our past for the symbols, encouragement, and even tactical wisdom that enables us to reaffirm, by creative variations on the revolutionary impulse, the age-old struggle against extrinsic control of community space.

(d) *Complementary Functions of the Future*

The revolutionary impulse gives the past a new status, for it is not valuable in itself or for its "pastness," but only because it is the springboard, the seat of promise, for the future. It is the future, rather than the past, that animates our national myths. Even our national heroes are often heroes of the future as much as of the past. Thus

George Washington, in the view of Margaret Mead, "does not represent the past to which one belongs by birth, but the past to which one tries to belong by effort." That is what the race toward success means in America: we strive onward and upward, "towards the world of Washington and Lincoln." Even the most dubious propositions can be accepted, says Goeffrey Gorer, if they square with the futurism of American society. And on the other hand, "no theory could gain widespread acceptance in America which did not concede that the child was the hope for the future, and that he could, given the proper start in life, go further and fare better than his parents."[43]

Just as we could discern three positive functions that the past plays in the formation of American manners and morals, so we can see that, in rough symmetry, the future has its positive role in each of the same respects. First, the future does not recall the symbols of promise, but *calls for action* upon the promise, often revising and redefining the promise in the very moment of action. Action is the preferred mode of establishing the real, and it enjoys a special status in the American armory when compared with pure remembrance. Remembrance establishes a past reality that is hoped for now, but action establishes an expected reality and makes it a present reality. Second, the future protests all cases of nonunfolding of the promise, pointing hardheadedly to the newly visible injustices of the present. That is why those among us who are purely future-oriented are so often impatient at attempts to seek encouragement from gains made in the past. These gains were not good enough, as the existence of present injustice testifies. The newness of the incoming time reminds us that the main task is to make further gains. Third, the future complements the past tactically by furnishing imaginative, unprecedented new departures in situations where sanction, precedent, or past wisdom have been unable to get the new challenges answered. Just now, for example, the old rules that have governed human relations seem not to be up to the challenge. What may be needed is a future-oriented set of tactics, including "a surprising openness in personal relations, a new intensity of personal commitment, a radical shift in the morally admissible, an expanded definition of education, a whole new array of learning techniques and a heavy reliance on direct action and direct experience rather than theory and talk."[44]

In truth, we cannot discuss the functions of history and of the future separately. Finally, they merge. Not since the beginning of the republic have we been able to judge who has the real revolution by simply equating revolution with up-to-dateness and liberality, and antirevolution with conservatism and love of country. Resisting such easy typing, but ever capable of breaking out anywhere, always distorted, but visible even in the bad manners of both camps, the revolutionary theme lives on in our tradition and in our daily lives and still sets the bias for the American attitude toward time.

7. Manners Oriented by the Equalitarian Sense of Space

"Equality of conditions turns servants and masters into new beings, and places them in new relative positions," Tocqueville observed of the Americans.[45] The end of revolution is only partly the overthrow of despotism. Revolution has less dramatic consequences that reach beyond the political realm into the world of manners. This more extended end is to reorganize the space of the community to provide larger participation for hitherto excluded groups and persons. There is, in a short, a permanent bias toward equality in American life.

Almost immediately we notice a division of opinion over the way in which this bias toward equality is to be expressed. One branch of the equalitarian mythology takes the individual as the locus, and personal freedom as the dominant value that is to be expressed. Another branch, by contrast, holds that the primary datum is the whole of the community, an entity that overrides the individual identities of the members, even though within this whole, the principle of equality still prevails. The dominant value here is the will of the majority, arrived at, however, on a one-man, one-vote basis. There is more to be said about each of these versions of the equalitarian bias, but that will best come after we have examined the manners that belong with them.

(a) The Self-Appointment Syndrome

At a fairly early point in the life of the American nation, Emerson discerned a certain tendency among his countrymen and remarked on the sort of manners it would lead to. Any man worth being called a "gentleman," says Emerson, will be "lord of his own actions" and will express "that lordship in his behavior, not in any manner dependent and servile either on persons, or opinions, or possessions."[46]

To be a gentleman, according to this conception, does not entail accepting a previously sanctioned code of manners, or even agreeing to be bound by current manners. Emerson understood, already, that manners in America would be quite different from manners in Europe. "There is nothing settled in manners," he insists, since "the laws of behavior yield to the energy of the individual." When people first enter society—say, the young woman at her first ball, or the man from the country at a dinner in the city—they too often fear that they must master a preexistent ritual, "according to which every act and compliment must be performed." Later, they learn better. The individual, if he has good sense and character, will expect to decide for himself which forms are appropriate. Manners, for Emerson, should not be performed out of "deference to a Chinese etiquette," but they should be signs or emblems pointing to the substance and dignity of the person. Manners should express "the grandeur of our destiny." In the long run it is the "heart" that shapes and reshapes fashion and courtesy, taking as its criterion the sense of regard for other men. But this concern for others can be expressed only out of a manner that springs from manhood, only from a community in which every man is to be "lord of his own actions."[47]

Emerson, like Montesquieu, is here describing republican manners under conditions of "virtue," in which the will operates with initiative toward other men and the commonwealth. Alas, as we have seen, virtue does not always operate so reliably. What happens in practice is that this lordship of one's own action is transformed, under American conditions, into something of an exaggeration. It becomes an urge not simply to be lord of one's own actions, but to take oneself to be the coach, advice-giver, or spokesman (although not the outright master) of the whole vicinity in which one acts. When the status of the individual is exaggerated, the trait of self-reliance becomes enlarged into the vice of self-appointment to superintend the affairs of the immediate space. We are still dealing with the notion of equality, but we are seeing it now when it is captured by the magnetic force of individual initiative. The upshot is that every individual is assumed to have the capacity to perform, speak, and lead in reform of the space around him; and if his own gifts and powers are sufficient, he may extend the orbit of this activity past the circle of his own personal acquaintances, reaching right on up to his assertion of the right to appoint himself a spokesman for the country itself.

"If an American were condemned to confine his activity to his own affairs," says Tocqueville, "he would be robbed of one half of his existence."[48] This urge to volunteer one's services to superintend the space is at the root of the garrulous patriotism that Tocqueville, Mrs. Trollope, and other observers have noted at all times and periods in the American experience. It is not just that the country itself is deemed fit to boast about. One more ingredient is required, the assumption that the private citizen himself is qualified and worthy to do the boasting. Thus with the cant of the past-embalmer goes the boasts of the individualist. As Boorstin has shown in his study of the birth of the nationalist spirit in America, the booster spirit characterized not just our "national" consciousness, but was in a sense built up out of local boosterism and pride growing out of the smaller units of American community in the nineteenth century.[49] And we see this spirit even in the most intimate situations of collateral personal relations, in the competitive brag that women engage in, for example, describing the achievements of their sons and daughters in winning membership in college fraternities or sororities. Although the counterposed American regard for conformity, groupiness, or "team spirit" also explains much of the booster talk (we will come to that presently), our point at the moment is that whatever the object of the talk might be—family, town, the local waterfall, country, Judy's status as cheerleader—the talking-up must be done by a *spokesman*. And the American spokesman is self-appointed. That is the heart of it. He is a spokesman in a new tradition, a tradition that has little in common with the European tradition which insists that a duly constituted official—father, *Bürgermeister*, minister of commerce—must be deferred to. However battered the ideal of equality is in a space where the aggressive individual may feel called upon to "take over," yet the ideal is honored even here: for there is no preappointed hierarchy; the right to volunteer is there for all.

A second feature of individualism, along with this tendency toward self-appointment, is the necessity of guilt denial. I am convinced that past analyses of the American character have misled us when they made too much of the "assumption of innocence" as one of its ingredients. On this view it has typically been claimed that Americans, coming to a pristine wilderness and reorganizing its space free of the tyranny, state secrets, priestcraft, feudalism, and wars of Europe, imagined themselves an innocent people, and that this monstrous pretension of innocence continues in the American psyche. But I think this is to misread the American psyche. There is, to be sure, a faint wishfulness about American manners that would have us stand at arm's length from the affairs of Europe, and a wistful dream that would have America a new, clean world, glossy and, I suppose, innocent. But, I submit, all this was only a wish and a dream—not the reality. Americans have not only found it easy to yield to the temptation to manage the affairs of other peoples, they have also had to deal, from the start, with their own patent noninnocence. Not even the first inhabitants of the wilderness, the Puritans and the Virginians, saw themselves as innocent or (what is the same thing) void of experience. What they supposed about themselves was not that they were innocent, but that they were righteous, which is a very different thing. An American is never innocent, for his world is a world of experience and doing, and no one who experiences reality and, worse, *acts* on it can ever think of himself again as innocent. But he can be righteous, if his acts and his judgments conspire to the verdict that his experience, on the whole, has lifted the community, and has helped matters more than hurt. The Puritan jeremiads of the seventeenth century, the Edwardean theology and the constitutional doctrine of separation of powers in the eighteenth century, the frontier revivals and the bloody war over slavery and the union in the nineteenth century, are none of them based on the assumption of innocence. They testify to the opposite—that in finding ourselves, and in transforming our dreams and wishes into acts and community, we had shaped all too often crookedly and unworthily and that our duty was to reshape all things again in the direction of what is right and just.

Nor has the American mind viewed unretouched nature as innocent. Unspoiled nature in America is, if anything, regarded as a mark of unrighteousness, for unshaped nature is a sign of human passivity.

We sin by leaving nature be. We may also sin, it is true, by reshaping nature according to our designs, which may betray a fair amount of inordinate passion and selfishness. But we do far worse by not shaping nature at all than by reshaping nature and only partly succeeding at it.

The secret of the capacity to reshape, and of the movement toward righteousness, is the capacity of the individual to work with others—and appoint himself leader. Thus the man whom American experience has cast as its hero: the rugged individual, the man of self-appointment writ large, really the successor to the aristocrat in the new world. He is Montesquieu's proper democrat, the leader who can lead without becoming outright master, and who can make followers of his equals. (The cybernetics age is apparently killing this hero, and the bias toward individualism is doubtless going to be expressed in other channels in the future; but this is an issue that must await our examination of the group-affirming tendency, below.)

The worst condition of all for an American is then not wrongdoing, but lack of confidence, the feeling that one has no center, no initiative, the failure to esteem and know oneself as an able individual. That is the most culpable condition of all for an American. Wrongdoing is not a mortal sin, but not-doing is. More exactly, it is not not-doing itself that is the worst thing of all, that doesn't quite take us to the abysmal heart of things. What is worst of all is not having a *warrant* to do; it is to be lacking the self-conferred credentials of self-appointment. That is the abyss that the American black man has now discovered that he is in, two hundred years after his white fellow countrymen discovered it and began climbing out.

From this point of view, the nonindividualist is a not-self or a nonperson. He is in need of redemption. He is in need of finding the strength to appoint himself a person. We see this sickness of the not-self not only in our actions (or nonactions) but also in our talk. The language of the not-self is the opposite of our normal American boasting talk. It is the language of apology. The apology is the very opposite of the boast: it is a denial of one's ability to make good on our common promise. The boaster may not make good either, but he claims to be able to, which shows his heart is right. The apology-maker is either cunningly humble, or worse, unable to do.

One should be able to consume, for example. That is an obligation imposed by the project of transforming the environment on every able-bodied citizen. "We're sorry but we just came for a sandwich" was the pathetic apology struck by a pair of bourgeois matrons at a motel restaurant in their own town. Their assumption was that to live up to their achievement handicap they must order chateaubriand at every sitting. At the airport restaurant one Christmas Eve as I waited for a plane to join my family in Florida, I noted couples recognizing each other at neighboring tables. Each apologized to the other for being there. They were, to be sure, performing ably at consuming. But they had violated a more primordial requirement of self-appointment: each able-bodied family is supposed to make its hearth the center of things on such a date. So they apologized to each other. Each couple felt they were letting down the rugged American ritual of Christmas by not organizing their own observance. To eat out on Christmas Eve was to fail to be hard at the center. It was to admit to a porous selfhood.

The thirst for individuality explains a whole set of manners that we could call "scavenging." These are acts and deeds done in a desperate search for the trappings of aggressiveness, that are to be packed in to stuff or cover over the vacuum of a suspected nonself. It is in evidence when a hostess asks if we like her meal. It can exist in a strange back-to-back twinship with self-appointment, because we are complex creatures who are justified and sinful at the same time: *simil justus et peccator*. Thus the hostess may *aggressively* ask if we liked her meal.

Just as boasting is a promise exaggerated and not lived up to, so apology-making is a promise not believed in and hence not unfurled. The name dropper is someone who doesn't believe in his own name, and who must cover up the absence of prospects here by ringing down the curtain of a substitute truth. The white supremacist is another instance of the person without a confident center: so desperate is he for the substance of selfhood that he must construct a kind of artificial vacuum into which he can enter without fear of self-destruction. If he sets up the black man as a subself, then he, whatever his demerits, must appear by default as a self.

Already, in considering the status of the individual, and asking why he must take himself to be righteous rather than innocent, we have brushed back against the conceptual model with which we are organizing the whole discussion of equality: space. The myth of American innocence, which we have rejected as an explanation of very much about the American character, was supposed to spring out of the fresh, new-world space that American life inhabits. We must seek a different understanding of what is unique about American space. For this space does not and cannot remain fresh, new, and innocent. On the contrary, this space must be organized, cut up, rearranged, furnished, and lived in. Nature must be shaped and reshaped for it to become worthy of being owned.

Accordingly, we may expect to find the individual in America strongly tempted to express himself in an urge to occupy personal space and organize it. It seems clear enough that every greater community has coined its own version of personal space. We have already noticed Edward T. Hall's study of this phenomenon, and his view that the model of personal space differs markedly when we compare Americans with Germans, Englishmen, Arabs, and Japanese. The German shows some preference for closed-off space of his own, for example, whereas the American is likely to keep his office door open in the wish to share (or perhaps exhibit) his personal space. To take another example, the Frenchman, too, will be on guard against "too close contact" and has evolved a code of manners aimed at shielding him. If this code "keeps the other at arm's length, the imposed distance permits a kind of frankness in social intercourse that might cause misunderstanding in the less stylized patterns of American conversational exchange."[50]

I suggest that a peculiarity of the American attitude toward space is not simply the urge to share it or exhibit it. There is a prior feature: this is the urge to rework one's space, to transform it into the current image of humanity. Thus the motif is not simply the craving for property or real estate. It is predominantly an urge to have a space to remake rather than simply to claim. That may explain the American's apparent willingness to share his space: it is really the handiwork he has done on it, perhaps, that he wishes to share. It is not natural, in this syndrome, to desire privacy, for that would be to conceal one's labors from view. Thus the "bubble" of personal space that every American carries around him is not to be understood as an opaque bubble affording privacy, as perhaps with classical European types. The American who seeks too much privacy is regarded as unrighteous by his fellows, as having something to hide, or better, as having nothing to show. The American bubble of personal space is a display window.

One can organize his space in simple and complex ways, in ephemeral and quasi-permanent ways. One of the more commonplace ways, for example, is the cough. Coughs indicate one's potential for self-appointment as master of the immediate vicinity. There is the imperious cough of the entrepreneur or magnate, signaling a strong presumption of leadership or priority. There is the bus-station cough of the underclass, really an anticough, indicating failure to conquer and announcing to all in earshot that no competition is to be expected from that source. There is the baroque public-library cough, open to rich or poor alike, laying claim not only to the newspaper one is reading, but also to a second one lying on the table not yet actually in the physical grip of the cougher, but claimed all the same; this cough also warns that the same ground rules will prevail tomorrow. But there are many other ways of announcing one's claims to priority in organizing space. Many a young tough who would never dream of using the cough achieves the same effect by the noisiness of his motorbike.

One may organize a space symbolically or fragmentarily to indicate that his powers of self-appointment are ontologically alive, although they have been forced by circumstances into a strategic retreat or period of lying fallow. Such is the game of the elderly apartment dweller who spends, seemingly, hours each day on the parking lot, with the trunk lid of his car raised, fussing and fiddling with the contents of the trunk. This opened trunk with its plunder is his altar of space. The car trunk is for him a kind of eucharistic celebration, its contents the medicine of immortality. He cannot organize the space of his apartment, for both his wife and the manager have appointed themselves co-leaders of that enterprise. There is no job offering space to furnish any more, for he is retired. But there is the car trunk, where he keeps his most sacred artifacts—fishing gear, carpenter tools, copies of *Popular Mechanics,* and other items for toying with space.

One may perform the ritual of preemption of turf even on a space that he does not actually own. (This is another reason why we deny that property rights, any more than the appeal to pure conscience, represent the proper focus of the moral struggle in America: the disposition of space is the issue that determines the value of property on the one hand, and gives embodiment to conscience, on the other.) A citizen of sound mind and body may for all that come to regard the state park near his home town as his own space (and that of his contiguous peers), given over to him for psychic management. He is thus prepared to resent strangers and under some circumstances even neighbors when they intrude. This close guarding of expropriated state space is especially evident in the waiting line for lunch at Paris Landing State Park in Tennessee on a Sunday, when there aren't enough tables for all the genteel townspeople to dine at once, and they are reduced to the extremity of eying each other hostilely, out of apprehension that a family that entered at 12:06 might be seated, somehow, before one that entered at 12:05 and set up a prior claim for preferred space. Both families, insofar as they are in parity and in tandem as locals, join in balefully regarding the teachers from Nashville who were spending the weekend there on a retreat and perforce preempted the churchgoers—they had been there from breakfast, ready to move into the dining room, committing the mortal error of blundering from the outside into space psychically reserved for the insiders.

Behavioral scientists are beginning to make much of the phenomenon of urban overcrowding as a factor in stress and antisocial conduct. They are prone to liken such spaces as Grand Central Station during the Friday afternoon rush hour to "behavioral sinks" among animals in which sheer compression of numbers into an inadequate space leads to various forms of pathology and erratic activity.[51] I strongly suspect that overcrowding as such need not be the only conditioning factor among human beings to drive them into campaigns of hostility, and that one need not limit his observations to sites like midtown Manhattan. Nearly every good restaurant in the United States is a behaviorial sink, at least during certain hours.

Lines of people waiting to board buses or planes (unless seats have been assigned in advance, and even then at times) are behavioral sinks. The second floor of the building in which I have an office is a behavioral sink, even though there are only twenty of us and twenty offices to be occupied. The trouble is, nine of the offices are large ones, and the others are pretty small—instructor and assistant professor size. There are more than nine professors here whose professional space-bubble is larger than that. But it is doubtless the politest behavioral sink in the country, much, much more so than Manhattan's Pan Am Building.

The limit of the expropriating drive, I suppose, is seen in the two classical antisocial habits, that of littering and that of looting. Actually these are two underground motifs for space disposition, and they work in counterpoint. As for the litterbug, he organizes space with antiartifacts, partly out of the urge to reshape nature, even if the reshaping is dysfunctional (that is better, let us remember, than not shaping nature at all), but also out of the competitive urge, another vector of individualism: littering can be understood as a way of competing with the others for disposal rights over all of the space there is. Despite its outlaw standing, littering is an extremely common form of spatial organization. One of the reasons may be precisely that it is antiestablishment. In any event, nearly all Americans commit it from time to time. A classic description of the manners of littering is given in John Hersey's novel, *Too Far to Walk*. John Fist, walking out to Humblesmith, remembers hiking across New Hampshire. He recalls, with a tinge of fury, a glimpse of Mt. Madison,[52]

> . . . a natural picnic spot with a broad view of green and purple hills, huckleberry bushes close at hand, iron-wood, outcroppings of gray lichened rocks—and a litter of Schlitz beer cans on the pathside, Saranwrap blown into sprigs of juniper, an aluminum pan for Sara Lee brownies left beside blackened stones set up to grill Roesseler franks, as the carton lying there testified; the filthy, selfish carelessness of those who thought the American mountains were simply theirs to enjoy and besmear.

In such manners we are at the furthest point from Montesquieu's "love of country," and yet we are not dealing with an absolutely contrasting behavior. For even the litterbug, in all his depravity, shows some spark of the will to organize space. And he does stretch the expanse of the Gross National Product a bit, in that the artifacts of littering come from the right-side-up forces attempting to organize the environment, the forces of the technostructure (who are thus revealed to have a left hand as well as a right). The litterbug, I fear, is as good an example as any of secular American man.

Looting is the second underground form of space disposition, but it works quite differently from littering. Whereas littering consists in organizing space with antiartifacts, looting consists in disorganizing space by removing artifacts. In the decade past it was natural to think of the ghetto riots—Watts, Detroit, Harlem—as the prime, definitive instances of looting. Television programs almost made a cliché of scenes showing looters making off with whiskey, suits, and television sets. Whole grocery stores were sometimes rifled by hordes of children and teen-agers.

But there is no need to take these riots as the chief examples of looting, for looting in one form or another is a deviant variety of self-appointment and of preemption of turf that erupts, like littering, in every precinct of the national ethos. One of the lingering memories of my days as a small-town newspaper editor is of the wholesale food-looting that occurred among good, decent, starched, conservative country folk each year at a family reunion (to which I, as editor of the local paper, was always invited). Christian women in large bonnets would dart in, snatch at fried chicken and Cokes, and make off to their subtribal base again. Originally, I suppose, there had been a communal lunch for the members of the reunion at large. Later, the lunch became an enterprise for each family to pursue on its own—an incursion of individualism and competitiveness into the loving-kindness of family remembrance. The looting is a newer attempt to reorganize the space, or rather to disorganize it further.

Significantly, the artifacts gathered in looting rarely suffice to organize one's own space, even when they are brought back into it. The fried chicken is gone in a moment, the suit does not fit. The dominant motif here is self-appointment at work to disorganize a threatening configuration. Looting is an underground copying of the proper work of the democrat, since it is aimed at disorganizing space that does not furnish equal sharing. Looting is a sign of pain, of illicit reaction to space felt to be organized in contravention of the equalitarian bias. But it is not, after all, a democratic form of disposition, since it subjects the organized space to a new version of extrinsic control.

The looting drive in milder form is even more widespread. Even the ads of resort hotels that say "complimentary bottle of iced champagne served in your room" can bring out, ever so faintly, the feeling that here we may be redressing the balance against us a bit. It is all a trick, of course, and we pay for the champagne in the hotel bill. But it is a trick that works, and works because the looting instinct within us is never quite stilled.

It is but a step from these subterranean forms of space organization to the outright uses of violence. The issue of the day is improperly framed when it is limited to the question whether students and black men are to be allowed to get away with violence. The issue concerns not these special members of the society, however active they may be at the moment in testing novel forms of space organization; the issue is how a society committed from the inauguration of its being to equality may control and contain the dysfunctional tendencies toward self-appointment and space-claiming that are endemic, not far from overt expression in any of us.

This brings us to a final feature of individualism, the antiauthoritarian bias in Americans, another of those traits that have been persistently observed throughout the entire run of time of the republic. In another of those reduplications of the primoridal republican features in everyday life, "The typical American attitudes toward authority have remained substantially the same as those manifested by the framers of the American Constitution" (Goeffrey Gorer). These attitudes take it for granted that authority "is inherently bad and dangerous." To be sure, survival of the nation requires that some be handed authority, but this authority is circumscribed and restricted by ingenious legal measures, and officeholders are regarded with suspicion. This distrust and low estimate of authority, says Gorer, is a key "to the understanding of American character and American behavior." And these attitudes are "far more than political"; despite the political element in them, "they are above all moral: people, or institutions, who 'push other people around' are bad, repugnant to decent feelings, thoroughly reprehensible."[53] Thus the high school football coach, clearly in charge of the scrimmage session, ostensibly gruff and irascible ("Can't you run, boy," he snorts to a lumbering fifteen-year-old back), still cannot function as an outright *authority*. He can represent himself as an expert on football, yes. He can prescribe the drills as "coach," viz., leader of the team. He can chide a blundering quarterback as one who in his day was more dexterous. But in the end his credentials are those of a fellow devotee of sports—not those coercive warrants of a master.

The same *a priori* resistance to constituted authority is present in the recent student protests, and explains, in part, the alacrity with which the cry of "police brutality" is raised (this is not to deny that the cry is also explained, in part, by police brutality). It is present in another form among the clutch of suburbanites (critics of students and black men and patrons, to a man, of law and order) who realized that an interstate highway being constructed in their neighborhood was not going to have an access road near them. An existing road leading to the freeway from their neighborhood was ordered cut. Highway department workmen dug out a three-foot ditch at the end of the access road to keep traffic from going upon the freeway. Residents of the neighborhood that night filled the ditch, used the road anyway, and announced to the press their intent of repairing the road every night, if necessary.

When the equalitarian bias is expressed in the modality of individualism, we are able to discern a number of pathological elements, summed up as the "self-appointment" syndrome—the tendency to volunteer one's services and act for those around; boasting talk (also seen inversely in apology-making and scavenging); assertion of righteousness; preemption of turf; littering and looting; and reaction against constituted authority. All of these patterns of manners at once express and betray the bias toward parity in the sharing of space.

(b) The Conformity Game

Individualism produces one set of manners in America. Thoroughly mixed and mingled with the manners stemming from this motif, however, is another set derived from an alternate modality of

the equalitarian impulse: the manners of conformism or majoritarian-
ism. If, on the one hand, I in my individual self am as good as anyone
else (and therefore able to do and to speak aggressively), on the other
hand, I can concede that this whole community—ultimately America
itself—is a fusion of such folk into a larger whole. Equalitarianism,
in short, also takes a community-affirming form. And this form
amounts to a counterpoint of the individualistic themes. Alongside
the boasting, competitive, self-congratulating talk of the individualist
exists the team spirit, cooperative pep talk of the larger group. Alongside the self-reliance of the individualistic motif thrives the participa-
tory motif of the communal spirit. Alongside the sharklike preemption of turf that characterizes individual initiative comes the collective
mastery of the environment that is exerted in our technological
solidarity. Alongside the antiauthoritarianism and bellicose garrulity
of the individual we know of the populism, anti-intellectualism, and
conformist thinking of majority rule.

We see these antinomies intertwined at every point in American
history. That is why the Puritans can be portrayed both as an existentialist folk who would pit the saint, isolated in all his moral responsibility and ethical individuality, over against the supreme individual,
Yahweh himself; and at the same time as corporate exemplars of a
holy, social, political, theocratic commonwealth. That is why the pioneer of the West can be pictured both as a gun-slinging privateer and
also as the loyal member of a wagon train who has subordinated his
ambitions to the highest ideals of community life. That is why, in the
ascent of capitalism following the Civil War, it is possible to speak of
a "Gospel of Wealth" and a "Social Gospel" flourishing simultaneously, each a plausible specimen of American piety. That is why our
own age seems at once the most individualist of times (*item,* the
autonomy of our younger generation, the permissiveness of our educational process) and the most collective of times (*item,* big government—or big labor or big business).[54]

According to David M. Potter, these are the only two significant
alternatives that have developed in America as expressions of political equality.[55] For Potter, the individualist option is allied with the
libertarian sentiment in a most salient form. This option has been
definitively expressed, he says, by Thomas Jefferson and later by

Frederick Jackson Turner, the historian of the frontier thesis. On the other hand, Potter sees the "conformist" or "majoritarian" option as less expressive of liberty and idealism and as characteristically allied with equalitarianism and materialism. Tocqueville, he suggests, has given us a memorable description of this option.

Potter's analysis, I think, has some flaws. It overemphasizes the affinity between liberty and individualism, on the one hand, and that between equality and conformism on the other. A better scheme avoids this categorization. For equality is a dominant motif in both the individualist and the conformist options. At this point it might be well to remember another memorable chronicle: Mrs. Trollope finds that Jefferson's doctrines are intolerable, in part, because of the arrogant pretense to equality that goes along with individual liberty. Jefferson wrote "with more perspicuity than he thought," she says, "and his hot-headed democracy has done a fearful injury to the country." For Jefferson's teachings, as unsound as they are, "are but too palatable to a people, each individual of whom would rather derive his importance from believing none are above him." In such a society, soon both law and gospel are replaced by the kind of self-rule that begins with the "darling" thought, "I'm as good as you."[56] On the other hand, there is no inherent contradiction between group-mindedness and liberty, as long as liberty is understood as a possible aspiration of groups as well as of individuals. One of the leading motifs of voluntary association in this country has been to combine forces in order to resist extrinsic control: that is a leading reason the thirteen colonies combined; it is a leading reason for the emergence of such contemporary movements as "Black Power."

Nevertheless, it is accurate to perceive in American life a fundamental split between individualism and conformism. It is doubtless a dilemma of democracy that will never be finally solved. For once the locus of power is removed from the prince and taken over by the community itself, contention will always arise over which design of equality is to be preferred: that which organizes community space around the locus of the singular person, or that which understands participation (hence equality) in corporate style.

Let us then turn to the manners induced specifically by conformity. Immediately we encounter further confusion. A battle is going on not just between individualism and conformity, but between competing styles of conformity. At this point, we may serve clarity, if not science, by borrowing a concept from physics—that of the simultaneous action of "fields." Several kinds of forces operate at once in the physical world. There is the nuclear field that holds atomic particles together in nuclei. At the same time, an electromagnetic field is exerting influence over the same atoms. Still another field, that of gravitation, also acts to bind matter into larger groupings. The nuclear field holds sway in the smallest sphere, although its effects are very powerful within that sphere. Next, according to physicists, is the range of the electromagnetic forces, which are most influential on bodies ranging in size from atoms to stars. Gravity, finally, is dominant over bodies of all sizes "from planets and stars up to the clusters of galaxies."[57]

Our corporate life is similarly pulled by the competing influences of several spheres. A tight nuclear force is exerted on us by the field of family life, gang life, and those close-knit associations that influence and constrain us in personal relations generally. A second field is that of the more impersonal groups we belong to: here our manners are influenced by our professions, our regions, our neighborhoods, urban, rural, or suburban. Finally, the largest fields that exert influence on our manners are those that characterize the greater community itself, the cohesive forces that taken together account for what is culturally dominant and distinctive.

It is the manners induced by these larger fields that interest us, though we grant the intensity of the short-range fields. And that means, essentially, that we have to ask the question: what are the manners produced by technology, automation, and cybernetics? For the technostructure has become the dominant field over American life today, the principal structuring and tincturing force upon community. It is no longer love of country in the classical sense, no longer rural mores, no longer the discipline of assembly-line life that magnetizes or corporately gathers up Americans. Now the prime field is that of the "new industrial state." We increasingly carry the manners and mores of the technostructure around with us, even when we are engaging in the group life of the smaller fields. To live in the new American industrial culture is like receiving a dose of radiation: even when we enter the comparative shielding of home and leisure life, the radiation is there. We do not go to cocktail parties to meet persons any more but to encounter emissaries from the industrial complex. We cannot even go out on the tennis courts for a quiet sporting session any more: we play with a fellow Jaycee, and what we toss back and forth is not a bloated, fuzzy white ball so much as the challenges of production and consumersmanship. Other fields of force may take up more time but carry a less lethal dose of radiation. An hour's stay at church involves very little irradiation today. A whole week's life with family doesn't fatally mutate our conversation. But a declining work week is not accompanied by lessening of the industrial radiation: on the contrary, it stays with us all the time, no matter how much or how little we are directly exposed.

The chief characteristic of individualism in the field of manners, we found, was the "self-appointment" syndrome. Conversely, the principal style of manners induced by corporate magnetization is the surrender of one's right of judgment and decision to the group. Much of everyday morality, as we all know, is simply a kind of withholding of self-appointment, a checking over of one's autonomy to whichever group dominates the field forces exerting influence on us. John Updike's adulterous pairs in his novel, *Couples,* are constantly subjected to such field effects: "For much of what they took to be morality proved to be merely consciousness of the other couples watching them."[58] For the moment our most conformist norms are still those of the nineteenth-century industrial surge, which is now in its endgame as an organizing entity. The new organizing field, as we have suggested, is not so much the assembly-line sort of industry as the new industrial regime of cybernetics with its monitoring and radiating arms in the mass electronic media. Whichever larger corporateness exerts its effect, the result is the same, and has been since Tocqueville found himself repelled by American conformism. "Men are not apt to change their characters by agglomeration," he thought; it was just as wrong to check over absolute power, then, to a majority, or a mass, as to a powerful individual.[59]

The receding set of manners, by and large, is the set constraining us toward good production habits—thrift, discipline, rectitude, sobriety, and all the rest. But this set is rapidly being replaced by a new set, the manners that conduce to good behavior in the day of a cybernated economy. With near unanimity all of the sanctions in this set of manners drive toward one goal: consumersmanship. If Veblen were alive today he would no longer be able to write about "conspicuous consumption" any more than an observer of American manners seventy-five years ago could have spoken of "conspicuous production." For the worthiest service to the society now is not in work, but in nibbling off one's share (and, if possible, even more) of the G.N.P. As Galbraith succinctly puts it, the American today "serves the industrial system not by supplying it with savings and the resulting capital; he serves it by consuming its products. On no other matter, religious, political or moral, is he so elaborately and skillfully and expensively instructed."[60] In past ages, the origin of manners was in the way of life of the landed, or of the nobility. Later, in America, as we have seen, it was in the way of life of the factory town. In contemporary America, manners are now coming to be definitively shaped by the necessity to consume.

Older people—those whose consciousness was fixed no later than the Cold War—are dedicated enough to the goal of consuming, but their technique is either obsolescent or awkward. It is obsolescent in their view that consumption is a sport for the comparatively few. It is awkward in that they understand consuming only rationally; having grown up in the only slightly slacked-off heyday of the production ethic, they still cannot consume smoothly, intuitively, or naturally. It is for the younger generation—those born after about 1945—who are truly casual consumers, to reintroduce polish and assurance. With the elders, once the point is borne in that consumersmanship is a higher activity than producersmanship, the simplistic thought occurs that the more one consumes the more worthy he must be. But the old thrift ethic is still there, and the result is the backbreaking feat of consuming prodigiously by making use of everything. The younger crowd does not fall victim to the quantitative fallacy, in the first place. It consumes symbolically, for the most part, although there are exceptions (clothes and cars are still quantitatively consumed). It consumes by waste as much as by use (tires burnt up in fast starts, breakfast ham left untouched at bedside). And—discovery of discoveries—it consumes services and intangibles, rather than hard goods, as its great contribution to the G.N.P.: its good works are high telephone bills, airplane travel tabs, tuition charges, dental fees.

We are not surprised to find out, on observation, that the language of conformity in America today is heavily infiltrated with the language of consumersmanship. Nonsmokers, with never a wistful dream of following up a good meal with a cigarette, nonetheless wake up of a morning unable to quit singing "You can take Salem out of the *country*, BUT . . ." And one's kids, "riding shot-gun on the shopping cart, may not know a stanza of *The Star-Spangled Banner*, but they can rap out several verses of 'To a Smoker, It's a Kent.' "[61]

The most obvious linguistic effect of consumer conformity, then, is to skew the notion of what a noun or substantive is: in American English the normative noun is now a commercially produced product of some kind. Verbs less and less denote man as a worker, master of his material, transformer of nature. More and more they picture him as a craftsman of knowing what to do with finished products. Thus a second great linguistic shift away from the classical European is to be seen here. The first shift was to differentiate the active, revolutionary, nature-transforming American from "the traditional attitude of peasants, for whom the land and its products are, as it were, part of themselves, of their ancestors and descendants, so that their histories and fortunes are conceived of as intertwined, so that there is at least a measure of identification between man and material." In this great shift, our speech pictured man as an ingenious reworker of the natural, the American as completely dominating his material.[62] Now the new language removes *Homo Americanus* one step further from the peasant: his environment is no longer a hard-scrabble nature that he is up against and constrained to conquer; now his background, his environment is the mosaic of goods and services turned out by the technostructure, and the function of speech is to relate him conceptually to them. Nature is now at two removes from most of us.

An ominous effect is to drive American speech toward a capability only for expressing pleasure with consumption (or, conversely, the plaintive wish for more refined consumption), and to deprive it of the words and sensitivity to reveal crisis and misery. "It's fun to be nice to people," is the slogan on an automobile dealer's customer-service truck. "If there's anything that Carol and myself can do for you this morning, please let us know," chirps an airline stewardess. Related to this is a clumsy attempt not to be peremptory, even in enforcing safety regulations: nature is kept at least one environment away. Thus the stewardess does not order you not to smoke when the plane is landing, or even request you not to. She invites you to read: with a detached retreat from the sought-after compliance itself, all that is suggested is that you "observe the 'No Smoking' sign when it appears."

In the final analysis, the entire environment becomes material for consumption. American tourists nowadays go to Europe, not to see Europe, but in order to read their travel guides. At a little canalside hotel in Amsterdam, we were always served a breakfast of boiled eggs, two kinds of cheese, three kinds of bread, with butter, marmalade, and all the coffee we wanted. But that, of course, is what the travel guide said we would get. The American guests would bring their copies of Frommer or Fodor or Fielding to the breakfast table. Instead of taking hints from these authorities about what to see that day in Amsterdam, they regarded Amsterdam itself (like the breakfast) as a kind of three-dimensional color supplement, to be consumed purely by way of illustration of what was said in the guides. "Today we're supposed to go to the Rijksmuseum and see Rembrandt's *Night Watch*." "Then tonight we have to go to Hollands Glorie Restaurant—and let's see, what dishes are we supposed to try there—oh yes, the roast." "I forget now, we've already made the canal trip, haven't we; or am I thinking about Copenhagen. Anyway, we have to go to the Enclosing Dike tomorrow." "Yes, but we're not supposed to go to Haarlem—Fielding says to skip it."

Here are experiences that, divorced from the consumersmanship of the tourist industry, might offer great diversity and range of significance. A visit to the great National Museum, for example—but now its treasures were to be largely disregarded except those few paintings mentioned in *Europe on Five Dollars a Day*. A sampling of another people's cuisine—but in the shape of a crowded, second-rank restaurant, which the proprietress of our hotel described as existing largely for the consumption of the American tourists: "We Hollanders don't go there, or to any of the other restaurants you had in mind." A tour of the great canal system of Amsterdam—but now embroidered by the guide with the Dutch version of blarney: when the boat passed our own hotel, the guide identified it as the site of Amsterdam's first diamond polishing house—a piece of simple fiction, as our host later assured us. A visit to a truly astounding twentieth-century technical wonder, the great enclosing dike across the body of water formerly known as the "Zuider Zee"; and if we had been even good nineteenth-century Americans, we could have appreciated it on its own terms, as a marvel thrown up against the extrinsic control of nature. But we could appreciate it only as consumers. It was an illustrated part of the travel guide. I found myself, when we returned to the hotel at night after a day of adventuring around Amsterdam, nearly irresistibly tempted to check the guidebooks and find out what I should think about what we had seen that day.

When the bias toward equality takes the form of participation in the dominant group rites, the result is consumersmanship. Like individualism, however, the American conformity game, for all its pathology, betrays the knowledge that salvation depends on joint action and communal being. For all its depravity, the conformist sentiment in America reveals an elemental awareness that "binding and promising, combining and covenanting" are the means by which the power to be and to become is preserved.[63]

(c) The Unfinished State of Equality

American space, it is now obvious, has by no means been fully or even satisfactorily organized as yet. The physical space is in a much more advanced state of restructuring than the communal and existential space. We could very well now designate "unfinishedness," "immaturity," or even "nonbeing" as a continuing and potent ingredient of the American character. Within the context of our present examination of the republican mores that have stamped American life, we can distinguish at least two major aspects of incompleted equality.

First, then, we can say, numerous sectors of American life are still managed by extrinsic control—as the insistence on self-propriety among the blacks consciously proclaims, and as the surrender of intellection and judgment to the technostructure among nearly all of us unintendedly testifies. America is as yet literally riddled with empty, unorganized existential spaces run from without—not without the commonwealth, but without the subcommunity and without the self—spaces in which there has not yet been a viable movement for structuring the terrain with the furniture of self-governance and self-determination. In a good number of these empty spaces, even the primitive struggle between "climate" and "morality" is repeated and refigured in contemporary permutations: what is the life of an urban slum today but the lagging persistence of a marginal standard of living, perpetuated by absentee ownership and the indifference of nonaffected citizens, and made more hideous than the worst either raw nature or human nature could do if these forces were acting alone, without mutual reinforcement? Rats still bite children in Harlem and in the run-down sectors of the most advanced cities. Where this primitive struggle has been proximately won, there is still the tyranny not just of consumersmanship, but of finding oneself reduced to a consumable commodity that can be the fate of the richest and most comfortable.

The struggle to reorganize such spaces goes on. Reverting to our time symbolism, revolution goes on: there are two revolutions in progress in this country today, each aimed at one form of tyranny, and each laden with the seeds of its own failure. There is the cybernetics revolution, which is overseeing the movement of our culture from a nineteenth-century society of factories and long hours and predatory individualism to a more ingeniously controlled system of automated plants, leisure, and electronic interdependence. At the same time, there is rising dissent, especially from the young, against the cybernetics-consumer world. "Yes," say the dissenters, "we are ready for a new world, too. We don't like the nineteenth century, either. But instead of a locked-in system, we want the freedom to disagree, the freedom not to consume. We want to use our leisure for self-identity, not for expanding the Gross National Product. We want no part of the 'system.' " There is, in short, a growing disjunction between the functional side of society, and the personal culture of many members of the society. "This tension between the 'technocratic' and the apocalyptic," says Daniel Bell, "may be one of the great ruptures in moral temper" of our day.[64]

The recency of the one-man, one-vote approach to representation in our courts suggests all too well how primitive and inchoate as yet is the republican ideal of participation by the people in the organization of their own space. In this sense, America has barely begun to realize what its identity is all about.

Much more pressing for our study of public ethics, however, is the second question that we must consider, that of the structuring agencies that must serve in our greater community until the distant day when the space is finally organized on a truly participationist basis. It has not been so organized as yet, and will not be for some few epochs at least! Thus we have to ask which institutions are most appropriate for America in this "transition period" from extrinsic control to genuine equality to replace the "intermediary corps" in Montesquieu's tempered monarchy. Evidently, we must be prepared to address ourselves to the question of which analogous institutions are actually present in the American commonwealth, as well as the question of which ones *ought* to stand in the breach. But let us defer the second question for a moment, and confine ourselves to a glimpse at the extant American "intermediary corps."

Let us be clear that we are dealing with an analogy and not a reduplication of Montesquieu's monarchical Europe. Even so we can make a compelling case that the United States today is to some extent not only a very unfinished and roughhewn republic, but that it is, worse than that, an imperfect replica of the European absolutism, minus at least one of the indispensable tempering institutions—an aristocracy—that at one time flourished as a check on the erstwhile absolutist monarchy.

First, setting aside the industrial community for the moment, we can take passing notice of the power of the federal executive in America: that is where we logically ought to start if we are to pursue the analogy with monarchical forms. And it is no bad place to start. According to the perceptive British student of American politics and character, D. W. Brogan, "The first truth to be asserted about this great office is that the President of the United States is a monarch." The Constitution entrusts the President with "the whole executive power of the Union" and the separate office of Commander-in-Chief "with complete control of armed forces." The President enjoys such great power not only in virtue of the stated structure of the office in the Constitution but also out of the potent force of tradition, for in our national history, the actual functions of the executive have evolved to fill this form dynamically and convincingly. Although this development does not make of the American President an "absolute monarch," Brogan says, it is nevertheless important "to insist on the monarchical character of the American presidency." The President holds a kinglike office not only because of his powers, but also "because he, more than any other institution (and every President is an institution), embodies *'We the People of the United States.'* In the President, in any President, the American people see their embodied power and see their own driving force personified."[65]

The separation of powers doctrine in the Constitution, we might note, may have been strong enough to encumber the chief executive in the performance of his duties—but it has not been able to inhibit the development of his power in the ways Brogan describes. Sensing this growth of presidential power, perhaps, the people have responded by entrenching themselves behind a set of critical manners and morals. Both right-wingers and left-wingers, for example, have reacted to the shocking discovery that in the twentieth century the chief can, in effect, deliver the nation into a state of war without the consent of Congress and for other than purely defensive reasons. One wing shows its apprehension by protesting our involvement in Southeast Asia and by virtually forcing an incumbent, Lyndon B. Johnson, to retire. Another wing reflects the same fear of the executive with a different style of protest, as in the conservative penchant for bumper stickers reading "Kennedy for King," and (with Johnson as target) "Caesar Bird." Some citizens derived ironic pleasure from finding monarchical overtones in the marriage of one of President Johnson's daughters. The groom, by this version of things, conducted himself entirely as prince consort—acted as a straight man, said little, played his role even more unobtrusively than Prince Philip or Lord Snowden. The largest Catholic church in the country was the scene of the wedding, which again indicated the royalist style that was being deployed.

Worst of all, this is not mere irony. As a people, Americans want the President to be strong, not to say a strong man. It is only when he takes an unpopular course of action with his power (as in the Vietnamese adventure) that they begin to make office untenable for him. At other moments, the American people show an unrepublican yearning for an executive to take the burdens of willed initiative off their shoulders and solve for them, let us say, the problem of violence in the streets. Americans thus turn out to be latter-day Troglodytes who find the burden of rearranging their space for common participation in governance much too onerous.

The Presidency, in short, because of the Constitution and history and human nature, "unites power, drama, and prestige as does no other office in the world." The President is, in effect, "a head of state as well as a head of government, a king and a prime minister rolled into one."[66]

Despite our democratic forms, then, we can say that the American republic bears much of the character of a tempered monarchy—and that the laws and manners will be dependent to that extent not only upon willed initiative, but that contemporary forms of rank and "honor" (appropriate to monarchy) will also be found to prevail. The next question must be to ask rigorously: what are the tempering institutions that will organize the space on behalf of the people to restrict the inroads of government? And the first matter that comes to notice is the gaping void in American culture left by the absence of a seasoned, time-binding aristocracy.

Tocqueville is aware of the great possibilities that formerly lay in government tempered by aristocracy, and he is sharply pained with the democratic excesses that he sees in America. But Tocqueville is poignantly aware that aristocracy has squandered away its opportunities. In France, aristocracy has become senile, in step with neither the people nor the times. On the eve of the French Revolution the nobility, which would fall along with the crown, still had the possibility of being more than a functionless caste; it still had the chance to serve the country as a critical voice against the excesses of royalty. Doubtless it could have served in this role more effectively than the more popular elements of opposition. One could still sense some of the great qualities of the aristocracy, Tocqueville thought, and one must always feel regret that instead of being brought under the laws of the land, the nobility was isolated and killed off. That solution deprived the nation of a part of its very substance and dealt a blow to liberty in France that would long be felt.[67] The nobility is a class that over centuries has developed leadership, fierceness of heart, natural confidence in its strengths, a habit of being looked up to which made of it a strong point in the social fabric. And not only did it realize a range of virile mores and manners in itself; it strengthened the virility of the other classes by example. Extirpated, it can never be reborn, yet nothing can replace it completely. Even if it could recover its titles and its goods, it could never again realize the lost spirit of its fathers.[68]

Whatever this memory of what the aristocracy could have been, it could not be the means of tempered government for new commonwealths. For Tocqueville, the solution appropriate to American time, space, and quality lies in the realm of voluntary associations, which were to replace the European forms of intermediate powers. These are important not only for political purposes, since in America there are no hereditary bodies that can be employed "as checks upon the abuses of power." They also organize into potent, if voluntary groupings, the will of the people to accomplish nearly everything else. The voluntary association, then, is for Tocqueville the great vehicle of manners and morals for "Americans of all ages, all conditions, and all dispositions":[69]

They have not only commercial and manufacturing companies, in which all take part, but associations of a thousand other kinds,—religious, moral, serious, futile, extensive or restricted, enormous or diminutive. The Americans make associations to give entertainments, to found establishments for education, to build inns, to construct churches, to diffuse books, to send missionaries to the antipodes; and in this manner they found hospitals, prisons, and schools.

Here we come to an extremely important qualification that must be made on our notion of space organization and that of virtue. Willed initiative, when it aims at equality, cannot be directly turned upon the state. It must be expressed by way of voluntary associations that have taken piecemeal responsibility for supervising various facets of the quest for public order. Such groups, themselves demanding a kind of virtuous, willed commitment from the citizenry, replace in America the corps of intermediary powers of European polities.

Now, we must ask, what are in fact the chief and most ponderable of these tempering institutions or associations in America? We wish to propose three, in descending order of importance.

We already know well enough what the first is. Aristocracy is replaced in America by the business community, better referred to in its contemporary form by Galbraith's term, "the technostructure."

The church is replaced in America by a loose coalition of the ethically oriented voluntary agencies (including present-day denominations—far cries and shallow heritages from the churches of yore; but also extending to welfare and educational agencies; and importantly including the universities, to the extent that they remain free of retainership by the technostructure, since they have replaced the churches as the voice of critical judgment against the society's baser tendencies).

Third, the local *parlements* and other political bodies are replaced in America not by state legislatures, as logic might dictate, but instead by political parties and urban machines, both apparently undergoing a time of troubles that may see them replaced with new power structures.

Here we will confine our remarks to what is by far the most powerful and influential of the mediating agencies in America, the constellation of business and technological forces.

If we want to point to the typical or representative American, we should of course have to point to the businessman, says D. W. Brogan. "If there is a class or an individual to whom the nation should turn, it is assumed to be the business class." This reliance on the businessman is of long standing and has proceeded so far that the government itself is ordinarily judged not according to political standards, but commercial standards: government itself is finally taken to be "merely business magnified or, if you like, . . . an inferior form of business." When he launched *Fortune,* an expensive, ambitious journal of commerce, Henry R. Luce declared that business "is obviously the greatest single common denominator of interest among the active leading citizens of the U.S.A." If there is any replacement in America of the European aristocracy, it surely lies here. "Our best men are in business," Luce proclaimed. Business is "the distinctive expression of the American genius."[70]

And it is true that the business establishment in this country has now and then taken on some of the attributes of an aristocracy. Tocqueville points out that the very notion of courage—a prized trait of the aristocrat—found a special, indigenous expression at the hands of commercial men in America. In Europe, courage was a virtue that had received its connotations from a long past of military engagements. In the United States, on the other hand, it is not so much "martial valour" that is most prized; "the courage which is best known and most esteemed is that which emboldens men to brave the dangers of the ocean, in order to arrive earlier in port."[71] This special kind of boldness and initiative has since been repeated in endless variations by the American entrepreneur.

Rossiter pictures the late nineteenth-century business community that managed our industrial development after the Civil War as consciously realizing a sort of natural aristocracy. This new form of *noblesse* combined "the twin doctrines of equality of opportunity and inequality of ability," a distinctively new-world approach. But it was not called a natural aristocracy, even though that might have been an accurate title. This theory of aristocracy was understood in quasi-religious terms and was known as the "Gospel of Wealth." Under this doctrine, the natural aristocrat, "elevated above his fellow men by his superior energy and ability," yet recognized an obligation to them. It was his privilege and at the same time his duty to offer them able leadership. This view was best expounded in the writings of Andrew Carnegie, Daniel S. Gregory, Russell Conwell, and others, and in them "we discover an aristocratic ideal as full-bodied and functional as any that has served the ruling classes of England and Europe."[72]

With the growth in the twentieth century of the giant corporation and of the complex technology on which our cities now utterly depend, we can virtually say that the industrial sector has become the ruler, and that it is the state that serves as an intermediary agency or tempering institution. The growth of governmental regulatory agencies illustrates the latter role, while the sheer massiveness and momentum of the technological planning, producing, and distributing process becomes the evidence of the near takeover of national values by the industrial system. Only the naïve, says John Kenneth Galbraith, will from now on ask the question of "how they are governed" in the context purely of Washington, the state capital, and city hall. "Others will ask also for an understanding of the goals of industrial planning."[73] The technostructure itself—that body of technical masters who initiate and oversee this planning process—has become a primary agency of governance.

Galbraith thinks that the mature corporation has become not just a *de facto* influence but that it has openly emerged as "part of the larger administrative complex associated with the state. In time the line between the two will disappear."[74] And industrial values have become part of the concepts of citizenship, manners, and mores, siphoning off commitments that in theory are due the commonwealth itself. One cannot really go about any more as a simple, unattached citizen. It is much better to be able to identify oneself as, say, a General Motors or Western Electric man. "The question automatically asked when two men meet on a plane or in Florida is, 'Who are you with?' " The fact is, says Galbraith, the organization man is willing to make this drastic identification with his company because it can do more for him than he for himself.[75]

Now the great need is to search out new agencies to arrest, temper, and criticize the imperium of the corporate ethos. Governmental regulation may accomplish some reforms—as the new safety-device regulations for automobile manufacturers may illustrate. But what government agency can take into account the kind of skewing of moral commitment that stems from this kind of radio commercial (one I have just heard as I sit here writing): "This year look out for Number One, and put yourself first"? The task before us is to seek transcendence of this ethos by developing ethically critical countervailing agencies. Perhaps churches and the universities can yet be enlisted, and part of the press. Perhaps our obsolescent political structures— the national parties, most urgently—can be transformed to allow more choice, and wider participation in the choosing, of national leaders. We need a new aesthetics to enter in contention against current technological verdicts of what is beautiful and pleasing. Certainly we need a new individualism, maybe even a new conception of an elite that would take up the fight for excellence. And yet, the technological conformity game is not a pure disaster. Beyond the depressing values we have looked at, there is the solid reality of triumph in the struggle over an imprisoning nature. For all its pathology, America's new industrial community does represent the victory of human initiative, and it does hold out a large promise of some of the necessary ingredients of the good life: affluence, leisure, and intercommunication.

Meanwhile, the republic will continue to divide its allegiance between individualism and community as the loci of equality, and it will doubtless continue to develop manners at each point of focus that express pathology as much as health. But one sign of health is the ongoing debate and dialectic between these loci. The self-appointment syndrome is countered, as it were, not only by the promise of a more genuine individualism, but by the restraints imposed by the supervening reality of community (even conformist community). And the worst excesses of conformity are constantly put to the test by the strident voices of personal dissent among us. Between these modalities, let us hope, the struggle will go on to recover the right to organize and dispose of personal and communal space free of extrinsic control.

8. Manners Oriented by the Voluntary Sense of Quality

By now, the pattern of dialectical breakdown is clear. The revolutionary impulse, under actual conditions of existence, splits apart into a zealous freezing of the status quo under the dead labels of a past revolution, on the one hand, and into a blind futurism without regard for the gains of the past, on the other. The impulse to organize the space under the banner of equality breaks down into a virulent individualism, on the one hand, and a thought-numbing conformism, on the other. In the same way, the motivation that drives a republican government—Montesquieu's *vertu*, Tocqueville's voluntary association, our own category of "willed initiative"—also falls into its own peculiar dialectic under the pressures and temptations of daily existence.

We have already discerned that the notion of willed initiative entails a double-sided motivation. The quality of manners and morals in a republic, we found, depends, at one point of focus, on the capacity to commit oneself to the commonwealth: one believes in the republic and gives it one's hand not out of the wish for status or external compulsion, but out of a voluntary passion, out of consent. This commitment eventuates not simply in feeling, however, but in positive action, for in a republic it is not only the laws and the work of the legislator and executive, it is also the conduct and manners of the citizen, that move the commonwealth toward its goals.

The best of all conditions for a republic is when these two aspects of willed initiative function in concert to make up one movement. Things are at their worst when these two aspects fall apart and when each, deprived of the complementarity and tempering of the other, becomes reified and is then disported *alongside* the other, artificially separated from it. Thus they appear in the American ethos as compartmentalized, hard-shelled entities, giving us the typical American traits of pure sentimentality and bathos, on the one hand, and a furious activism, on the other. Taken together, these partial versions of willed initiative conspire to raise the specter of the loss of quality under the factical conditions of American life.

(a) *Activism*

If there is one feature of American life that nearly all observers from abroad have been unable to miss, it is the furious activity of the inhabitants, an activity often devoid, apparently, of meaning or purpose. "The political activity which pervades the United States must be seen in order to be understood," Tocqueville reported to his fellow Frenchmen. "No sooner do you set foot upon the American soil than you are stunned by a kind of tumult; . . . Everything is in motion around you."[76] To this very day the same restlessness impresses itself on the observer:[77]

The American spends his spare time whacking golf balls to better his score, or slamming tennis balls to best an opponent, or climbing mountains, skiing, sailing, camping, or hunting to prove his prowess. All of this reckless expenditure of energy strikes the European as slightly mad. He treasures moments of rest that the people of the United States cannot even comprehend.

What is the explanation for this activism? At one level we can satisfy ourselves, of course, by remembering that it took energy, industry, and dexterity to wrest a civilized community from the wilderness. Furthermore, the dominant Puritan theology and ethics, spreading out from New England and becoming a sort of new existential environment for the whole country, laid sanctions on both "preparation" and "response" as fitting roles for the man of faith, and these were invariably interpreted in terms of the contribution that deeds could make to community betterment. But our interest at this point is not so much in seeing how historical precedent has been set in this country for stress on action; what we want to look at now is the meaning of contemporary activism in America: why is there a whole subspecies of manners in America today—whacking golf balls, organizing car washes, making telephone calls for the church women, selling a third more carpets than in the same quarter last year—so obviously linked together by one quality: the ceaseless, bumptious, furious activity that goes into them? The manners of activism may not represent simply a rote repetition of habits burned into us by the past; perhaps they betray something of our current hopes and fears, our style and quality of existence in a strange new world.

As I have said before, I cannot escape the feeling that activism, however divorced in practice from our inner lives, is always in some kind of reciprocity with feeling. The manners of activism, I suggest, can at least in part be explained by three propositions relating activity to passion or feeling or commitment:

1. Beyond a certain quantitative threshold, further and more furious activism is embarked on to compensate for *lack* of feeling. That is, a certain amount of doing is necessary to express passion; but if the doing begins to fill the whole horizon, either in the frequency of activity or in the zeal for sheer action, we may infer a reciprocal lessening or absence of inner feelings.

2. Some modalities of activism point to a *misplacement* of commitment and passion. One's action seems inappropriate not because it

does not stem from feeling or inclination, but rather because it seems to implement feelings or inclinations that cannot be realized by the kinds of activism being undertaken.

3. Activism may be undertaken to *escape* one's feelings or passions. Much of the modality of activism that goes under the title of "mobility" is of this sort, and often the escape takes the form of refusing the invitation to participate in the organizing of space, or to seize the day of a revolutionary occasion.

First, let us look briefly at activism that betrays a lack of feeling or commitment and is thus amplified and made all the more frenetic as a compensation. It is found at every level of conduct from personal to public and in every orbit from the local circuits of friendship to the larger issues of statecraft. It is often the man or woman with the most friends who seems to have no friends; it is often the couple most active on the cocktail and party circuit who seem most desperate, when one takes them unaware, for serious closure. The use of activity or voluble talk as a substitute for communication is, of course, an utterly familiar problem to psychotherapists and the directors of various sorts of "sensitivity training groups." Such manners are almost a cliché in the new cinema of human relations: the thirty-five-year-old spinster finally breaks loose, has a fling, decides to leave her widowed mother and move to the West Coast, where she can be herself, free of the inhibitions of the home town. She tells all this to mother. Mother does not want to hear it and shuts her mind to it precisely by doing things: fiddling with her handbag, looking for her glasses, concentrating on a bottle of pills. Contrary to a common impression, we cannot get very far in sorting out such manners by any attempt to classify activity as pro- or antisocial. One can avoid any commitments either by unleashing a hurricane of activity upon his friends, hustling them to plays, introducing them to each other, coffeeing with them, never pausing for anything painful with a one of them. Or one can lose himself in his work, or his jogging, or his boxwoods, quite without anybody's assistance.

On a more public plane of manners, one of the grand paradoxes of the American style is that the most unfeeling displays of activism should take as subject matter that about which we should feel the most deeply: love of country, that sentiment identified by Montesquieu as the very engine of a republican community. Commitment to the country, expressed in activism and steamed-up talk, soon becomes not a real commitment at all if we mean by that a qualitative passion, a sensitivity to values. It becomes instead a forced, quantitative creedalism, an end in itself expressed wholly in a parade of gaudy deeds and bullying talk. It becomes that garrulous, mindless patriotism that has shocked observers for a century and a half. "The Americans in their intercourse with strangers appear impatient of the smallest censure and insatiable of praise," says Tocqueville. "It is impossible to conceive a more troublesome . . . patriotism; it wearies even those who are disposed to respect it." And one simply cannot shut off the display, he finds. "I contradict an American at every word he says, to show him that his conversation bores me; he instantly labours with fresh pertinacity to convince me." Such patriotism is all external. It is completely expressed in show. It betrays inner vacancy, lacking feeling. And it is still celebrated in a wide variety of contemporary forms. It is seen in the bellicose declaration of the rightwinger that "actions speak louder than words." It is seen in an uncritical religious form in the affirmation (and here I quote a high school lad from my own congregation): "I don't care what you believe so long as you do something about it." It is heard in movie houses at the climax of John Wayne's film about the Vietnamese war, *The Green Berets.* At the premiere, according to one reporter, "The audience often erupted into spontaneous applause when air strikes devastated Viet Cong waves; there was a deafening roar when an explosion illuminated a grisly row of guerrilla bodies impaled on a barbed-wire fence." Another reporter remarked that applause is rare in movie houses today, "but everywhere this film is playing you get the same kind of reaction when the gooks get greased. You wonder who these people are."[78] Some critics of this kind of conduct would want to call it an excess of emotion. I think of it as a lack of it—as insensitiveness, a callous and mindless show, altogether devoid of inwardness. What is excessive is the outward show. If there is emotionalism here, it has been captured by activism, by the need to overreact. There is no compassion here, no qualitative commitment to republican values.

The crux of the matter is that the American view of experience, with its stress upon doing, tends to rob us of the ability to "see" reality in terms of telling, meaningful *symbols.* Everything has been turned into performance. Let me not be misunderstood. In the long run I defend this view of reality, this approach that sees in terms of constructive activity, for it is the only approach that lets man emerge from bondage to nature. Here, however, we are examining the pathology of this approach as seen in American manners. Americans think in terms of deeds, facts, and artifacts, and are all too little ready to see what these entities may *express from within* in the realm of feelings, values, and ultimate concerns. In other words, we are simply not open always to the symbolic character of the things we do, say, and build. There is a story about a group of American students who took passage to Europe on a ship run by Europeans. Continuing to practice their usual collegiate manners, the American students soon found themselves engaged in vigorous "food fights," and they were especially pleased with the hard round rolls served as bread. The rolls made excellent missiles. But to the Europeans on board such conduct came through as gross, devoid of feeling. To a European bread still retains its symbolic value, as that which binds men together around the table, and as that sacramental artifact which binds men both to a sustaining nature and to the giver of life.

Fortunately, we Americans are not always so insensitive. Even so, a second problem presents itself in the realm of manners. At times our ready resort to activity does not quite match up with the inner values or sensitivities that we do have. The commonest example of this mismatch between feeling and action is our misplaced emphasis on individual activity. More often than not, we agree that certain values that should be promised in a republic haven't yet come true for some people in the community, and that something should be done about it. So far, so good: commitment to republican values + action = realization of promise. The problem is that the actions we think of taking commonly don't really answer to the values we are committed to. It is easy nowadays to get wide agreement that justice has not yet been done the black man in America. But the commonest proposal for a remedy is that the same channels of improvement be opened to the black man that worked for, let us say, the Boston Irish, namely, the late Victorian ethic of hard work, educational improvement, and political aptitude. Moreover, all of these forms of action are commonly visualized in terms of individual expertise. The problem cannot be solved by these forms of action: the black man in the ghetto is not the Boston Irishman; his problem, besides, is that of the disenablement of a mass, and it will not be solved by the expedient of providing an escape route for singular individuals.

A particularly alarming variety of mismatch, one that is seemingly a special affliction of American democracy, involves the filling of public office. Too many gifted citizens, possessed of a strong public spirit, yet refuse to enter political leadership, preferring to express their commitments to the commonwealth through purely personal pursuits. We should remember, of course, that a good part of the public weal in America is served precisely by voluntary activity and by voluntary associations having nothing officially to do with the government. Yet if too many gifted citizens shun official leadership, the republican cause will suffer all the same. Much talent is inevitably wasted when this happens and too many offices, from the county courthouse up, are filled with second-rate public servants.

Another variety of misplaced activism occurs when we are tempted to borrow the technological skills that we have used to rearrange the physical environment and attempt to employ them in the resolution of political and social dilemmas. Let us grant that existentialists and theologians have been all too sensitive about what is distinctively human and have commonly ignored the continuity between humanity and the physical environment. It is not enough to reject the classical body-soul dichotomy; we might regard with healthy suspicion, as well, the replacement of this concept with a dualism of the external and the inward, especially when the motive seems to be to discount the importance of man's external, physical, natural attributes—which are just as much a part of him as his metaphorical "spirit," "inner self," "heart," or "inward existence." But we cannot reduce man to nature or to organic and neuronic functions, and we cannot reduce communities to matter amenable to efficient housing projects, better sanitary engineering, and wider freeways. Yet an entire segment of American activistic manners is evidently posited upon just such an assumption. To hear my fellow apartment dwellers tell it, about all that it would take to make their world completely livable would be for the manager to put in a quieter air conditioner (that would improve the quality of the talk at parties), get the squeak out of the sliding doors, change the angle of the parking spaces, redesign the room divider for the vanity bath in the master bedroom, and send the painters around to revarnish the front door.

We began by observing that activism can take the place of feeling, or become the means of compensating for the absence of feeling. Let us glance, finally, at an inverse use of activity: not to cover up an absence of feeling, but to escape from an overload of it; to repress feeling, to put oneself at a distance from the things one feels all too well. In terms of manners, this use of activism ordinarily involves running away from a painful piece of space, seeking out an exempt haven in space, or avoiding space ties altogether by some form of perpetual motion.

Let us begin with the fascination upon Americans that is evidently exerted by motels. Motels, somehow, seem more inviting than hotels, more transcendent. It is because they are deliberately planned as exceptions to the American notion of shared space. When one goes to a hotel in another city he may be understood to be entering the permeable space of that city, to be locating in the hotel as a way of affixing himself to the communal space of that city for a while, and of advertising his own accessibility. The central location of hotels, and the courtroomlike, public character of the lobbies combine to proclaim the hotel as such a center. Granted that one can find privacy and withdrawal in his room, yet the dominant characteristic of a hotel is that it is a transaction center at which one engages in positive acts that relate his own personal space-bubble to the ramified public space of the contiguous community. The staffing of hotels adds to this character, for the ubiquitous bellboys, assistant managers, and chambermaids provide a core of functionaries whose specialty is receiving and accommodating the visitor into the new spatial network. Going through the network of staff people at a hotel is in miniature much like passing through customs and immigration at a national boundary.

The motel, on the other hand, is a sanctuary, a place of refuge, a zone of transcendence, a bit of antispace in which one can disrelate himself from the public transactions of entering a community. The location is usually out of the center. But if it is in the center, means are taken to correct any misimpression about that. The lobbies do not look like courtrooms. One is not met by a retinue. One may go for his own ice. There are nonlobby entrances to the corridors. One may repair to a motel, in short, without giving his reasons and without committing himself to transactions in the new space. It is far too simple to account for all these private features of motels by saying that they accommodate our needs for irregular sexual activities: hotels have long served that function, too. No, the motel is distinctive in a far more profound manner: it is the American's refuge from the burdens of occupying communal space; it is the antiplace one goes to get out of existential space for awhile. Not even that great American institution of escape, sports, can compete with the motel as a sanc-tuary from day-to-day business. For sports remain surprisingly cap-tive to the oppressing space around one, most notably in the small-town Friday night football game, at which the business community simply regroups for a couple of hours, with commitments merely suspended for the moment.

The motel is the logical antispace made possible by mobility. But motion, mobility, or movement itself can be another form of avoiding the commitments that would be imposed upon us by communal space if we remained put. In this respect, America's westward settlement, the opening of the frontier, and the great restlessness of the American people have all been much overromanticized. Much of this motion proneness of the American spirit has undoubtedly been connected, as legend would have it, with the wish to get free of tyrannous domina-tion. But a good part of it, on the contrary, has undoubtedly flowed from the wish to escape commitments to organized space, from panic at the thought of the burden involved in willed initiative toward one's commonwealths, local and beyond. Any land in which it is so easy to move about, Santayana thought, must actually be a rather empty place—not empty in the mode of a "primitive physical emptiness," though that survives in some regions, but "the moral emptiness of a settlement where men and even houses are easily moved about, and no one, almost, lives where he was born or believes what he has been taught."[79]

Movement and activism become the American equivalents of the

Eastern resort to Yoga, motionlessness, contemplation, and quest for Nirvana. In America one escapes self, community, history, fate, karma, not by getting perfectly still, but by becoming perfectly active. All sorts of modalities of such activism will serve: from taking to the road in one's car, to spending the day at the golf course, to contacting five dozen prospects a day on the telephone. Running in place for twenty minutes is the exact American cognate of the classical Oriental quest for nothingness.

As with other expressions of manners, the activistic set in America is accompanied by a characteristic form of speech. Just as willed initiative degenerates into blind activism, so persuasion degenerates into cajolery or an overstrained kind of browbeating. It is an externally forced attempt at persuasion (external since the link with feeling has been lost or dissevered). It is based on extrinsic, circumstantial, often irrelevant considerations rather than on experienced reasoning. In the realm of law, for example, this cajolery often takes the form of blustering appeal to group mores or thinly veiled threats that stop just short of outright authoritarian talk. Mrs. Trollope observed a typical bit of such language in nineteenth-century Indiana in the form of a printed notice urging citizens to pay their taxes, which she offered "as a curious sample of the manner in which the free citizens are coaxed and reasoned into obeying the laws." The poster was titled: LOOK OUT DELINQUENTS. And the sheriff and tax-collector announced: "I am at a loss to know the reason why those charged with taxes neglect to pay." With heavy handed moralism, he goes on to the conclusion: "I should be sorry to have to resort to the authority given me by law."[80] Here is a leading example of what the Puritan theologian, Jonathan Edwards, had observed a century earlier: that his fellows often were constrained in one way or another—by pressure, cajolery, exhortation, awkward moral talk—to channel their activities toward excellent ends. But by doing such things for external reasons with no true "consent to being," their activities still lacked excellence.[81]

(b) Sentimentality

If pure activism hitched to no passion is one way of avoiding the ordeal of republican community, another is pure feeling hitched to no action. Here we descry two essential modalities. One can *withdraw* into a world of pure feeling, not to return to the world of space, time, and action. Or one can turn his feelings inside out, in some form of extrovert enthusiasm, bathing the whole world, as it were, with one's feelings. In both cases it is possible to avoid connecting one's passions to reasonable actions, in the first form by cutting oneself off from the world, and in the second form by imagining that one's enthusiastic sentiments obviate the need for action. In either case the result is an abdication of "critical passion" in the American ethos and the subsequent triumph of mediocrity in taste.

Withdrawal into feelings takes a number of exotic forms in American manners. Feelings can take the form of a marked self-consciousness to the point that the person restricts himself merely to observing his fellows, so fearful is he that his actions will seem inappropriate, or that they will draw unbearable attention to him. Many such persons are taken to be nonfeeling when they are actually so sensitive that they have effectively severed themselves from intercommunication. They walk past a restaurant entrance one, two, three times before summoning the will to enter. They risk being thought unfriendly rather than overwhelm an acquaintance with cordiality. They carry around feelings that simply cannot find an outlet in the form of normal, aggressive American "heartiness," which is a feeling that begins in the heart but is projected outward by activism.

American society includes a wide assortment of dreamers, romantics, moody people, hesitant types who "think too much," folk who, in the cliché, "live in their own little worlds." They are very different among themselves: some are good-natured, some terribly angry. But all have one thing in common. They thrive on their own feelings, passions, and inclinations. They do not link up their consciousness with the public world of community transactions. Perhaps most of us have our moments of such withdrawal into our own worlds, as when we retreat into moodiness and refuse to communicate.

Much more common, however, is withdrawal from the public arena based on self-interest. Here we are no longer in the domain of the exotic personality, the rare type who knows himself too intimately. Rather we have moved into the larger world of typical human emotions and temptations. There is no sharper contrast in American life than that between the intensity of feelings one may direct at his own private circle of concerns, and the apathy which characterizes his view of larger matters. The closer a matter to one's own interest, the more passion one puts into it. The smaller the orbit of concern, the more intense the feelings. That is an axiom governing American manners, morals, and politics with relatively few exceptions. Contrary to the teachings of Marxist orthodoxy, such intensity is not always or even predominantly governed by economic motivations. Considerations of status and comfort, and above all the wish to dispose of one's own space, whether justifiably or not, tend to govern. Economic motives are common receptacles and vehicles of feeling, of course. After the late President John F. Kennedy made a speech at American University advocating a treaty prohibiting nuclear testing in the atmosphere, one week's mail brought in 896 letters on the subject—861 favorable to the President's position, twenty-five hostile to it. In the same period, says Arthur M. Schlesinger, Jr., 28,232 people sent letters "about a freight rate bill." The President concluded in disgust: "That is why I tell people in Congress that they're crazy if they take their mail seriously."[82] Even here, economic motives did not explain some of the letters, since a lobbying effort was obviously responsible for the volume. Some people were persuaded to write for other reasons. Nor was money directly at the root of a strange concern displayed by a downtown church in the spring of the year not long ago, at a time when riots had marred the city's peace and the fires of racial controversy were still burning brightly. The church made the news not by saying anything about peace and good will, but by coming to the rescue of the business community, announcing it would plan its $1,800,000 expansion to conform to a plan for extending a nearby street.

In such manners as these, feelings are contained within the walls of private or limited concerns—ultimately the walls of the self. It would be a mistake, however, to conceptualize the role of feelings in American manners as playing only this kind of limitary role. A more widespread phenomenon in the American ethos is to employ the feelings to extend oneself or one's community to men at large. In short, feelings can be either implosive or explosive. The classical example of explosive feelings in American life is the frenzy and enthusiasm of the religious revival: in this setting, unshaped passion expressed without reference to constructive action has been a notorious subject of comment, both early and late in the nation's history. Again Mrs. Trollope has a sharp eye out for such aberrations. She thinks of camp meetings, with their unguarded display of emotions and shrieked utterances of ecstasy as "trash," "hysterical," "maniacal," and "gross." Whereas American manners are often dreary, cold, and suffer from lack of enthusiasm (corresponding to the lack of feeling we have described above under activism), on some occasions, Americans go to the opposite extreme and behave with remarkable passion. In both religious and patriotic contexts, such as July 4 celebrations, she points to the American tendency toward "bad taste," "bad feeling," and bellicosity.[83]

Far more in evidence than outright belligerence is the sentiment of benevolence. The most pervasive emotion in the whole pantry of American manners is a diluted, sentimental loving-kindness. Good intentions spread at large are the usual substitute in America for action, law, and the operations of justice. One can reasonably argue that the worst enemy of republican government in this country is not ill will or outright selfishness but the sentimental good will of too many Americans, who assume that a vague aura of amiability and frequent creedal resort to slogans about loving one's neighbor in his heart are all that is demanded.

And it is here, at the point of sentimentality, rather than at the point of action, that we encounter the typical American language of optimism. Action (as distinguished from mere activism) engages us with the unyieldingness of the environment, with false starts, and with the reality of small steps. The language that describes honest action is the realistic, sometimes pessimistic language of pragmatism. It is with the counterpoint of stress on sentiment that Americans are so easily tempted to incorporate the spirit of "Pollyanna" into their speech and manners. It is the language of sentiment that takes for granted all the things that are not so: it "feels" in advance that we love all our neighbors, we all do, that we enjoy our space with unalloyed comfort, that we will see our dreams come true. And the traditional Christian focus upon love as a special virtue has unfortunately had the effect of exaggerating, in the American ethos, a false reliance on sentiment and unjustified optimism.

The net result of sentimentality is to shift the American psyche away from a critical approach to the problems of community and to the standards of quality that should obtain in the community. For the question of quality is in large part a question of taste, and questions of taste are largely based on measured emotion, gauged passion. When feeling is either held all inside, or is turned upon the world in a flood of anger or love (more often love), no measure, no matching-up, no critical test is possible. Americans for the most part cannot tell good music from bad, good art from bad, not because of unintelligence but because of the overkill of diffused, generalized sentiment. To the last item, they will take the sweet, the maudlin, the childlike: crude souvenirs of JFK, such as a blue dinner plate bearing his head; sweet wines toward the start of a meal rather than a California Sauterne; humdrum praise of baseball players, child artists, and ornate chandeliers. Whereas good music may be heard on ordinary days on a good-music station, such as the public library's FM outlet, the quality degenerates into *kitsch* on Christmas Day. American culture is fundamentally anti-intellectual not because of the absence of intellect but because of the ubiquity of sentiment.[84]

But poor taste has more ominous consequences than the overloading of American coffee tables with pathetic pieces of bric-a-brac. Lack of taste is but a form of lack of judgment. It may be harmless enough, this absence of critical standards for the family that goes to a resort, puts up at a plush hotel, and gratefully accepts the advice of printed cards on dining room tables bearing instructions to guests on how much to tip. But this syndrome extends far beyond poor taste in etiquette or bad judgment in tourist matters. In truth, poor political decisions stem from poor taste, boredom, lack of inner standards for judgment, the wish to be told how to behave in the absence of definitive feelings of one's own. Bad politics is also a question of taste and quality.

What is worst of all is that action-without-feeling and feeling-without-action can coexist in the republic, often in the contradictory manners of the same person or group. Under healthy conditions, these two aspects of "willed initiative" should, of course, continually interact. Under the perverse conditions of factical existence, they fall apart and move the republic toward mediocrity. Even so, we can see the elements of health, however altered by this compartmentalization, in the activism and passions of American life. We must finally ask about the prospects that a healthy cooperation may be achieved.

(c) *The Prognosis for Willed Initiative*

Our qualms are sufficient enough to lead us to ask the question whether willed initiative can really be expected to produce, by a fusion of motive and action, a future realization of quality in a republic.

First, we might return to a fundamental question that Montesquieu raises: any republic that is too large, he suspected, simply might not be amenable to willed initiative. Is our problem the sheer massiveness of the United States? Does its size account for the failure of quality that we have observed in the republic? After speaking on the attitudes of college-age draft protesters at a college in Lincoln, Nebraska, I was taken to a workingmen's saloon by a genial pacifist and several of his student adherents. They wanted to argue with me. In my lecture I had criticized students who moved to Canada to avoid military service; one should remain with his greater community if only in order to criticize it, I had suggested.

"There's a reason for moving to Canada that transcends that kind of argument," the pacifist countered. "This country is just too big. It is good for it for some of us to move away—not just good for us, I say, but good for America."

This view echoes Montesquieu, who thought that the only decent republic (barring a resort to federalism) had to be of "only a small territorial extent."[85] Strangely, it is an argument that unites for the nonce the most improbable allies. For my pacifist friends, in arguing that the country is too big, are saying somewhat the same thing as some of their foes. Much right-wing grumbling in America today about "big government" is actually frustration at the vast scale of the country itself, with its mass-produced opinion, food, and fashion.

We cannot answer so complex a question here. We suspect, however, that America is condemned to largeness, whether for good or ill. Our Federal system has probably been successful enough at the level of survival to condemn us to continuance. It may thus be that its size both guarantees existence for America and sentences it to a future of mediocre taste. What is open to us, in any case, is not a readjustment of the size or scope of the republic—the Civil War closed that option —but a reconsideration of the character of activism and sentiment. Whatever is done in America will have to be done through, in, with, and under the technostructure and the opinion-shaping media.

In a sense the problem is not that America is too large, but that it is too small. The sights of Americans are all too restricted, as we have seen, to what is intensely local, tribal, and "patriotic." One reason to reflect on the manners and morals of the American greater community is to free our allegiance—through actions rather than vaguely universalist sentiment—by reminding us of our own limitations, "the dangers of too excessive a concentration of interest on the uniqueness of the American and the American way of life."[86] Youth need to know of the society that bred them—its pathology as well as its hope—but they also need to know of the great world of which this greater community is only a constituent part. Americans in Detroit need to be reminded "that the internal combustion engine is not an American invention."[87] All Americans need to be disabused of the conviction that "America's wants and values are universal" or that American democracy, property rights, or cybernation "provides a prototypical solution for the world's disorders. This is a belief of nearly theological intensity, and it is no exaggeration to label it an American ideology."[88]

Another set of qualms about quality in American life clusters about the uneasy suspicion that *education,* on which republican governance depends in principle, does not really evoke judgment and taste. Dwight Macdonald has summed up this fear in speaking of the American failure to appreciate art, but it is a concern that applies to the whole realm of manners and morality:[89]

> We have, in short, become skilled at consuming High Culture when it has been stamped PRIME QUALITY by the proper authorities, but we lack the kind of sophisticated audience that supported the achievements of the classic avant-garde, an audience that can appreciate and discriminate on its own.

For this more difficult enterprise, we shall need what we very well may not get for all our four million college population: a cultural community.

It will scarcely do to have guardians supervising our artistic taste, but it will not do at all to yield governance over existential and communal space back to despots, or even to caretakers who might see things through despite the indifference and boredom of the people. Besides, a republican community is committed to a modality of action that surpasses browbeating. From the very beginning, as we have repeatedly observed, governance in America depends on the persuasion of an educated, decision-making populace. "The communication of understanding," says Bernard Bailyn, "lay at the heart of the Revolutionary movement." The great expressions of revolution in America were thus embodied in argumentative pamphlets. "The reader is led through arguments, not images. The pamphlets aim to persuade."[90] In other words, the organization of political space in America was to proceed through the colloquy of citizens who had been through an educational process that honed the capacity to willed initiative. This does not necessarily mean that all Americans must have the benefit of a formal, higher education: willed initiative has come through in both a Jefferson and a Lincoln, in the Montgomery seamstress with tired feet who wanted a seat on the city bus as well as a Martin Luther King, Jr. (Ph.D., Boston University). Whatever the mode of education, what is requisite are the gifts of commitment and initiative, good judgment, the ability to make decisions with the commonwealth as well as one's own self in view. These gifts are unquestionably nourished by the talent of reason, by historically coached wisdom, by the sort of world view that leads one beyond mere vocational and family concerns and succeeds in imparting a kind of vision and a kind of good taste. And the question, quite simply, is this: what if the American populace proves unable to bring forward these gifts?

Montesquieu, in a sense, is rather less demanding than we are. For him, it would appear, the mere presence of reason is enough. He does not say that everyone must be educated to the constant, effective use of reason. That would be to demand the impossible. What is necessary to the quality of a republic is the possibility of reason, its freedom to appear. In a free nation, he says, it does not really matter whether given individuals reason well or poorly; what counts is that they are free to reason at all. For from the very existence of that opening toward reason spring the conditions that guarantee the republic. By the same token, in a despotic government, it is equally dangerous whether one reasons well or poorly. If there is the possibility of any reasoning at all, good or bad, the despotic principle of government is undermined.[91]

The quality of life in a republic depends squarely on preserving and evoking this capacity to reason, then. But it is a hard requirement despite the simplicity with which Montesquieu states it. Althusser has put it well. Montesquieu's notion of willed initiative requires of the citizen, in his ability to make judgments, "une véritable *conversion* de l'homme privé dans l'homme public." If this does not quite mean turning men into angels, it does mean turning them into citizens, which is after all not far from the same thing, since the good citizen is "l'ange vrai de la vie publique."[92]

We can compile impressive evidence that this spirit of awareness, of informed participation, and in general of "conversion" to the cause of the republic is not widespread. A John Bircher, himself a college graduate, picks up the telephone and rings a talk-back radio program. He offers the view that the mayor's human relations council borders on Communism, or that fluoridation of the city's water is a Castroist plot, or that the World Council of Churches is antiflag. How does the ordinary citizen—nay, the above-average citizen—deal with these charges except on the basis of his intuition and his gastric juices? Few citizens, even the educated, have the equipment, time, or will to go to the public library and track down the facts about fluoridation. All too many would not know which source to believe, in fact: the *Encyclopaedia Britannica,* the *Reader's Digest,* or Mrs. Jones down the street, who said . . . Few hearers, like the spreader of such word, could give anything approaching a reasonable and accurate definition of Communism. The mass media, far from coming to the rescue, seem to fill up this vacuum of public empty-mindedness not with reflection or aids to judgment, but with diversions from the whole problem. Nor is the problem just one of lack of information. It is sometimes a problem of fear. Blacks in the South, though now firmly in possession of a fundamental instrument of self-interest, the vote, have not as yet managed to use it to elect very many of their peers to public office. Sometimes it is a problem of apathy numbing one's own sense of urgency. In many areas, where residents of poverty sectors have been urged to vote to elect their own representatives to community action boards, pitifully few have taken advantage of the right. In one such election in Los Angeles, for example, fewer than one per cent of those eligible to vote actually bothered to do so.[93]

Other qualms could be mentioned. Is the principle of equality itself the problem? Was Montesquieu right when he opposed putting the power of governance into the hands of "low people"?[94] (His standards would exclude not only illiterate sharecroppers, we judge, but the run of John Birchers as well.) Is Arnold Toynbee right in suggesting that "democracy, so far from having been one of the sources of the Western peoples' power, has been one of the luxuries that their power has enabled them to afford"?[95] Is Herbert Marcuse right in his protests against "tyranny of the majority"?[96]

> Well, if it is a crazy idea to suggest that people qualified to rule should rule, and not movie stars, tap dancers, and cheap politicians, then, yes, perhaps I am in favor of an elitist rule. I think this kind of elite is the hope of a free society—those with education, training, and capability to rule.

In the end, all of these qualms fade when we consider yet one more: that America will not only fail in the means to its end, but in the end itself; that America will miss its promise. The quality of a republic ultimately rests on its promise to give back to the people their own space—to wrest it from the domination of outside control, and to reorganize the community through the participation of the residents of that space. At its deepest level, this promise must be understood not just as a political phenomenon, but as a religious faith. Whether willed initiative can bring off the promise of the republic is finally a question of existential, community, and national "salvation." We should not really be nauseated, as we so often are, at the way religious and political symbols are linked in public spectacles in

America—at the way some preachers in the Southwest invoke the deity at football games, with mayors and governors called upon at half time. Beneath the hubris and pretense of this athletic, religious patriotism, there is a truth, discernible ever so dimly. Action and passion in America are sacred, because they are the loci of the quest for salvation. With that discovery, we can profitably break off this inquiry into public ethics, and reapproach it from another angle. What light can American theology throw on the quest, inaugurated in revolution, and purposed in willed initiative, for the right to dispose of personal and communal space?

Part Two

The Role of Theology
In Public Ethics

CHAPTER IV.

TOOLS

Although we have proposed that the outlook and methods of the theological ethicist may appropriately be marshaled for the study of American manners and morals, we now come to an embarrassing hiatus in our study. Contemporary theology and theological ethics in America are today in very poor condition, as intellectual disciplines, for engaging in any professionally mature study of the American ethos, or of "public ethics" as we have defined this venture. For our theologians and Christian ethicists, by and large, have simply not been very interested in such inquiry. We have not developed the necessary conceptual tools and norms for sustained examination of the American greater community. We have not really taken very seriously the prospect of genuine interdisciplinary study. In a decade of one moral crisis after another, and of the demise of classical theology, we have continued to debate the most arcane, sectarian, intradisciplinary matters imaginable. Even the debates over "situation ethics" and the "death of God" have produced, *within* the disciplines of American theology and ethics, not the excitement that such discussions have elicited on college campuses, but a time of protracted, stuffy, repetitious quibbling.[1]

This new scholasticism is not only a pity, it is a departure from a great tradition in American theology and ethics. In past eras, American divines were more venturesome, more ready to address themselves to large public questions. To cite only recent examples, we may mention the liberal theology and the Social Gospel at the end of the nineteenth century, and the American version of neo-orthodoxy as it was shaped by Reinhold Niebuhr, a profound public ethicist. Whatever public concern we theologians and churchmen now display over such issues as civil rights, peace, and economic justice is largely a heritage from these movements. Sadly, we have done little rethinking of our own to enter the insights of theology and ethics into the new context of revolution, campus upheaval, cybernetics, the new moral sensitivity of youth expressed with blithe disregard of what churches or theologians used to say or still say to each other.

It is our intent in this closing part of our study to make a start in what seems the necessary direction. It will certainly be a very tentative effort. And it will be an amateurish effort, for I see no way to move beyond the classical limits of one's discipline and to take up problems that conventionally belong to other disciplines—political science, sociology—without risking this kind of approach.

In the present chapter we will outline some of the problems and issues that contemporary American Christian ethics must now rethink, if it is to make common cause with other ethics-oriented fields in the study of manners and morals. We will suggest some of the historical, cultural, and intellectual resources from the American experience that might now helpfully be brought into the "conceptual workshop" of the American ethicist. In the final three chapters we will attempt to put some of these tools into practice.

1. Space as a Theological Datum[2]

The first task of the theological critic of culture, says Julian Hartt, is to discover "what civilization is up to"—that is, to get a picture of "what the key structures are through which human energy must flow in that time and space—or against which it must recoil—if the human spirit is to reach significant expression." This does not mean for Hartt (any more than it has for us) that the theologian looking at his community will expect to find truth, beauty, and goodness unambiguously exemplified there. Indeed, that is not what he is looking for. The calling of the Christian is, among other things, critical in respect of the world. He is thrown into conflict with "the negativities of civilization." Every day he must contend and live with institutions and powers that suppress the human and distort creativity. "Accordingly, the first strategic aim of Christian criticism is rightly to identify these negativities."[3]

The theologian who undertakes such study, we now propose, must do so by adding one dimension to recent theological study of man and culture. In the most general terms, recent American theology, while well enough aware of the warrant (and mandate) of cultural criticism, has not approached it in terms of the special negativities of extant greater communities. It has much preferred the generic approach to frailty that was the contribution of existentialist analysis from Kierkegaard to Heidegger. This way of analyzing human and cultural structures saw man as a time-binding or historical creature, but not as a space-disposing or geographical creature; it saw the link between "being and time" but said little or nothing of "being and space." Our claim is that both dimensions of cultural existence must be examined in respect of their capacity to bend, shape, refract, and warp the human spirit: we must be students not only of the threat of time for Dasein, but of the finitizing impact of space upon human existence.

Let us understand recent North Atlantic theology, all the same, as having advanced in the right direction. For the neo-orthodox divinity of the generation now just behind us had the considerable merit of seeing acutely the effects of at least one of these dimensions, that of time or history. Some strands of antique Greek thought, we might recall, were obsessed with the timeless. Such thought "disparaged temporality and change as hallmarks of an inferior realm; truth was said to be outside time and salvation was liberation from time."[4] For too many generations, despite the introduction of a time- and history-sense with Augustine, Christian thought still understood its world in a way that discounted the temporal. Indeed it was only yesterday, so to speak, with the advent of enlightenment belief in worldly happiness and with the somewhat less eudaemonistic nineteenth-century liberal theology, that time became accepted and understood as an essential dimension of the inquiry into human culture, belief, conduct, misery, and promise.

After some fugitive tendencies to withdraw from historical studies as a burnt child from the fire (the Great War seemed a sorry temporal outcome), early neo-orthodox theology soon bravely returned to its new task and vision. Much of the creative theology of our own era springs directly out of the heady experience of wrestling with time, or of setting time over against eternity. One need think only of Karl Barth's celebrated revision of the Calvinist doctrine of election. Here was a drastic reworking of dogma that, for all its Word-of-God pietism, describes the only kind of deity contemporary man can consent to—"The Being of God as the One Who Loves in Freedom" (*Church Dogmatics,* II/1). This Barthian God is a God of our time, and only a Barth overhauling Calvin, we might speculate, could portray him.

At the same time, we must concede that neo-orthodoxy was somewhat less comfortable with the pull of space than the Victorians were with the fact of sex—this despite its acknowledgment of theology as a historical phenomenon and of cultural phenomena as temporally transmitted. Why was theology so much more chary of the other side of human relativity—the forces of space, of geography? Toward space, neo-orthodox thinkers sometimes adopted almost a Manichaean stance. Paul Tillich charged: "Tragedy and injustice belong to the gods of space; historical fulfillment and justice belong to the God who acts in time and through time."[5] Neo-orthodoxy's nay-saying attitude toward space was owing, I conceive, to the special, demonic space in which its best early thinkers lived: Hitler's Germany. The Nazis could not be allowed to equate the Word of God with the will of the German *Volk.* Hence the desperate *non sequitur,* superstitiously echoed even in America, that there is and can be only "Christian" theology. The fact that "Christian" theology had varied enormously with time, and even with creedal and denominational groups, never swayed the point: there could be no variations in theological substance according to national terrain.

And yet if the task of the Christian critic is to lay out the *negativities* of civilization, we are perhaps much more obliged to attend to spatial configurations than to the temporal ones. Let us grant with Tillich and others that space distorts being, tempts it more than time, as it were, to live unto itself in private systems. If provinciality (pride in a special space) is more indicative of fallenness even than secularism (pride in a special age), then we could well bend our talents toward the development of more incisive theological tools for inquiry into the ways in which the temptations of space, and of spatial communities, blind and limit us and distort our promise.

It can be argued, on the other hand, that time is the more terrifying of these two partners: less amenable to being conquered by human technology than space, and thus more able to pose itself as the more ultimate threat to being. We have pretty well mastered global space, this argument runs, and can now think of ourselves as dominant in principle and to a large degree in fact over the earth's surface. At the same time, the threat of time remains unsubdued. We have no prospect of living forever. Death, time's agent, is still going to win out over our temporal existence, and that is the more fascinating and dreadful and unavoidable challenge for the mind to dwell on.

Perhaps this is a sound argument. But we might observe that technology is fully as devoted to pushing back time's threat as to conquering space. The whole class of medical advances of our epoch, for example, can be understood as stunning victories over time, gaining additional life-spans for men and extending the promise of vastly elongated life for the human species generally. And the argument that space has been even proximately conquered falls to the ground when we turn to the microcosmic and macrocosmic dimensions of the universe. We have barely begun to probe the inner world of the atom.

Despite the successful American effort to land men on the moon, the unknownness of outer space yawns just as threateningly as the unconqueredness of time. At least comparable in drama to our knowledge that we shall die is our knowledge that we shall never traverse the universe, and probably never communicate with extragalactic life that is perhaps equal or superior to human life as we know it here.[6] Furthermore, our communal and existential space, nominally conquered in the technical sense, still continues to defy us. The cities, those compact spaces that are supposedly our highest monuments to spatial technology, are at this writing the parts of our civilization closest to chaos and most productive of misery. Thus we must understand the challenge of space not in terms of advances in transportation, but rather in terms of the possibilities for expression of the human spirit in the "conquered" spaces.

Ultimately time and space, these two quanta of the unknown, merge into a master threat and mystery. For in the final analysis, not being able to conquer space is a paraphrase of our time-boundedness. And our short-range prospects, temporally speaking, are but another way of stating the finitude and limitations that characterize earth-man in the universe.

The result is perhaps a standoff between time and space as threats, limits, and media of our existence. But what this means is that theology must seek parity between them. In sum, life as it is now known is constitutively organized, especially where the "negativities" of civilization are concerned, into spatially distinctive communities. And these communities, to date, have not been the object of attention from theologians.

One result is that such indispensable studies as those of the American character in its ethical aspects, and "American theology" itself, have largely been ignored in America by theologians and ethicists, although literary critics, church historians, and devotees of American studies have attended in their own ways to these areas. "American theology" and "American ethics" have had to be prosecuted, perforce, almost in a vaccum. That is still the situation and promises to remain so for the immediate future, since little or no methodological guidance is available from the preceding generation of theologians.

There is some evidence, however, that theology in America may have turned a corner, and that it may now be possible to think, for the first time in many decades (indeed, since shortly after the Civil War), of the challenges of undertaking a definitive American theology and ethics equipped to inquire into the beliefs, conduct, theological folklore, and popular morality distinctive to the American greater community. An interesting study that points in this direction is entitled *Toward an American Theology,* a collection of five essays by Professor Herbert W. Richardson. Predictably, it has been too little appreciated by Richardson's fellow theologians. Some are put off by its irreverence toward Reformation themes and other quasi-eternal verities. Others seem to take offense that it actually undertakes interdisciplinary study, as opposed to merely advocating it. Whatever Richardson's problem of accreditation with the establishment, I have found his venture so useful in my own reflection on public ethics that a summary of his position is appropriate. His main propositions (apart from one essay on the philosophical problem of unity that seems to me not central to the concerns of an American theology), I take to be as follows:

1. Protestantism is dying because it is tied to an outmoded individualism and has no appropriate form of either a personal or communal ethic for a "sociotechnical age."

2. What is needed is a new theology that participates in the rising imperium of cybernetics and technical systems and can share in the new forms of knowledge and authority that are coming to dominate society. We require an ethic that can affirm social good and at the same time find an appropriate place for technical values. This means overhauling the traditional Christian ethic that sets man as person dualistically over against machines, nature, and social wholes.

3. A necessary feature of the new theology will be a reconception of faith that takes *relativism* as one of the chief challenges of the age (in contrast to the gnosticism, rationalism, and skepticism that in turn challenged Christianity in earlier epochs). Apart from the implication that a good number of New Testament scholars and historical theologians are working on dead problems, this proposition aims at a special, appropriate version of faith for our own time: a form of reconciliation that "works to unite the many relative perspectives and to thwart ideological conflict."

4. For better or worse the leadership and motivation for this theology will come from America. "For the spatial center of the next period of world history, that center from which the technological innovations will stream forth to reshape world culture, will be America," which "has created and continuously promulgated social technology."[7]

5. A new principle for organizing the community of faith will prevail, for the new American theology will be ecumenical, neither Protestant nor Catholic. It will reject the dominant Reformation standards (which overemphasize the New Testament, sin, redemption, and the second person of the Trinity) and it will restore the doctrines of creation and sanctification.

6. The outline of the new American theology is to be commenced by stating a "normative doctrinal system" exhibiting the characteristic emphases of American Christianity. In this pursuit we are to avoid the kind of systematic theology that takes European categories

to be decisive for all religion and thus is bound *a priori* to find American religion seriously deficient. Bonhoeffer, for example, explained away American religion sociologically, while presenting German religion theologically. As a result, the only "real" theologians Bonhoeffer found in America were those who reiterated "European doctrine."[8]

What is the content, the "teachings" of this new theology? That Richardson's approach to the substance or the characteristics of "American theology" varies considerably from our own is immediately evident. He claims that the chief item in American theology is sanctification, or the reflection of God's own holiness in the human community. He rejects the idea that the fundamental perspective of theology and ethics is deliverance from crisis, for the concern of his kind of theology is not primarily redemption or salvation. For him, "the idea of sin is unnecessary to the Christian understanding of God, since the incarnation and the indwelling of the Spirit do not presuppose it." The main focus is rather the notion of God glorifying himself in the creation. The work of the Holy Spirit is the unique preoccupation of Christianity in America, and this feature points not so much to the death of Christ as to the theocracy of God, and to the vision of "holy worldliness, the sanctification of all things by the Holy Spirit."[9]

Richardson proposes that an indigenous American theology must begin with some signalization of the theme of sanctification, and he suggests that a fitting symbolic starting point is the Puritan doctrine of the Sabbath. He wishes to begin here rather than with Christology because the Sabbath nicely symbolizes the end God has in mind for man and creation, the exhibition of his holiness or dignity. Christology, on the other hand, is too tied to the idea of rescue, repair, redemption from sin. Accordingly, Richardson undertakes a major restatement of the doctrine of Christ. Jesus Christ now becomes the God of heaven himself present in person with men, instead of mediator or rescuer. Only such a Christology, Richardson argues, "is adequate to the requirement that God in person be present with us in space and time."[10] In the meantime, we are challenged to reinvest the symbol of the Sabbath with the positive meaning that stands for man's happy situation before God: he exists not as an object of divine pity, not as a miserable creature whose shortcomings are to be forgiven. Man is rather to be understood as God's own chosen reflection of himself, and man's role is to manifest God's being, dignity, and holiness. "Now, in fact, keeping the Sabbath holy is nothing other than the way that a man lives to the glory of God."[11] And only American Christianity, this child of the Puritans and of the radical Reformation, has fully embraced this new, positive relation between God and man.

I have already suggested uneasiness with an approach to theology or ethics that would substitute a sanctificationist scheme for a problematic that views the human situation as shaped by its predicament and by its responses to predicament. Furthermore, I do not see how any approach to theology or ethics that claims to read the *experience* of the American ethos can come to any other conclusion than one that allows for the primacy of crisis: for what the American experience seems to deliver to view is the story of emergence from crisis and triumph over reverse. This is not the story of sanctification in any direct sense but of struggle toward promise by a people who make mistakes, follow wrong leads, learn by trial and error, divide in conflict, but finally triumph. In the following chapters I shall defend this crisis-and-response view as the best depiction of the forming of American theology and ethics. At this point, however, we must deal with certain other questions that should be raised about Richardson's approach—questions that must inevitably be raised about any venture as innovative and bold as his:

1. I am not sure that Richardson gives us the right reasons for setting out an American theology. While he does not flatly claim that American Christianity is better than European Christianity, he comes close to it. Christianity in America is full, balanced, ecumenical, not reductionist and one-sided as is European theology. Except for Eastern Orthodoxy, American Christianity is the only really trinitarian religion around.[12] I doubt if it is profitable to get into this kind of game, especially since European theologians are so much more practiced at playing it than are Americans. Anyway, there are better reasons for delineating an "American theology." The first, as I have been suggesting, is that it is important to understand the beliefs, morals, and manners of the American greater community. It is useful

to know which theological and ethical presuppositions are actually operative. From this point of view it does not matter whether these presuppositions add up to a better or a worse theology than Europe's. The important thing is to cease trying to explain American religion and ethics by means of theology imported from another greater community and another era, and to see what it is like in itself.

2. This brings us to the question of what is normative in theologies and ethics of greater communities. I am not sure what Richardson means when he says that he is setting out a *normative* American theology. I hope he means, as I have just suggested, that he is identifying doctrines that do in fact describe what is operational (and in that sense "normal") in American religion. As we shall discover more convincingly in Chapter VI below, the attempt to describe what a community *takes for itself* to be normally expected of its adherents is a necessary part of arriving at a more transcendent, critical set of norms. What I am afraid Richardson may really mean, however, is that the perceived operating doctrines in themselves, once described and assembled, are then to be *commended*—proffered as a normative theology rather than as a description of what, in fact, seems to be functional. In short, he seems to suggest that what he describes is also to be believed. All I would say about the same set of doctrines is that they represent what *is* believed (and practiced), reserving the question of what *ought* to be believed and practiced for further deliberation. This tendency is most obvious when he takes up the Christology-without-tears that he says characterizes American religion and then advances it as an integral part of his system.

3. In some ways Richardson himself is still too bound to classical European thought. At certain points he falls back on extrinsic norms patently derived from European theological experience. His highest accolade for any form of Christianity is that it is trinitarian.[13] American Christianity is to be appreciated not really as a new emergence, on this view, but as a form that meets the patristic norms. But are we really bound to such norms? Perhaps we are, but then why? I would say, as already suggested, that what is missing here is attention to the character of misery, lostness, and predicament in America, a category that Richardson consciously omits on the ground that the true character of theology is sanctificationist or even perfectionist rather than

redemptionist. If we begin with the predicament and ask what promises of the Gospel come to relieve just *this* predicament, and not some other community's predicament, we will have gone a long way toward establishing a program for validating standards and norms, *whatever* their origin—antique or contemporary, Old World or New.

4. A related difficulty is Richardson's reluctance to venture outside the world of Puritan New England to define American religion. Though he deals imaginatively with such nontheological disciplines as cybernetics, his intramural religious conceptions seem notably delimited by the Puritan experience. It is true, of course, that the American Puritans transformed European theological thought seriously, particularly in such realms as church polity and the characterization of the believer's experience of grace. It is true at the same time, however, that the New England fathers were not innovative dogmaticians. They took for granted, by and large, the teachings of the Westminster Confession of Faith. Profound changes begin to appear with the work of Edwards, and a considerable adaptation of the notions of the sovereignty of God and the free will and ability of man was performed by Edwards' successors. When all that is acknowledged, the fact remains that the New England divines from Hooker all the way down to Edwards' apostle Bellamy were still, in general, comfortable with the European understanding of what theology was. But in the nineteenth century out on the great frontier such men as Charles G. Finney did much more than just change around European theology. They understood religion not as theology primarily, but rather as *experience*. From that point on, American religion cannot be plumbed by beginning with too European a notion of theology, or even too "Puritan" a notion of it (the Puritan doctrine of the Sabbath, for example). Instead we must begin with experience (and I would press the point even more closely to specify the experience of existential and communal crisis). From that point we must then go on to see which doctrines must be recalled (or devised outright) to explain, and also to ameliorate, the experience.

In short, American religion on the frontier became a national axiology, even a national soteriology. It was no longer a European-style theology at all, and could not be approached as reworked European doctrine. Or, as we have put it in Part One of this study,

American morality cannot be understood without seeing it as a particular version of "republican" experience, shaped and transformed by the struggles of the American greater community to dispose of its own communal and personal space. Proceeding out of the Puritan seedbed, to be sure, American beliefs and morals have been decisively affected by the republican venture that begins in modest revolution, seeks to overcome extrinsic control of the community in favor of some form of equality, and operates more or less imperfectly by the willed initiative and voluntary association of the citizen.

5. Finally, Richardson does not pay sufficient attention to the dialectical quality of the American experience, or of the relation of this experience to Europe. He is doubtless right in asserting that European theology has laid too much stress on human error and sinfulness. It does not follow, however, that a corrective theology (American or other) must therefore reduce or eliminate redemption from the corpus of doctrines. To cite confidence in man's ability and goodness is to pick up only one side of the American experience. The great revivals, in New England as on the frontier, emphasized the predicament of man and his need of a champion in Jesus Christ. It is true also (viz., dialectically) that American religion has stressed the human capacity to act and to overcome misery and lostness. Similarly, the great tradition of American philosophy (culminating in James and Dewey) has emphasized crisis, predicament, and suffering as the basis of consequent human action. Our literary tradition is highly dialectical, with a notable strand of dissent and pessimism, and also rises at times to depicting the American experience as a quest for redemption (Thoreau, Melville, Faulkner, Salinger).

Given the extratheological character of American religion, and the paucity of such studies as Richardson's, the would-be student of "American theology" may have to attach himself for awhile to the domain of American studies, consorting with historians and littérateurs rather than fellow theologians. This temporary exile may be the best way to get at the complexity of the American moral and religious heritage, and to find seasoned help for assessing the continuities and discontinuities between America and Europe. In the meantime, he should take the view that a rightly done American theology will show in the end not something remarkable about America, but rather something tangible about the human condition and man's encounter with the divine, concretely illustrated in space as well as in time.

2. Contemporary Christian Ethics and American Manners[14]

Let us turn from the issues relevant to an "American theology" to those proper to the more restricted subject of an "American ethics" and the role of Christian ethics in inquiry respecting it. We might expect to find the study of moral phenomena as elaborated in this discipline a useful point of contact for our project of seeking the relation of Christian values to public ethics. And indeed, we may well attend to certain debates that have lately taken place in American Christian ethics. There has been a heated discussion over the nature of moral principles or rules—whether they are obligatory or permissive, socially sanctioned or legitimated by personal decision. This discussion, although it has not been consciously set in the framework of American moral tradition, nevertheless gives us some intimation of the current condition of "willed initiative" (or something very close to it) among reflective American Christians. Tied in with this discussion has been much debate over the importance and character of the "situation" in which ethical decisions are made. What role should circumstances play in our minds as we weigh the meaning of rules and principles? Finally, there has been an ongoing argument about the nature of norms or motifs that should govern decision-making in the American community: is love the only ponderable norm, as some parties to the discussion have held, or must we accredit such alternative standards as "justice" a relative autonomy, particularly as we address public questions?

These discussions over rules, situation, and norms have been gathered up in a protracted debate over what has been called variously "The New Morality" and "Situation Ethics." Often centering in a consideration of revised or emergent standards of sexual behavior, the controversy has all the same echoed some of the issues that we were earlier concerned to delineate as elements of "republican morality." Proponents of the more permissive morality have seemed to embark on a "revolutionary" course by declaring an end to moral principles that have extrinsic or automatic authority. They have seemed to favor a form of the bias toward equality by insisting that every thoughtful citizen is able to make moral decisions, if he reflects according to some such norm as the Christian obligation of love. They have seemed to argue for a radically personalized form of willed initiative by stressing the importance of decision by the participants in a given situation, say a couple of college students faced with the temptation to engage in premarital intercourse. It will assist us in our search for theological and ethical tools if we briefly review the latest stage of this debate in American Christian ethics, and then suggest ways in which these issues might be redefined more helpfully in terms of the American moral experience.

To visualize the debate over "Situation Ethics" or "The New Morality" in the proper context, we need to repair briefly to the years just following World War II. In 1950 an American theologian published a rather good book on Christian ethics. One of the crucial chapters is entitled: "Christian Liberty: an Ethic without Rules," and in it he declares:

> Christians are bound by Jesus' attitude of sticking as closely as possible to human need, no matter what the rules say, as the primary meaning of obligation, . . . Strictly speaking, this is a new "principle" for morality only in the sense that here all morality governed by principles, rules, customs, and laws goes to pieces and is given another sovereign test. . . . Human need and man-made regulations (indeed, as Jesus devoutly believed, *divinely* promulgated law) are never to be compared except to the infinite advantage of the former. . . . While love itself never submits to external rule and does not proportion its benefaction according to some rule, it never becomes unruly, since the needs of other persons are the rule of love and quickly teach such love what to do.

These lines were not written by Joseph Fletcher or any other true believer of "The New Morality," but rather by one of this movement's most ardent foes. They come from Paul Ramsey's *Basic Christian Ethics*.[15] It is well to begin here because it will be necessary presently to take the measure of what has happened in American Christian ethics since 1950. Thus our point is not to demonstrate inconsistencies between *Basic Christian Ethics* and Ramsey's more recent book, *Deeds and Rules in Christian Ethics*.[16] Anyone who thinks (and Ramsey is one of the few serious American thinkers in his field) will want to restate the issues nearly twenty years later, maybe severely if the situation has changed. Moreover, Ramsey is not concerned in his later book to *deny* the possibility of need-governed acts apart from rules, but rather to assert, against the stream in popular morality, that there is a place for rules, including general, binding rules (not just permissive "guidelines" or "summaries") in the Christian life, and that there can be no "doing of Christian ethics" without such rule-making. He urges, often convincingly, sometimes archaically, that the expression of Christian love in general rules "covers a good part of the moral decisions and problems in the midst of which the Christian life must find its direction." He upholds the "freedom of *agapé* both to act through the firmest principles and to act, if need be, without them" and that our ethicizing must account for all of these modalities instead of promoting an acts-only (or a rules-only) method.[17] In our own terms, Ramsey argues that personal decision-making takes place, among other modalities, by affirming or reaffirming community sanctions previously coined, and that "willed initiative," accordingly, finds an outlet much of the time through law-accepting rather than through innovations. It must be added that all the stress in Ramsey's new book goes toward the bracing and staying of these "firmest principles." And so the emphasis is certainly changed from 1950; whatever he said then, in his later judgment, the forces of "The New Morality" must be confronted, restrained, and if possible, routed.

Ramsey selects three positions to criticize: First, he rejects that of the English theologian John A. T. Robinson, Bishop of Woolwich, who in *Christian Morals Today*[18] argues that love expresses itself in acts but also in general "working" rules of less than general obligation—in *guidelines,* we commonly say. To settle for this kind of rule-making, replies Ramsey, is to refuse to allow agape to reach certitude, to deny love's constancy. One should be able to affirm also that "in and from love, there *are,* or there may be, unbreakable rules, and the question to be relentlessly pursued is what these rules are."[19]

The second target is the contextualism of Paul Lehmann, with some of the same arguments repeated, and with many additional criticisms of Lehmann's *koinonia* ethics as elaborated in *Ethics in a Christian Context*.[20] The most recurrent of these is that Lehmann's contextualism reflects assumptions that are "precisely those contained in the American ethos, which came to fill the vacuum" (this of Lehmann's views on war), and that "however much no Christian today should be rigidly bound by the conclusions of the past, the task is to try to see with the eyes of faith and love *at least as deeply* into what is entailed in Christian ethics itself for and into contemporary political realities."[21] Thus, on this view, decisions that depend for content too much on the context, even when the context is the church community (in Lehmann's words, "a laboratory of the living word, . . . a bridgehead of maturity, namely, the Christian *koinonia*"[22]), reflect the waywardness and perversity of ordinary, uncritical American manners and morals.

But the chief enemy is Joseph Fletcher, popularizer of an act-morality taking agape itself as its only principle, and usually called "Situation Ethics." The enthusiastic reception given Fletcher's paperbound book, *Situation Ethics: The New Morality*[23] by churchmen, collegians, and others, says Ramsey, "makes nothing more evident than the parlous state of Christian ethics in church thought today." With Fletcher's understanding of ethical decision-making, "there is really nothing that can be said and nothing that can *not* be said about the moral life." In an ethics "where everything may count for loving, then nothing can significantly count for loving." Analyzing the cases in Fletcher's book (which mostly illustrate suspending moral rules if love would be served thereby), Ramsey concludes that Fletcher's method operates by foreclosing the discussion of the significance of moral acts. Fletcher, he says, names the act in passing, then quickly "re-describes" it in terms of its consequences for loving, turning our attention away from the gravity of the act itself. Thus Ramsey objects when Fletcher justifies an instance of euthanasia as " 'a particular case of loving-kindness,' " holding that this is an arbitrary redescription that irresponsibly shunts us past the compelling moral issues that are involved in any act of killing. Nor may we characterize " 'killing nascent life' " as " 'saving a mother's life' " until we have engaged in proper moral reasoning about the question of abortion. Ramsey is especially critical of Fletcher's redescriptions of sexual intercourse, which "is properly termed fornication, adultery, rape, incest, or an act of marriage; but not as maximizing pleasure or administering therapy or curing souls. . . ."[24]

All in all, situation ethics has become "an arbitrary subjectivism and existentialism, . . . or by another name a non-ethics," Ramsey concludes—unless it "takes the other turn and joins a community of ethical discourse that is seeking to determine what pieces of behavior count or do not count as loving."[25]

As the foregoing suggests, the book is decidedly a return to that old theological style, still known in Jonathan Edwards' day, of extended, polemical review of the tracts of the day. But it makes a contribution on the constructive as well as the critical side with its introduction into theological ethics of some clarifying categories from philosophical ethics.[26]

The rules-versus-acts debate is only the latest phase of an old struggle in American Christian ethics, one that was known in an earlier form a few years ago as the "principles-versus-context" debate. Classical Christian ethics insists on the primacy of norms, and even more or less precise cultural translation of these norms into binding principles and rules. But the sea current of a republican ethos, as we have seen in Part One of our study, is perennially toward criticizing "extrinsic control" even in personal morality. When the norms, principles, or rules begin to be felt not as living sanctions but as imposed compulsions, the familiar resort to morality by "self-appointment" appears. But the result is to encourage the professional ethicist to reinstate the force of norms, either by giving them new relevance or by giving them new coercive specificity. The "Situation Ethics" debate in which Ramsey and Fletcher have been engaged comes at the end of a long tug-of-war of this sort. There has been a hardening of the battle lines over the years, and a reduction of the scope of each position, so that the leading exponents on each side pay little attention, in their latest writings, to the claims of the other side. Ramsey grants the importance of "knowledge of the situation" and recognizes the freedom that should characterize an act of love; but all the weight is on rule-keeping. We see clearly this drawing of sharper lines in his refusal longer to allow the possibility of a middle-ground, mediating position, such as the summary-rule or "guideline" agapism of the Bishop of Woolwich.[27] Similarly, the situationists, committed to the decision-making capacities of ordinary men and women provided they are guided by Christian love, continue to resist what they think of as legalistic intrusions into the life of freedom.

Though Ramsey seems to think of himself as a combination-agapist, reserving a place for acts, summary rules, and pure rules, nowhere does he enter upon a methodological disquisition to show us how these are related. Whatever position was represented in *Basic Christian Ethics* (his critic Frankena says it was act-agapism), *Deeds and Rules in Christian Ethics* is, to all intents and purposes, a vigorous manifesto for rule-agapism, with pure-rule agapism visualized as the only "non-slippery" variety.[28]

I should like now to propose the hypothesis that both rule-agapism and act-agapism, in their latest forms, are competing American reductions of the Christian ethics of neo-orthodoxy, and that in the last twenty to thirty years the republican biases that we have discussed in Part One have made increasingly untenable the classical Christian approaches to rule-making, decision-making, and moral action. If I am right, it follows that we cannot "do ethics" for the next generation from either side. We must hope for a new start, based on a deeper appreciation of the American experience, that can transcend this hopeless sundering of two elements—moral sanctions and the freedom to act—necessary to *all* serious ethics, theological and public. By way of some suggestions about this new start, I can best proceed by raising three questions about Ramsey's position in *Deeds and Rules in Christian Ethics*: Can agape or Christian love stand as a suitable norm for a Christian ethics that is relevant to American manners and morals? How do we handle the problem of changing the rules when the moral environment changes? Does the American ethos impose a peculiar bias on our conception of the "situation"?

(a) *The Problem of Agape as Norm*

It is worth notice that the argument we have been considering is between two kinds of *agapism*—one kind that says agape is expressed primarily in acts, and another kind that says it is expressed primarily in rules. I wonder if it is not time to ask whether it may not be the enthronement of agapism as such, rather than the respective merits of the varieties of it, that should be inquired after. This question may be posed on two grounds—first, those of a distinctively theological ethics; second, those of the relevance of Christian motifs to public ethics.

What are the theological reasons for concentrating upon love as a norm? It may be significant that mainline Reformation thought, though favoring Christology as the central locus of theology, yet retained some buttressing doctrines to bear some of the responsibility for thinking about man and his condition—the doctrine of the Trinity, for example, which permitted in turn a powerful richness of complementary themes in understanding God's relation to man: the judging, righteous God of the law, and the loving, faithful God of the Gospel. By contrast, the American reappropriation of Reformation themes in the last generation was almost overwhelmingly Christological. (By the process of observing trends a generation later, we can see this Christological bent in stylized form among the God-is-dead thinkers, who are as much the inheritors of neo-orthodox dogmatics in America as the agapists are of its ethics.) The results for moral reflection are seen in terms of the narrower motif that is apprehended as giving rise to the Christian life. For Luther and Calvin, that motif was unquestionably *faith,* not love. For American neo-orthodoxy and its successors, that motif is just as unquestioningly *love,* not faith. Such vital countering notions, bound up with the classic understanding of faith, as law and justice, having no other place to go, are perforce redescribed as forms of love.

Ramsey chides Fletcher for simply and without ado redescribing justice as love ("Love and Justice Are the Same" is the title of one chapter in Fletcher's *Situation Ethics*). But I submit that ample precedent was set for Fletcher by Ramsey himself and other neo-orthodox thinkers some years ago in the process of enthroning agape as the only *distinctive* virtue of the Christian faith. It was Ramsey who insisted in 1950, along with other establishment Christian ethicists, that "the Bible knows nothing, or little of any conflict between justice and love."[29] To be sure, this point is much more subtly stated by Ramsey than by Fletcher, indeed with enough subtlety to free him of the charge of simply equating the two. As Ramsey now explains, replying to Frankena's classification of him as an act-agapist, he was arguing that agape is "primary and distinctive," which is not to deny that there may be "independent secondary and non-distinctive principles," one of which would be justice. Ramsey seems to be saying here: "No, I was not so just an act-agapist; I had a place for rules also." But that is not the issue. What I want to argue is that being an agapist of *any* kind, act-, rules-, or combination-, does not give enough independence to the reality of justice (which seems to me, to the extent that the groanings of mankind today are revelatory, to be just as important *for our time* as love, and certainly not to be confused with it in the pious fashion of last generation's biblical theologians). Ramsey also has a reply to this point, agreeing that one cannot just flatly rule out the possibility "that there may be rules, principles, or precepts whose source is man's natural competence to make moral judgments." Yet he takes some of this back by insisting in the next breath that his "mixed agapism"—a combination of agape with "man's sense of natural justice or injustice" is still internally asymmetrical, for love is always *transforming* natural justice.[30] So far, so good—so long as natural justice is transformed into *a better justice.* But if we are being told that this "transforming" in principle changes justice to love, then we are no better off with Ramsey than with Fletcher.

I do not myself regard love-enthroned as all that crucial to the distinctiveness of the Christian faith. What is distinctive about it is the "good news" of man's redemption in Jesus Christ. This redemption *may* mean the saving relationship of love, but it may *also* mean the saving accession of justice. That love is a "higher" virtue than justice I grant, if by that we do not understand ourselves to be signing away the complementary self-standingness of justice. Just now, for example, unquestionably the unloving emergence of what Leveller Richard Overton long ago called "self-propriety" is crucial to the black man's becoming a redeemed person. That he will become loving, too, is a promise of the Gospel—but he cannot become loving *instead* of self-proprietary, and that is why justice is a moment of salvation infected by love but by no means swallowed by it.

To turn to the relevance of Christian norms for public ethics we may say that agape corresponds closely to what we have been calling willed initiative, at least in terms of human motivations and actions. Both express commitment to neighbor and action on his behalf—the first in the context of a community of faith, the second in the context of a republican ethos. More profoundly, the first stems from God's love of man and man's answering response to God and neighbor. The second stems from the republic's freeing of the person from extrinsic control and his subsequent answer in terms of "love of country" and acts of voluntary good will toward fellow citizens. For the Christian the two loves are even closer, for he considers the freedom and benefits of republican governance to be gifts of God and aspects of that wholeness of men and nations that is promised by the Gospel as an ultimate sequel to our present disordered and partial realizations.

Just as willed initiative cannot be understood as the whole of public ethics, so the theme of love is inadequate as a singular norm. Willed initiative springs out of a revolutionary time occasion and aims at reorganizing the space of the community to permit self-disposal of space and shared space. In this sense, willed initiative, while "resembling," as we have said, the classical Christian notion of love, is much better thought of as a program to achieve freely disposable, shared communal space. In that sense, love points to justice, and is only one of at least three imperious norms that must be consulted in public ethics, the others being the temporal and spatial norms that we have already mentioned. For public ethics, the Christian motif of love certainly has its relevance. In the final analysis love is a lively symbol of the way to redemption: it reminds us of the spirit and action-form that willed initiative should take. But it is not redemption itself. Maybe love does transform justice into itself—sometimes. For *public* ethics, just as often it transforms itself into justice or, what is the same thing, refines "natural justice" (more aptly, "*cultural* justice") into a new justice, productive of shared space.

(b) *The Problem of Changing the Rules*

Neither Ramsey nor his situationist foes give sufficient attention to the necessity of replacing one set of rules with another, given shifts in the salvation crises men face from age to age and from greater community to greater community. To be sure, the situationists are ready enough to discard obsolete rules, and presumably they are willing to grant a place to more relevant replacements so long as the new principles, whatever they may be, are properly subservient to love and the needs of the situation. And even Ramsey allows for the reform of "practices." A practice or institution, he tells us, "may be compared to a game with its established rules. If one wants to play a game, he doesn't treat the rules of the game as mere summaries or guides as to what is usually best in particular cases." One may never appeal directly to agape to override the rules of practice in a particular case. What one must do, rather, is to try "to reform the accepted practice as a whole in some fundamental respect."[31]

And yet life isn't a game. Let us consider the formerly accepted "practice" of segregated facilities in the South. Ramsey is right in suggesting that no baseball player, in mid-game, would demand that he, next time at bat, be given four strikes instead of the customary three. That is no way to change the rules—of a game. But the "practice" of segregation gave the white man four or five strikes, so to speak, every time he came to the plate in education, public accommodations, and everything else—and the black man was often called out before coming to bat. The black man was right to insist, *in the course of "play,"* that each side be given the same three strikes per inning.

The public ethicist must do more than simply provide for the honorable possibility of someone else reforming the rules of practices. He must lead in this enterprise himself, for if there is one lesson about the human community we should have learned, it is that its history is characterized by rise and fall, by crisis after crisis in the struggle to dispose of its own space: its history, in short, is characterized by upheavals and discontinuities in ethical conceptions. One reason Ramsey doesn't spend too much time with the possibilities here is his puzzling mental blockage against any and all teleological models in Christian-ethical theory. He has the impression, derived in part from borrowing category labels unreworked from Frankena, that "agapism" is somehow incompatible with "teleology" (though not necessarily with "deontology"). I would argue, on the other hand, that men must be understood all the time, at every time, *across* time, to be receiving the benefits of Christ, at least in part. The Gospel, it seems to me, is therefore teleological *as a matter of form,* i.e., God's promise to renew man may be understood in terms of the future.[32] One has only to look at the contemporary revolution in human values, involving such moral fields as civil rights, economic dignity, the big-power consensus against nuclear war, the equality of women, or the cruelty of capital punishment, to see that some rules, at least, do change, and possibly for the better. It is the business of the theologian as public ethicist to delineate the criteria for appraising and governing these changes and for connecting them with man's pilgrimage.

Ramsey is ultimately right, however, in insisting that it is rules of societal practices *as wholes* (the same thing we mean in this study by "manners") that must be the subject of reform. The kind of *ad hoc* direct appeals to conscience, agape, and higher law that has characterized the recent civil rights and peace movements was justifiable only as a series of emergency measures and cannot take the place of careful reflection upon, and studied revision of, societal practices, institutions, and customs as such.

I venture to suggest, then, that what must be *held on to* from one generation to another as a matter of ethicizing is not a set of "rules" at all—these come and go with crisis and response—but rather one's *moral tradition,* with all its conflicts and ambiguity. The two primary elements in any ethical issue are the *saving tradition* that has nourished the making and observance of rules in the past, and the unique *unsaved situation* of new crisis that may call into question the old rules. Rules are necessary, but secondary, the outcome of the mutual confrontation of tradition and situation.

Ramsey does not give us a program for rule-changing, perhaps because his project of confounding the elders of "The New Morality" forces him into the use of examples largely drawn from the field of sex relations. (I am tempted, but refrain from concluding, that *all* forms of agapism bias the selection of examples in the direction of personal sex ethics.)

It is significant that with most of the common topics of ethical concern today (say, open housing, nuclear nonproliferation, anti-poverty programs), our problem is not to put up barriers against change, but to promote community reorganization in the face of seemingly insuperable social, institutional, and cultural resistance. But Ramsey has chosen sex as his main topic for illustration, and it is just in this area that the problem seems to anyone of moderate or prudential tendencies to be to hold the line *against* change rather than to promote it. Thus Ramsey's rules respecting fornication and adultery (both of which he classes with rape and incest over against marriage) are not very revelatory for the problems of social ethics in other areas, or for the methodology of "doing public ethics."

Ramsey is fond of charging the devotees of "The New Morality" with simply reflecting uncritically the going assumptions of bourgeois society which so easily tolerate flexible sex standards and sometimes discourage marital fidelity and perdurance. We can as easily charge that Ramsey's strictures on sex are just as culturally conditioned. Over a hundred years ago Tocqueville had already raised the question why Americans seem so tolerant on a variety of moral subjects and yet treat "all those vices which tend to . . . destroy the conjugal tie, . . . with a degree of severity which is unknown in the rest of the world." His conclusion was that public opinion in this country "especially condemns that laxity of morals which . . . disturbs the internal order of domestic life which is so necessary to success in business."[33]

In a republican ethos, any responsible citizen (and thus every responsible Christian) stands under a mandate to be not only morally literate, but to become what we might call an amateur metaethicist, or an informed decider about which rules are binding. Because of the historic bias in America toward the revolutionary republican symbols commending overthrow of extrinsic control of one's own space, the classical Christian motifs of obedience, servanthood, and deontology —concepts dear to the European theological mind—seem to miss the mark almost entirely. Americans will win fulfillment not through any passive version of Christian "obedience," but through seizing the day, through reorganizing their own space for shared existence, through willed initiative. They will therefore not win fulfillment by being mere obeyers of past general rules. The distinctive tasks of an American Christian ethics that leans into the republican ethos include, then, not only clarifying what our obligations may be, but also outlining a historical framework within which we arrive at a properly safeguarded program of changing rules to take into account the unfolding promise under which, we believe, every human community lives.

(c) The Problem of the Situation

So far we have argued that "agape" is not so basic a category as "Gospel" taken as response to a greater community's contemporary predicaments; and that "rules" are not so basic as a greater community's "moral tradition," which supplies materials and motifs for the making of new rules. Now we must say that the prevailing notion of "situation" must be rethought and deepened and given a more substantial spatial context.

The situation, as defined by some existentialists, is to be understood in terms of our decision-making "moments." It is at that point, "in the deed of decision," that "man's being is at stake . . . in the *moment* whose content can never be deduced from the universal, but which is always a concrete, individual moment that demands action, decision."[34] As a countermotif to the older insistence upon obedience to community norms without independent reflection, this stress upon the decisional moment has been salutary. Moral action is a personal responsibility, to be approached in one's own time and place.

Yet this same situation in which responsible men decide what to do is more than the moment. To take up another existentialist metaphor, it is rather one's "world." An existentialist moment may be the *occasion* of decision, but it cannot be the basis of decision. A moment is like a subatomic particle in physics, or a phoneme in semantics. It is a submeaningful unit, necessary in the construction of meaningful time, but less than intelligibly real in itself. Particularly in the realm of moral values, what is most satisfyingly human tends to take shape across a stretch of personal or community time. Too many moral decisions involve colloquy, often hard, agonizing, extended debate between two or more parties to a situation.

The situation is thus one's history and his space and his engagement with others in his community. It is his "world." It is his greater community with its own peculiar pilgrimage, tradition, memory of crises, and sets of rules that have kept men on the right road in the past.

All of this Ramsey knows and helpfully affirms against the situationists, who are all too little aware of the historical and traditionary resources that form an input into our present situation. He suggests, for example, that Fletcher's method of dealing with sex ethics, far from representing a revolt against our "Puritan" morality, is in some ways nothing more than a retouched, competing version of it. Some of the old landmarks are turned around, to be sure; Fletcher's new morality is a "reversed" Puritanism—but a Puritanism nevertheless. For we need only recall the kind of moralizing that went with the stylized Puritanism of, say, Cotton Mather's *Essays to Do Good*. Here and in countless later quasi-Puritan tracts of our American moral tradition, the value of Christian action is to be measured purely by the consequences, by the *good* it does. Just so for Fletcher and his method. As Fletcher himself has it, in a quotation Ramsey gives: "Nothing is right unless it *helps* somebody." Against this view Ramsey argues that "Sexuality has present, immediate meaning *in itself* . . . sexual love . . . is not a good secondary to progeny, or to someone's consequent integration, or to some cure of souls, or to espionage."[35]

But the situation also includes the new, the different, the cutting edge of the present. Truth-seeking, for Americans in the twentieth century, must now be defined inescapably as direct participation in experience, and in that sense, as grappling not so much with rules as with testing the meaning of situations and seeking new openings to the future. Finding the truth must be characterized as participating in a series of experiments and experiences, some of them painful, some of them discovered too late to be destructive, others redeemingly discovered to be redemptive. There is no way of knowing the truth by remaining pure or idealist, or by remaining inexperienced. This discovery, summed up in far too simplistic terms by the architects of "The New Morality," nevertheless portends a wholesale revision in our understanding of what it means to be moral. We can never be moral henceforth by remaining innocent of experiences. We may have to be moral by making mistakes and committing sins and acquiring guilt—although the winning of moral quality comes only when we can relentlessly appraise our experience and be prepared to criticize it in these hard categories.

What a more critical inquiry into the American ethos would show is that this approach to morality has long since been normative. In this sense not only the situationists but Ramsey, too, overlooks his own American tradition. Throughout his book, but especially in a satirical (and heavyhanded) last chapter entitled "A Letter to John of Patmos from a Proponent of 'the New Morality' " Ramsey is critical and contemptuous of what he thinks of as "contemporaneity" in Christian ethics. In a way it is a delight to see him inveighing against the fads, the "in" clichés, and the posturings of contemporary theology and ethics. Let us have more of his forthright kind of polemic against "dialogue," "encounter," the wonders of secularity, the much cried-up hermeneutical problem, "cheap *koinonia* ethics," and the spirit of "relevance."

At the same time, we must not make the mistake of supposing that it is only just now that the Christians in our midst have become infatuated with innovations and have lost interest in rules, tradition, and reflection. Nor should we think that if a few of us just keep the faith, it will all someday blow over. The problem is not one of "contemporaneity" as such, but, if I may use the expression, of "Americaneity." One has only to read Tocqueville, as we have already seen, to discover evidence that Americans have always been commercially bent, earthbound, and committed to furious activity, innovation, and practical ways of finding their destiny. In America, Tocqueville observed, men are "in constant motion . . . precedents are of little authority and laws but of short duration, resistance to novelty is languid, and the fabric of society never appears perfectly erect or firmly consolidated." Much of the change so celebrated in our time is actually foreshadowed in American history, argues the historian Marcus Cunliffe—urbanization, for example, has led us into a crisis today, but the seeds of the crisis are already visible in the last century's patterns of industrialization and settlement. Isolated from the past, we have no chance to reckon fully with the outcomes of our own actions.[36]

3. Guidelines to Recovery of the American Moral Tradition

It is apparent that contemporary theology and ethics in America, despite promising developments, have not yet broken through to an awareness of the American greater community as a context or framework for conceptual and constructive thought. The motivation and excitement are sometimes there, as with Herbert Richardson's essays on the new task of outlining a distinctively American theology. The basic ingredients of an "American ethics" are there, though split asunder in the competing claims of two camps—the situationists or act-ethicists, and the principalists or rule-ethicists. But much is still lacking, especially acceptance of the American experience as a coherent reservoir of symbols and historical themes for thinking. In an effort to suggest some of the ways in which the resources of this experience might be marshaled, I wish to turn finally to the question of the major components of the "American Moral Tradition."

(a) *Saving Symbols and Historic Predicament*

The American moral tradition stems from the application of "saving symbols" to practice (manners and morals) in answer to a peculiar historic sequence of predicaments.

In the first part of our study we have already explored the character of the primordial predicament that inaugurates the moral experience in America and influences the remainder of American history. This primary predicament is extrinsic control of personal and communal space. A revolutionary break with the past is justified by realization of this predicament. The agents are then constrained to seek a new constitution of the community that provides for reorganization of the space on a participating, shared basis. We participate in community space by willed initiative and voluntary association, although these terms do not imply the absence of a binding constitution and laws, which are the first object of public will following revolution.

This formal description—compressible here only because we have elaborated it at length in Part One—would seem to comprehend most of the great crises in American history, from the American Revolution itself through the Civil War, the twentieth-century worldwide conflicts with totalitarian regimes, down to the civil rights struggle of the mid-twentieth century. The same formula would seem to apply to a wide variety of personal moral crises in American life, from the anguish of the college students in our decade insisting on self-determination in the university to the sex revolutionaries insisting on the right of persons to express mutuality that defies the heteronomous rules of a past era.

Now we must approach the whole subject from another viewpoint, the perspective of the accumulated symbols that give impetus to these revolutionary movements in American history.

Ethics, from this point of view, may be understood as that discipline of reflection meant to provide guidance and criticism for human actions in accordance with some continuing experience of crisis and deliverance. The emphasis may be either upon a positive hope for some new blessedness toward which the community is to be led, or it may be a more negative concern with a pressing predicament from which the community yearns immediately to be rescued. Or the experience may partake of both positive and negative elements at once, giving rise to a balanced ethics. In any case, this continuing experience and the hope of deliverance is communicated from one generation to the next through an evolving set of efficacious "saving symbols," and ethics is radically dependent for its content upon both this input or past environment of saving symbols, and a situational response to it.

A saving symbol may thus be defined as a historically efficacious, specially remembered and often strikingly expressed representation of what rescues from crisis or predicament and tends toward blessedness. It may take the form of an object, creed, slogan, story, person, or act, but what counts is not the bit of the environment that forms the sign itself, but the insight and the power that have been present in, with, and under the sign in the past. The dimensions of what constitutes "crisis" or "predicament" and "blessedness" or "deliverance" depend upon what forces threaten the life of a given community. Thus the Eucharist is remembered well up into the middle of the second Christian millennium as the "medicine of immortality"—the symbol of rescue from the predicament of mortality, and the miseries of temporal existence, of the yearning to pass through the travail of a cruel, secondary natural existence into the impassibility of supernature. To take another example, if the priest who dispensed this saving medicine was the savior figure of one age and great community in Western history, it was Robinson Crusoe who became the savior model of later Western man, for Crusoe represented the individual who, by his temporal actions, could deal with and conquer nature. Saving symbols henceforth could be not so much aimed at rescuing man from his finitude as at enabling him to live with it.

Two corollaries may be laid down:

1. Saving symbols, and hence the discursive directions of ethical thought, are significantly organized within the boundaries of greater communities, and do not necessarily retain their numinous or extraordinary quality when a decisive community boundary in time space is crossed.[37]

2. Though saving symbol sets migrate across communities, great and small, their theological "genes" or constituent symbol bits vary with the differential predicaments of communities, with varying apprehensions of what constitutes the threat to life and rescue from it. This factor accounts for some of the shifts in symbolic elements in the transmission of legends, fairy tales, and other pieces of folklore. Thus tales concerning the dire character of "trolls" that originated in Scandinavia were transferred to England with much of the meaning intact; but the "trolls" themselves, not representing an image of threat in the popular mind in England, disappeared from the stories, and were replaced by human villains. Similarly, "The vampire stories of the European East become, as they travel westward, more and more 'neutral', more and more 'washed out', until even the vampire is replaced by an indifferent robber."[38]

There is, to be sure, a persistence across space and time barriers in saving symbols, for there is something perduring and perennial about both saving vision and the human condition. Thus, in the upheavals of the Protestant Reformation, involving a shift from a Latin to a Germanic understanding of some elements of faith, the essentials of the Christian message are preserved. But the shape of the crisis changes from age to age and from greater community to greater community, and the saving symbols that orient ethics are reconstituted in each greater community. Thus Luther's conception of justification by faith leads to a rejection of the monastic program of the Christian life and the substitution of the view of the worldly vocation of the believer.

In short, a special history or tradition concerned with "salvation" lies back of every greater community in the West, based more or less on the Christian heritage but also more or less on secular, political traditions (such as the evolution of legal rights in the Anglo-Saxon countries). In each greater community it is a complex tradition rather than a unitary, rigid history. It is an accumulation of saving symbols that have in fact saved in past crises. In any new affair of either crisis or blessedness, some of the perennial symbols continue to be adaptable and still point to salvation. Others become "period trash" and must be discarded (the symbol of the Virgin Birth, for example, to a great many literate Europeans and Americans). Sometimes new symbols arise to commemorate a new crisis and vision (the symbolism of the Civil War in America, for example). Or old symbols are commandeered to serve new meanings (one need think only of the new usages to which the early Christian community put the past environment of Hebrew saving symbols). Each greater community in a phylum of communities thus may share some of its saving symbols with the other communities, in the same way that a family of related languages, such as the Indo-European tongues, share ancient and primordial features. But each greater community has its own special saving tradition that stands in both continuity and discontinuity with the others and with the parent tradition.

(b) *Demise of the European Symbols in America*

In America, the European symbols have been undergoing modification to meet the historic line of march of moral predicament proper to the American greater community.

From our present point of view, the American Revolution raised a decisive question about the viability of the unmodified European set of Christian saving symbols. The American colonies became a new theological subcommunity of the West, principally because of a shift in the experience of predicament and in the corresponding notion of what constituted salvation.

It is often argued that it was the "wilderness" that constituted the definitive predicament of the first Americans, as the imagery of the Puritans frequently insisted, and as the factical, ontic misfortunes of the Jamestown settlers seemed to demonstrate. But the wilderness—

the real one or the wilderness as broader symbol of the hostility and cruelty of nature—was ceasing to be a deep threat to Western man once the idea (or countervailing symbol) had broken through: man could master nature—a realization that was dawning and beginning to be celebrated by the whole of the North Atlantic community, ultimately including the American colonials. In this study we have consistently understood the resistance of nature—whether of the American wilderness and its threats to the seaboard settlers, or of the inland frontier with its seeming potency to reshape our very character as a people—as real but subordinate. What was of more moment for the distinctiveness of the American salvation struggle was the realization that a properly organized community could triumph over despotism, or extrinsic control of political space. The "tyranny" of nature was, of course, included in this vision, and the image of Americans as masters of the physical environment continues to be powerful. But the crucial, comprehensive struggle was that for the establishment of the right to space disposal through a community built on willed initiative.

To the extent that nature does play a role in the American dream, it does not play the romantic role usually assigned it. Americans did not come to America to fix it in amber as an unspoiled Eden or to conjure up idle dreams of pastoral salvation. That is both to underestimate the uncomfortable, dangerous conditions imposed by unconquered wilderness and frontier and to disregard the active, transforming aspects of human nature as they were evoked in America. From the very outset, the Americans understood nature as a challenge to be transformed and subdued. Nature was a secondary despot, to be sure (only in tribal days had it reigned supreme), a threat subordinate to that of the overbearing political ruler. As Tocqueville acutely sees, the wilderness was neither an "Eden" to the Americans nor a threat to be obsessed with:[39]

> In Europe people talk a great deal of the wilds of America, but the Americans themselves never think about them: . . . Their eyes are fixed on another sight: the American people views its own march across these wilds,—drying swamps, turning the course of rivers, peopling solitudes, and subduing nature.

It may be, as Leo Marx argues, that the Americans deceived themselves to some extent, continuing to entertain pleasant Jeffersonian
visions of a rural landscape with its green garden. Such a sentimental
pastoral ideal remained long after the beginnings of industrialization,
he says. It allowed the country to go on thinking of "the pursuit of
rural happiness" while it was in fact bent on "productivity, wealth,
and power."[40] I would accept the contradiction implied here, but
argue that this rural vision of happiness was never a dominant theme,
whatever its persistence in some of the art and literature and oratory
of the nineteenth (and twentieth) century. We have indeed insisted
earlier in our study that every ponderable ideological theme in the
American experience is liable to a dialectical interpretation, or a
breakdown into two seemingly opposed versions; thus nature could
have been at once regarded sentimentally in America and yet taken as
mere matter to be mastered. But this has not been the dominant
dialectic. The controlling vision has been the dream to dispose of
community space freely, rejecting extrinsic control. Is this vision
amenable to technological methods or to political methods? That has
been a more persistent, and painful, division in America. In neither of
these possibilities is nature to be preserved as an idyllic still-life
scene. It is to be subdued either industrially or politically (that is,
either the factory will replace the farm or the city will replace it).

Shortly we shall posit another key role that the wilderness played
in the American moral tradition. If it was not the chief threat to
community, as we have been arguing, it did pose a serious problem in
an entirely different realm, in its impoverishment of our ability to
think critically, to nourish the symbols of salvation at the conceptual
level. Here let us reiterate that the principal salvation goal in the
American experience has been to clear the space of extrinsic control,
whether of a resistant nature or of political domination. What was
most distinctive about the American experience was the discovery of
a method to go about this clearing and reconstituting of the community space. While leaving an opening for the dialectical aberrations of
"rugged individualism" and "conformism," America discovered "the
idea of the people as a constituent power." This was a new notion, a
new way of realizing the sovereignty of the people. It avoided both
the weaknesses of direct democracy and of rationalizing political

power as something wrung from a monarch. The ideals of liberty, human rights, and equality were already familiar in Europe. But the American Revolution produced, in the constitutional system, a new approach to political community. The people retained ultimate power at the level of higher law or of a constitution "that only the people could make or amend, through constitutional conventions or bodies similarly empowered." The worst effects of direct democracy were avoided by drawing from this reserved power "a statutory law, to be made and unmade, within the assigned limits, by legislators to whom the constitution gave this function."[41] Here was a victory not over the wilderness but over the most perplexing of political challenges. It was a victory for what we have called "willed initiative."

This new implementation of governance in America, offering participation to every citizen in reorganizing the community space, amounted to a new program of salvation. Thus it was bound to entail, sooner or later, a reevaluation and reworking of all the received European saving symbols, Christian and secular, that had taken root in the New World. Here was an advance over the classical Christian hope of blessedness in the next world. But here was also a decisive advance over even the Enlightenment discovery of worldly *bonheur,* for with the American political experience, not only did men grasp a new vision of happiness, but a way of achieving it. What was decisive, then, was not the ideas, but their emergence in "the novelty of the New World's political development," a discovery based on "the tremendous strength inherent in mutual promises" which saw "the intimate relationship between 'happiness' and action" (Hannah Arendt).[42]

For a salvation reality to become available ethically, it must be mediated by symbols that speak to its distinctiveness. From this point of view, the discovery of a revolutionary "political" salvation in America—aimed at equality and mediated through willed initiative—meant a massive overload on the older European Christian symbols. These older symbols were more religious than political. They were not adapted, at least at first glance, to a revolutionary program of salvation. They were not suited to commending personal and communal activism or initiative, since obedience, rather than initiative, had long been a primary category of both Christian and monarchical ethos in Europe.

We see the demise of European salvation symbols almost from the very first, as in the slackening of hope in New England that there could ever be a "Holy Commonwealth" truly in being in the New World, and in the subsequent transference of this early Puritan vision to outright political life, on the one hand (Benjamin Franklin is one exemplar of this shift from religion to politics), and to the advocates of an internalization of God's grace on the other, given the failure of the revival to spread this grace at large socially (Jonathan Edwards exemplifies this outcome). It is also true that a good part of the religious heritage continued to serve the new vision of salvation. To the extent that the preaching of new life, liberty in Christ, the holiness of cordial union, and other theological symbols served to bolster (and criticize) the political vision of spatial self-determination, the religious sector continued in lively service. But by the nineteenth century the unappropriated, unreworked European religious symbols had retreated into dogmatic reservations and theological enclaves, such as Princeton, or else had become so thoroughly pragmatized, as with Charles G. Finney on the frontier, that they lost much of their original meaning. In either case the symbols were lost from the arena of advancing ethical reflection.

Now we are ready to consider, as we announced we would, the real impact of the wilderness—its impact, that is, on this testing of the old symbols and the search for new ones. The wilderness was not, as we have seen, the chief existential threat, except to the extent that as a subordinate form of tyranny it, too, had to be mastered, along with human perpetrators of extrinsic control. More pertinently to our present concern the wilderness was an *intellectual* barrenness; and thus it loomed as a threat to discourse, to conceptual work, to that upkeep, maintenance, and care of symbols that depend on a "workshop" of conceptual activity. Perhaps New England, with its Puritan divines headed by the great Edwards, and its literary tradition, was something of an exception, and did offer something of an intellectual workshop. But one reason, as we have already suggested, is that the New England life could still draw its nourishment from England. When the national experience began to draw away from Europe, the New England house of letters, like the classical Christian symbols, could no longer speak for the whole or for the new hour.

"A democracy cannot derive substantial benefit from past experience," Tocqueville observed of nineteenth-century America, "unless it be arrived at a certain pitch of knowledge and civilization." It seems clear that outside New England America had not yet arrived at that pitch. Only with advanced civilizations, later scholars have observed, do we find sophisticated manners; art forms in which the "ideal image—not to mention the tensions—of a people are explored"; or "distinctive theologies and philosophies" which can examine and criticize the values of a people. This kind of intellectual expertise can be found only in societies that have gained some stability, can confer leisure on part of its citizens to permit them to become reflective, discriminating, and critical, and has generated enough creative and psychic capital "to encourage spirals of development and synthesis of cultural forms."[43]

It is not surprising, on this view, that students of more than one discipline have noticed a failure of discourse in early America, a seeming inability to go beyond the transferred European intellectual capital and to engage in much conceptualization of the new reality in human affairs represented by the American experience. Hannah Arendt, as we have seen, celebrates the political advances in the New World, but laments that there is no corresponding "liberation from the conceptual, intellectual framework" of the past. "The novelty of the New World's political development was nowhere matched by an adequate development of new thought." The men of the American Revolution made history in their deeds, yet "remained bound to the conceptual and intellectual framework of the European tradition."[44]

We see the same pattern in other attempts to plumb reality—in the field of folklore, for example. At first, European folklore styles prevailed in America, as exemplified in the persistence for a time of belief in witchcraft and of the frequent attempts to explain physical phenomena by stories of "remarkable providences." But these European folk symbols were patently unsuited to strike the mood of reality as it was apprehended in this active new world. "After a century and a half in the New World, Americans began to center their folk invention upon themselves."[45] In the arts, the same loss of vitality of European themes is noticeable. Tocqueville describes a drastic transformation in the office of poetic imagination from what it had been in aristocratic Europe. What he sees happening in America is what we called above "the demise of European symbols" or what theologians today would call "demythologization." An aristocratic people, he says, is always tempted to posit intermediary powers between God and man—angels and demons, for example. But in democratic ages, a more realistic, earthbound outlook prevails, and the imagination of poets is confined to the real, visible world. In a democracy, poets will not seem convincing, Tocqueville thinks, if they attempt to picture the old world of gods, demons, or angels, "and if they attempt to draw them down from heaven to dispute the supremacy of earth." In a democracy, tradition means less, and thus "poetry will not be fed with legendary lays or the memorials of old traditions." What the people believe in is not a supernatural world of semidivine beings or a past of legend, but only man—"and the poet needs no more."[46]

In short, the American world view "has dried up most of the old springs of poetry." Yet this demise of the European symbols was not soon compensated for by a replacement at the same level of sophistication and maturity. One has only to recall the painting and poetry of, say, the Revolutionary period. Charles Wilson Peale "depicted the Continental uniform in careful detail," comments Samuel Eliot Morison, "but unfortunately used a standard face so that his portraits of Washington and Lafayette, who differed greatly in physiognomy, look like father and son; and even John Paul Jones looks like a member of the same family."[47] Down to Hawthorne (and beyond) doubt prevailed about the richness and subtlety of literary materials in America. Hawthorne was much interested in the problems of the artist in America, but he shared the misgivings of other critics about the meagerness of "the available materials for literature."[48] Even when literary production was underway in America, educators with aspirations to quality long refused to teach such materials, preferring to stick to the corpus of European literature. For awhile, one could say, there was little or no literary class in America, and when a lettered tradition did arise, it looked to Europe on the one hand, and turned in the direction of a nonbookish approach on the other, settling for the popular magazine, journal, and newspaper. "Almost wholly dependent on London for their books," says Daniel J. Boorstin, the colonists "could not avoid borrowing English ways of thinking about many things, but they did not borrow the institutions of a literary

class." American men of letters were not *literati*. They were professional and commercial men: physicians, clergymen, lawyers, printers, leisured farmers. When artists, writers, and the whole machinery
of a literary culture did arise, it bore the marks of these beginnings.[49]

In short, the wilderness did seriously threaten our ability to handle
saving symbols by interfering with the development of a conceptual
workshop. At the very moment when America began to emerge with
a national consciousness (in the early nineteenth century) the literary
and imaginative materials that were needed to refurbish the store-
house of theological and ethical conceptions were scarce.

Consequently, America stands as that larger community in the
West representing the most striking ontic developments in Christian
ethics, but also as the larger community that has been least able
noetically to deal with this reality in the conceptual framework that
nourishes symbols into a formative tradition. *Homo Americanus* had
discovered the saving efficacy of mutual action, but he did not know
how to fit this discovery into the history of salvation, and so his
discovery drifted away from that guidance and coaching that historical tradition offers new reality in the human struggle for wholeness.
Here was the plight: How is moral action to be carried out *and
rightly tested* in the intellectual wilderness with only a fading memory
of the European analogies?

American whiskey makers, we might observe parenthetically, had
the same problem as American theologians: they had to use American materials and formulate, sometimes amateurishly, a new tradition
of quality control. By the twentieth century, it is clear that the makers
of American whiskey have triumphed. There will always be a place
for Scotch, but there is also pretty good bourbon around now. Dorson
speaks for American folklorists when he argues that by now "the only
meaningful approach to the folk traditions of the United States must
be made against the background of the American history, with its
unique circumstances and environment."[50] And yet in American
theology there continues to be genuine doubt that an "American
tradition" for the guidance of the theologian and ethicist can—or
even ought—to be sought. "It is a serious question," argues Michael
Novak, "whether American theologians, renouncing the only theolog-

ical languages they presently have, German ontology and German existentialism, have the resources to carry through an intellectual transformation of Christianity."[51]

(c) *The Continuing Evolution of Saving Symbols in America*

The American moral tradition continues to evolve saving symbols today, and students of humanity and society, including theologians, are challenged to reflect on them.

To pursue this line of thought, let us continue to reason from the analogy of the fate of folklore and its study in this country. By the middle of the nineteenth century, the irrelevant European folk forms had all but disappeared. But by now even the first wave of droll, ingenuous native folklore had flowered and begun to disappear— crowded out by the explosion of mass communications. The sentimentalities of romantic novels, the small-bore gossip of the penny press, the crassness of the industrial revolution in the manufacture of cheap household goods, all claimed their victims: "Eventually the maudlin taste of the mid-nineteenth century, when *Godey's Lady's Book* set the fashions, and the stultifying effect of factory production, withered the native folk crafts."[52] Legends and stories died out, too, surpassed by the popular press.

Thus folklore has already died two deaths in America, and we may possibly say the same for theology. But the folklorists in America have been more perceptive about this recurrent rise and fall than some theologians. If European folk legends and fairy tales have disappeared, if primitive American folklore has been killed off by the mass media, nonetheless folklorists are aware of a *new* eruption of *contemporary* legends, myths, and folk stories, concerned with the emergent fantasies, fears, and hopes of ordinary men and women living in a technological age. Dorson's researches illustrate this development with well-documented accounts of the origin of legends concerning automobiles and technological devices. Even as amateurs to folklore, we have all heard some of this—stories that deal, for example, with the theme that "the computers are taking over." Dorson has catalogued a number of those that deal with the automobile:[53]

Rumors spread about remarkable inventions which would improve automobiles. A carburetor that will give fifty miles to the gallon is being kept off the market by the big oil companies. But an experimental model inadvertently slips into a customer's hands, who informs his dealer with astonished delight about the fine mileage he has been getting. Hastily the dealer offers another car in exchange, saying this model was not intended for sale. Similar stories deal with the tire that will never wear out, and the razor blade that will last forever.

Religious belief has suffered somewhat the same fate in America as folklore: it, too, has been through a series of symbolic meta-morphoses—from European Reformed thought through Puritanism to frontier Arminianism to indigenous liberalism to imported neo-orthodoxy to late disaffection with all of these strata—and with the idea of God himself. But this history affords no basis for disillusionment; it offers, if anything, the liveliest challenge to the serious pursuit of religious belief in America. The symbols of "salvation" in the American community have continued to evolve through all of these births and deaths of religious and theological styles. Whether the artifacts of the physical world are "shadows or images of divine things" (Jonathan Edwards) or just "extensions of man" (Marshall McLuhan), we can still see even in the electronic age how our thirst for salvation continues unabated, but now symbolized in new ways: "The aspiration of our time for wholeness, empathy and depth of awareness is a natural adjunct of electric technology," says Mc-Luhan.[54] Yet American theologians, by and large, disdain any study of "folk religion." They have little use for bridge-building efforts to relate theology and the study of cybernetics, preferring to translate and promulgate the writings of European theologians who preach against such corruptions of the faith.[55] In this respect, they do not live up to the vision of some of their predecessors.

Aside from the current scholasticism and sterility of American theology, however, there is a more long-standing difficulty that has inhibited the development of a fully elaborated moral tradition. In traditional greater communities, the moral commitments of the past are ensconced in ethnic roots that go back to mythical origins of the community. For the United States, with its heterogeneous racial stocks and its destiny of pluralism, no such antique structure for holding together a moral tradition was possible, at least beyond the early period of British hegemony. That the white Anglo-Saxon tradition cannot be the vehicle of the American moral quest is now finally coming to consciousness, as demonstrated by recent decisions of the Supreme Court outlawing school segregation, sectarian (usually Protestant) religious practices in the classroom, and unequal apportionment among political districts. The old myth of the "American Way of Life" was all too dependent on the moral tradition of but one ethnic group, and if this group's traces, for better or worse, continue to play an important role in the forging of a new American moral tradition, built on the roots and ruins of the old, yet a new tradition, it is clear, is needed and is building.

The new American moral tradition will be built on ideology rather than on ethnic myth. The roots of this new tradition are already there in the Declaration of Independence, the Constitution, and the Civil War amendments. To date the chief guardians of this tradition have been dissenters, abolitionists, literary men, journalists, jurists, and philosphers, with frequent participation by crusading churchmen. The subject matter of this tradition must be the struggle against extrinsic control of community space. Its concern must be to keep reopening the questions of how communal space is organized and who participates in the reorganizing. Its aim must be to seek the widest participation. Since one of the emergent characteristics of American society is its diverse racial and ethnic mix, this new tradition will be unlike any conventional moral tradition, for it can have no agreed-upon base in some historic religion or tribal consciousness. What is required is the mythical reconstruction of a new notion of the "American Way of Life" that will allow not only for plural backgrounds, but also for conflicting views. And the role of participating groups, whatever their ethnic background, will be assured more by the evoking of "new myths" that point to participation in the American experience than by the remembering of their pre-American racial backgrounds.

Indeed, this building of "new American myth" has been underway for much of our history. In Europe, says Daniel Boorstin, the great national communities can look back to origins so far in the past as to come down in the form of legend, rather than of history. The same could be said for the great European national heroes—figures like Charlemagne, King Alfred, Alexander the Great. These founding fathers, coming into national consciousness as "misty legends," had eventually to be reconstructed as historical figures in order for modern European communities to understand them. But the United States, with its somewhat shallow reservoir of history, had just the opposite problem. Our Founding Fathers were known quite well historically: at the outset of the Civil War, there were men who could remember Washington, Adams, and Jefferson from personal acquaintance. The national problem was not how to make Washington and the others historical; what was needed, rather, and quickly, was a way of making them mythical. "What is most remarkable is not that Washington eventually became a demigod, Father of his Country, but that the transfiguration happened so quickly."[56] The new myths were needed to transmit the incipient American moral tradition, and just as this tradition is being reconstructed on a broader basis today, so the older myths of the "Founding Fathers" must be reinterpreted and supplemented. From this point of view, the problem with such remnants of the earliest American mythology as Parson Weems' story about young Washington and his hatchet and his inability to tell a lie is not Weems' inventiveness. It is rather Weems' Puritan values, which were vital ingredients of the moral tradition for the predicaments of the day, but which are inadequate to the challenges of postindustrial America.

That myth-making proceeds today among groups newly throwing off extrinsic control of their space is fully illustrated in the case of the black man. In the first place, since blacks have not long been able to participate with some semblance of equality in organizing community space, the older symbols that functioned for the Anglo-Saxon groups are not felt by the blacks as saving. This difference of feeling about symbols explains, in a word, the Black Muslim and Black Nationalist mystiques of recent years. "Christianity is the white man's religion," the late Malcolm X said, defending his entry into the Muslim movement. "The Holy Bible in the white man's hands and his interpretations of it have been the greatest single ideological weapon for enslaving millions of non-white human beings."[57] Not only were the white man's religious symbols inadequate. There wasn't enough carryover symbolic content in many of the early American political myths to include blacks, and thus additional mythic materials must be coined: a new conflicting mythology of space disposition (built, to be sure, on the pervasive ideological foundations of the American greater community) had to be evoked for this sector of America. In the instance of Malcolm X and his Muslim movement we can glimpse this myth formation in the very act of creation. Alex Haley, in his Epilogue to the *Autobiography* of Malcolm X, recounts just such an episode in a Harlem neighborhood:[58]

> I remember another stoopful of women alongside the door of a small grocery store where I had gone for something, leaving Malcolm X talking across the street. As I came out of the store, one woman was excitedly describing for the rest a Malcolm X lecture she had heard in Mosque Number 7 one Sunday. "Oooooh, he *burnt* that white man, burnt him *up,* chile . . . chile, he told us we descendin' from black kings an' queens—Lawd, I didn't know!" Another woman asked, "You believe that?" and the first vehemently responded, "Yes, I *do!*"

The evoking of new myth may be accompanied by the elaboration of ceremonies, rituals, and manners appropriate to the mythology. The affinities for African culture displayed by some black groups is not so much a direct tribal memory, or the attempt to reestablish such a memory, as it is an attempt to equip the blacks for space disposition in the American greater community.[59] The same needs for myth and accompanying customs are displayed by some religious sects. The Mormons added their own quantum of Scriptures to the traditional Christian Bible. The Christian Scientists added what amounts to the inspired interpretation of Mrs. Eddy to the same Bible. In the late 1960's, after two decades of inattention, the American blue-collar worker found a potent myth-maker in former Alabama governor George Wallace, whose assertions that factory workers and taxi drivers were as capable of deciding the country's future as "professors," "theoreticians," "bureaucrats," and "pseudo-intellectuals" struck a responsive note. Wallace mounted the most serious third-party presidential candidacy since Theodore Roosevelt.

What unites all of these supplemental myths in the American ethos is not the immediate content of the myths, and certainly not the ethnic and cultic backgrounds of the adherents. Indeed, there is obvious conflict among them. What unites them is that they all represent, in one version or another, the characteristic American search, through a break more or less radical with the preceding community myths, a protest against extrinsic control of existential and communal space. To some extent, these conflicting myths can go their way in a national community organized for pluralism and dissent. After the widest latitude for such divergent expressions of space disposition has been granted, we can still affirm the primordial and ultimate authority of the great national ideology, stemming from the epochal crises that tend to emphasize the common quest in these disparate subtraditions. Thus the Revolution and the Civil War remain definitive myth-spawning events in the history of the greater community at large, even though they must be supplemented and reinterpreted today in the light of new expressions of space disposition. It is these larger saving symbols that afford the norms by which the subordinate myths are finally to be judged.

At this point, the Christian faith plays a critical role. In the elaboration of the American moral tradition, both the input of the new myths and the criticism of these myths from the tradition must be encompassed. Christian theology plays its role by seeking to identify those elements in the tradition that express the Gospel, while it is at the same time open to those new elements in our contemporary situation that express new challenges and call for new expressions of the Gospel. We will carry this normative contribution of theology further in the next three chapters.

Now it can be seen that the American moral tradition, not just in its ultimate tendencies, but in its cultural artifacts, is also highly dialectical. Though we can cite certain "official" sources that are clues to the moral promise for America (Declaration of Independence, Lincoln's Second Inaugural Address, and so on), these documents can never be interpreted unequivocally, for the very promise that they are meant to secure is one that can be realized only by the possibility of dissent from the received, established view. Our tradition in this sense is a history of promises only partly realized, which means, from the viewpoint of those not yet taken in, a history of unrealized promises, even of betrayal. It is this failure that the strain of dissent within the tradition speaks to. Yet it is a strain that still honors the tradition in the very dissent by pointing to the promises that have not yet been made good. Staughton Lynd, an American historian who advocates a rereading of American history from a radical viewpoint, illustrates this dialectical tendency when he insists that such "New Left" activist groups as the Student Nonviolent Coordinating Committee (SNCC) in their advocacy of civil disobedience, take precedent "directly from long-standing American tradition." Or again, he cites a "position paper" issued by a group of white students supporting the "black rebellion." The students "simply reprinted the preamble to the Declaration of Independence."[60]

There are many such dialectical tensions to be encountered in any reading of the American moral tradition. Emerson posed in contrast the party of "memory" in this country and the party of "hope," enunciating in his own way the oft-sounded distinction between those who look to Europe and the past, and those who want a clean break with the past. It could be that the chief dilemma posed for moral reflection in America is something like that which confronted the earlier *philosophes* of Europe, who had to choose, according to Peter Gay, not between innovation and tradition so much as between incompatible traditions. "The philosophes' experience, I discovered," says Gay in his study of the Enlightenment, "was a dialectical struggle for autonomy, an attempt to assimilate the two pasts they had inherited—Christian and pagan—to pit them against one another and thus to secure their independence."[61] In America, Jonathan Edwards struggled to do justice to both Enlightenment currents and Reformed theology. Lincoln was much in debt to Jefferson for his views on equality, but he also subscribed to a countervailing commitment to the primacy of the federal union.

With this dialectical character of the American moral tradition firmly in view, we can now risk a tentative listing of the "places" or "loci" from which its strands may be gathered.

(d) Sources of the American Moral Tradition

It should be clear now that the locus of salvation has been displaced in America from its old setting in a specifically religious community and rebuilt upon a new center that partakes of the religious but is also public, civil, and political in its reality. As Robert N. Bellah argues, the older European religious symbols have been reshaped in America into a symbol set belonging to "civil religion," based on but by no means identical with the European Christian tradition.[62] The saving symbols are no longer purely theological but are now the property of the *pleroma*—the full ethically conscious and responsible political community. In the European and Near Eastern past saving symbols were cared for and handed on by religious specialists under a unitary rule in the community. These symbols were collected and validated by a central authority—the priest, the Jerusalemite editor, the bishop, or the seventeenth-century local "Parson" in England. But salvation in the American ethos is such a cooperatively pursued phenomenon that it behaves in effect as a "system" in the behavioral scientist's or technologist's use of that term:[63]

> The systems approach is dedicated to emphasizing the ideas which are common to the successful operation of somewhat independent parts in an integrated whole. Further, the successful operation of the whole is the primary objective of the system, so that although individual parts and equipments may not at a particular time be operating most effectively, in the balanced overall interest of the complete system, the action at one particular time is compatible with the overall system requirements for the entire period of interest.

Such a concept of knowledge—requiring complementary contributions from a diverse range of disciplines—may be easiest to visualize in the case of technological phenomena. Rocket technology, for example, requires the skills and knowledge of metallurgists, fuel specialists, electronics technicians, mechanical engineers, and (if human beings are to travel aboard) such professionals as biologists and psychologists. But the concept is equally applicable, we say, to any significant moral question today. Who among us is capable alone of definitively expounding upon or laying claim to the symbols dealing with *justice,* for example? We need the insights not only of the theologian, but also of the jurist, the civil rights activist, the political scientist, the cultural anthropologist, and a wide range of other specialists. We may say the same for the assessment of the qualities of love, forgiveness, community, equality, and in fact, for any of those desiderata men dream of today as saving qualities. If with the stoutly neo-orthodox we must hold that the Judaeo-Christian tradition has certain distinctive and definitive contributions to make to this symbol set, we must agree also with sociologists of knowledge that men know far too little all taken together—theologians and scientists, engineers and doctors—to heal the wounds of mankind. The existential problems, temporal and spiritual, public and personal, mundane and superliminal, of just one city like modern Calcutta, for example, "so swollen with unplanned and unimagined growth," so mired in wicked politics, so packed with filthy, homeless, hopeless transients, must defy the joint insights of all the resources we can muster.[64]

The "sacred places" of the American moral tradition are not churches or temples, but those arenas where we pursue these staggering political and social challenges and seek to advance. The sacred storytellers are not priests but all those who relate us, whether functionally or symbolically, to the greater community's struggle for justice and community. Just as the Hebrew Bible achieves a theological standing despite a variety of types of material that went into it, so the new American moral covenant will now be understandable as a composite entity, reflected upon by a coalition of students both offering and seeking insight.

How may we schematize the widespread sources of this American tradition? Let us proceed by analogy, beginning with an outline of the representative sources of the more compact European *Christian* tradition, and then asking what corresponds to these classical sources in the American situation. One reasonably comprehensive list of the sources of classical Christian tradition might be assembled as follows:[65]

1. Back of the Christian community, there is the parent community of Israel. Its sacred records are preserved in the Christian canon in the Old Testament books of history, law, prophets, and writings of poetry and wisdom.

2. The "new Israel," the Christian community, adds to this deposit from the parent community its own special writings—the Gospels, Apostles, and Fathers.

3. Authoritative interpretation of these writings plus, according to one view, additional elements of the Gospel, come from the *magisterium* or teaching authority of the ecclesiastical community.

4. An important supplement to the revealed aspects of Christian tradition, according to Catholic Christendom, is the preliminary truth that is delivered from natural knowledge—including the philosophy of classical antiquity and the Catholic subtradition of "natural law," itself enjoying official accreditation.

5. Above and beyond these inspired and official sources, the tradition moves through and acquires form from the folklore and myth of the new community—which in the case of Christendom means such resources from the peoples of Europe.

6. The tradition is also expressed at the symbolic level in the art and literature of the new community—the painting of the Italian Renaissance, for example.

7. To these conventional accounts of sources and media, we must add the history of "private judgment" or of conscience as counterposed to Scripture and community judgment—a source that acquires visibility in Christendom with the left wing of the Reformation.

8. Significant influence on tradition is exerted by the critical work of theologians and moralists, who seek to reshape the deposit, without necessarily altering the content of its teachings, to changed situations.

9. An often unrecognized locus of tradition is that spectrum of contemporary records and new myths that supplement, for the later history of Christendom, the official and inspired sources. Thus the emergent traditions of the "younger churches" in Asia add something by way of interpretation and content to the more antique sources.

10. Finally, the net effect of tradition is influenced by the pooling and comparative criticism of separated traditions that is realized with the ecumenical movement. In recent years, ecumenical theology and quasi-official statements of ecumenical bodies have become important vehicles of tradition, to some extent supplementing and replacing earlier media.

Let us suppose now that we were to translate this skeletal account of the sources of conventional Christianity, with the assistance of a bit of imagination, into the "cognate" sources of the moral tradition of the American greater community. The result might be something like this:

1. Writings of the parent community (England, Europe, Christendom), its history, law, prophets, and wisdom. Here we should include the classical Christian doctrines, which are a background input rather than primary sources for the newer American tradition. We should also include, to take only an example or two, the history of the struggle for political freedom in England, the development of jurisprudence and the concept of government by law that characterizes the British Constitution, and the prophetic dissent of the seventeenth and eighteenth centuries in England that was crucial to the ideological foundations of the American Revolution.

2. Writings of the new community—the "Gospels," "Apostles," and "Fathers" of the American Revolutionary period. Here we would include the Declaration of Independence and Constitution, the addresses of the Presidents down to the end of the canonical period (Civil War?), and other landmark official documents of that period.

3. Authoritative interpretation of these writings—the "magisterium" or "teaching authority" of the new community in its postapostolic history. Here we would include the inaugural addresses of the noninspired Presidents (those since Lincoln), the decisions of the Supreme Court, and the developing conceptions of republican government as viewed in the acts of Congress and of state legislatures, and in the executive leadership of the Presidency. Perhaps the twentieth-century American university should be included in the magisterium, since it has become the chief agency of indoctrination in the American value system for many Americans. A popularization of the magisterium has occurred with the advent of mass media. Now among the "teachers" are radio, television, the weekly news magazines, and other opinion-forming media.

4. Natural law—what may be known by "reason" apart from the official revealed sources. In the American ethos, reason is practical knowledge, and everyday experience, quite apart from our formal indoctrination into the meaning of democracy, teaches a kind of preliminary, common man's grasp of "space disposition." Like much natural theology, this natural knowledge in its raw, uninterpreted state leaves something to be desired: it consists of rugged, direct "self-

appointment," or of the most blatant "conformism" as we have already described these distorted manners in Chapter III above. Still, this everyday, untutored insight into the notion of equality when guided into the refined channels of willed initiative by the magisterium affords a genuine entry into the moral tradition.

5. Folklore and myth. We have already portrayed earlier in this chapter something of the affinity between religious belief and American folklore. Theologians and ethicists would do well to deepen their study of the subject of American folklore, from Davy Crockett to the myths of the computer, to understand how the American moral tradition is transmitted partly through these indigenous symbols. Logically, there is just as much need for the study of "theology and folklore" in theological seminaries as there is for the study of "theology and literature."

6. Art and literature. The role of the novel and other art forms in portraying the moral dimensions of the American ethos is already well recognized, as just suggested, for example, by the presence of authorities on "theology and literature" on the faculties of theological schools. Little attention still is paid to popular art forms as transmitting media of moral tradition, however, and most interpretations seek mainly the theological content of the moral tradition, whereas what is transmitted is mostly the existential, communal *civil* tradition.

7. The history of private judgment and conscience. To this locus corresponds the history of dissent and criticism in America—the writings of Tom Paine, Henry D. Thoreau, the abolitionists, and other exemplars, extending down to contemporary annals of the civil rights movements, the student protests, and the peace demonstrations.

8. The critical work of theologians and moralists. Here our cognates include not only the work of contemporary theologians concerned with moral analysis, but the best literature and writing at large that is responsive to such contemporary communal crises as the Depression, the Nazi and Communist totalitarian regimes of the World War II era, the black man's struggle, the era of assassinations (President Kennedy, Martin Luther King, Jr., Robert F. Kennedy). Literature that prophetically envisions the new community to be hoped for out of, say, the cybernetics revolution could also be included.[66]

9. The emergent tradition of the "younger churches." The counterpart for public ethics is the growth of new nations that have their own aspirations to justice and reorganization of community—the third world. Students of governance in America must be open to the visions and innovations of these incipient national communities for countercontributions (and criticisms) that will enrich the American moral tradition.

10. The ecumenical movement. The cognate here is the growth of common purposes among the nations, from the reciprocal trust that characterizes the American alliance with Canada to the cool détente that has lately seemed more or less possible with the Soviet Union. Such movements as the United Nations offer a visible, if somewhat pale, prospect of joint deliberation on the rights of man to his own time, space, and will.

(e) The Critical Function of American Moral Tradition

This moral tradition, no monolithic entity in either substance or media, should be brought forward as a basis for the criticism of contemporary American manners. More precisely, the function of moral tradition, as a reminder of the reality of the promise of shared communal space, is to disabuse us of pretenses, illusions, and conceits; to testify to and criticize our national bad manners and moral blindness; and to offer positive clues, and even new moral rules, all aimed at coping with contemporary moral crisis.

Every culture is, in one sense, a set of spectacles, but in another sense, and for the same reasons, it tends to be a set of blinders, blocking out all that isn't in the line of vision and at the precise point of focus of the cultural spectacles, shutting off the experiences of other communities, and often hiding the genuine insights of the past instead of transmitting them. In the American context we can illustrate this limitation by observing how easy it is to forget every distant environment, so concerned do we become in our "everydayness" with our own ready-to-hand manners, morals, and immediate experiences. Indeed, every greater community is overlaid with an opaque cultural patina consisting of easy morality, direct reward, veiled amorality, political obtuseness, and indifference to the generic human predicament.

Every people in every age and clime tends to understand salvation in the crassest, most tangibly short-run terms. Just as medieval folk, in Luther's discerning complaint, sometimes took the sacrament to be a means not of finding the favor of God, but of latching onto gains of a material kind, so our own people take the political covenant of their greater community not as a means of deepening the bonds and extending the frontiers of community, but rather as a means of closing themselves off into tight local commonalties that amount to a series of "private systems" (Jonathan Edwards).

Thus our quest for the "American moral tradition" should aim first of all at cultural criticism: the tradition is to be produced in the first instance as a scourge to the patina of self-interest, direct reward, everydayness. Indeed it should be capable of pointing to a great deal of what passes for American manners and morals as in fact an *antitradition,* the signs of which must be reversed if we are to align such conduct with the saving tradition itself. To take one example, America's everyday warlikeness may be traced back partly to the precedent set by an unruly nineteenth-century Tennessean, General Andrew Jackson, who on the basis of the kind of "self-appointment" syndrome we have often alluded to, set out on an invasion of Florida without real warrant otherwise and even drew a demand from the then Secretary of War John C. Calhoun that he be courtmartialed or reprimanded. This war proneness, like an unchecked virus, continues to infect the American psyche, and not even the malaise of the long, unsuccessful Vietnamese war could cure the fever of some Americans to drop still more bombs on that unhappy land. But this aberration, with its long history of bristle and arrogance, conceals another American attitude, the conception of war as a limited operation to be engaged in as a last resort when community space cannot be reorganized by political means. As Professor Morison observes, "Limited war is also in the American tradition. We did not go on fighting in 1814 to conquer Canada, we did not try to take over all Mexico in 1848, we did not attempt to annex the troublesome Caribbean republics."[67] Hence beneath the surface of contemporary bluster and world-management talk there is a strand of experience that reflective critics can ferret out and point to as authentic in American moral tradition, to be supported and enlarged upon today and regarded as ethically normative in sizing up our current world responsibilities.

American Christian ethics must both join this quest, letting itself be guided by the larger moral tradition and sharing in the critique of the public morals and manners, and seek to make its own peculiar contribution to the content of the tradition. One of its special tasks is to keep the channels of communication open with the critical theological symbols of other greater communities, welcoming them as a deepening, chastening, depatinizing influence. To mention only the European tradition, the impact of the Barthian theology on the culturally saturated and limp, liberal theology of early twentieth-century American Protestantism is a case in point of this cross-cultural impact. By the same token, American passion for ethical action takes the symbolic form of criticism of European dogmatic sterility in the transit of American symbols to the European milieu. When this kind of exchange of critical symbols is possible with Europe, American theology will have overcome its slavish dependence on European theology, won through to a maturity of its own, and found a much better role for "imported theology" than it now knows. There should be, in the generation to come, a thriving pluralism of world theologies, with frequent family reunions and even more frequent exchanges of "letters," first as among the Western cousins, America and Europe, but more largely among the greater communities that make up the wider world. Thus we may expect much critical and salutary impingement of competing symbols in the next generation not only from European Christianity but also from the various salvation systems of Eastern religion, which may have far more critical effect on the technologically skewed symbol set of the West.

The theologian thus has a series of peculiar functions in this larger process of remembering, criticizing the past, and of winnowing our contemporary manners and morals. For Americans, salvation is bound up in the general course of the affairs of the republican greater community. Even theologians agree that "all history is salvation history *in a sense.*" Yet there must be some determination of just what in "salvation history in a sense" is truly salvific, and this determination requires the work of "students of salvation history *without qualifi-*

cation," theologians pursuing the proper subject matter of theology. Knowledge of the divine promise in history does involve some conception of "trans-historical experience." And it is just in rounding out the study of a greater community's moral tradition with reflection upon this ultimate experience that the theologian finds his mission.[68]

It is to this distinctive, normative contribution of the theologian to the criticism and appreciation of the American experience that we must now turn. Let us consider, successively, and from a theological perspective, the familiar dimensions of the American experience that we have been describing.

CHAPTER V.

REVOLUTIONS

Mrs. Helen Givings, a real-estate broker in Richard Yates' novel, *Revolutionary Road,* recognized Frank and April Wheeler as the kind of couple one ought to take some time with, even if they didn't have much money. "They're sweet," she told her husband. "I think the boy must do something very brilliant in town." She quickly saw that the Wheelers wanted something out of the ordinary—a barn made over into a house, or an old cottage, perhaps.

She drove them through a housing development which bore the suggestive name of Revolutionary Hill Estates—"great hulking split levels, all in the most nauseous pastels," she told them, "and dreadfully expensive too, I can't think why." She sold them a house somewhere else. But we see a lot of Revolutionary Hill Estates in the book, for friends of the Wheelers live there.

This neighborhood was an improbable place for tragedy. It was too cheerful, something of a toyland. At night it seemed almost as if the houses cast no shadows at all and presented no darkened shapes against the sky. The neat front doors and the pastel automobiles reminded one of an ice-cream assortment. Yet there was a man running down these streets in desperation:[1]

> Except for the whisk of his shoes on the asphalt and the rush of his own breath, it was so quiet that he could hear the sounds of television in the dozing rooms behind the leaves—a blurred comedian's shout followed by dim, spastic waves of laughter and applause, and then the striking up of a band. Even when he veered from the pavement, cut across someone's back yard and plunged into the down-sloping woods, intent on a madman's shortcut. . . , even then there was no escape: the

house lights beamed and stumbled happily along with him among the twigs that whipped his face, and once when he lost his footing and fell scrambling down a rocky ravine, he came up with a child's enameled tin beach bucket in his hand.

This grief-stricken figure was the same Frank Wheeler, and the tragedy was an event in his own life. That climax came, novelist Yates has shown us, to a person who is surely one of the most unfeeling, impersonal characters in contemporary fiction. But it's not the picture of Frank himself that interests me just now. It's rather the picture given in the novel of American middle-class society as it existed on the eve of the most serious crisis in moral values since the Civil War. And even more importantly, the novel helps me to lay out the problem of facing a moral revolution.

I want to begin by ruling out two approaches to social crisis. These are in the nature of presuppositions, or a couple of rules for playing the game of appraising social crises. Both are depicted very well in Mr. Yates' novel, *Revolutionary Road*.

One approach to revolution that I rule out to start with is the one that most of us have in fact adopted. This is to arrogate the name of revolutionaries to our American selves, considering our history, and to admit no new revolutions to be valid. The other, also fairly common in American society, is to seek to revolutionize conditions only for ourselves, and to reject the society itself (or the "system," as we now call it).

1. The pastel houses and their pastel inhabitants in Revolutionary Hill Estates make suitable symbols for what has happened to America's own revolutionary heritage. The people of the Estates were about as revolutionary in their way of life as skim milk. It's all as Frank Wheeler told the Campbells, their neighbors from the Estates, one dull evening: "It isn't only the Donaldsons—it's the Cramers too, and the whaddyacallits, the Wingates, and a million others. It's all the idiots I ride with on the train every day. It's a disease. Nobody thinks or feels or cares any more; nobody gets excited or believes in anything."[2] Now Frank here is describing middle-class, mostly middle-aged people—but most of the people in this country under thirty, we might notice, can't be trusted to be revolutionaries either, for the

same reasons. Most of us, in a decade when great revolts are going on all around us—on the civil rights front, on college campuses, in our views about war—most of us are about as revolutionary as Frank Wheeler's friends.

2. Mr. Yates' novel also has a symbol of the other and opposite kind of pseudo-revolution, the activist who "revolts" only to take care of himself. Frank and April Wheeler, of course, didn't buy a house in Revolutionary Hill Estates. Instead, they chose a place up the hill. The Wheelers weren't going to be caught up in mediocrity, not them. They were people of promise. They would enact and define their own thing. Their revolt would take shape in a dramatic escape from the suburban and business worlds. They would go to Europe. Not that they could afford it, although letting the neighbors think they could was part of the plan. "The whole idea of taking off to Europe this way," Frank told his wife April, is "like coming out of a Cellophane bag." And of his neighbors: "You picture the whole cozy little bunch of them sitting around all snug as bunnies in their pajamas, . . . toasting marshmallows." And just think "how close *we* came to settling into that kind of an existence."[3]

The trip to Paris never comes off. Instead, April kills herself. And Frank never learns to feel, not even from such a tragedy.

Frank and April here in my own mythology stand for those restless young adults who want to rebel against the dullness of their lives, yet who want to do it by somehow running away from it. They also stand, I must add, for a good many people under thirty who just run out on the dullness and injustice of their society, or try to burn it, and call that a revolution.

We have already taken the first step, then, in our effort to set some criteria for appraising the revolutionary impulse as it seems to be manifested in our day. We have laid out the playing field on which we are to pursue the project of judging revolutions. Indeed, these ground rules are already implicit from our delineation of the revoluionary impulse for republican societies in Part One. In a republic, the people take up a new, special kind of time, we observed: the time of a new start, when extrinsic control of community space is overthrown. It is a time that may have to be reenacted. And it is a clearing-out process that extends across the whole of manners. Thus we rule out to start with two types of fraudulent revolution that often go, in this age of advertising, under the very banner of revolution. We cannot call revolutionaries those folk who simply want to freeze the benefits of the last revolution and to shut out further revolutions. We can't call revolutionary those folk who think that abandoning one's society is called for because the society may have relapsed into a species of extrinsic control. These are the opposite poles of inauthentic revolt.

1. An Expanded Definition of Revolution

Now we must turn to the positive, normative side of our inquiry and ask, first, what a revolution is. There are two elements, I believe, that we can agree on immediately—the element of *immediacy* and the element of *contagiousness*—and a third that is a bit harder to get at.

(a) *Immediacy*

Revolution is a sudden and violent overthrow of some previously organized communal space. It involves rapid change over a finite, relatively compact period of time. However deep our roots are in the past, a revolution lays the stress upon discontinuity. It seeks to create change through a "quantum jump" rather than through gradual, evolutionary, glacial drift. It begins, proceeds through one or more stages, and dies down. While it may seize upon ideals from the past and transmit gains and unimplemented ideals to the future, a revolution is characterized by innovation and preoccupation with the demands of the present. The call to act *now* is one of the essential features of a revolutionary stance.

(b) *Contagiousness*

A revolution is contagious. It is uncontainable. It is always a "shot heard around the world." It may begin at a definite place—Lexington, Concord, the Bastille, Montgomery, Greensboro—but if it is a real revolution it will quickly enroll and embroil the whole of a certain population set—that is, a whole group, a whole class, a whole community, perhaps a whole society or nation. Revolution moves across social wholes. Its contagion sweeps aside formal and artificial barriers. Thus, once we concede shoemakers the right to organize, we must expect schoolteachers and garbage collectors to demand the same right, in spite of the fiction that employees of the state may not legally strike. "A colonized people is not alone," writes Frantz Fanon in his emotional account of the Algerian revolt against France. "The great victory of the Vietnamese people at Dien Bien Phu is no longer, strictly speaking, a Vietnamese victory." Since that event, he says, the question that all colonized people have been asking themselves is "What must be done to bring about another Dien Bien Phu? How can we manage it?"[4] Once the sense of dignity and nationhood has been felt anywhere, we can expect rising peoples to act everywhere—and to ignore such neat distinctions as that between Communist and anti-Communist which seems to mean so much to Americans in the 36 per cent tax bracket.

These two criteria are not enough. For they let through our net several events commonly called revolutions that are not sufficiently interrogated for our present purpose. When machines replaced manual and bestial labor in eighteenth- and nineteenth-century Western nations, we underwent what is generally called the Industrial Revolution. Today, mechanical means for transmitting data are rapidly being replaced by electronic means, to the point that we are undergoing, society by society, another great upheaval—called the communications or cybernetics revolution.

These are revolutions of a sort involving technology. They do change us and our societies in violent and drastic ways. There are also more gentle overturns that could be and are called revolutions—those revisions in manners and fashions, say, that meet our two criteria—in which all of the women suddenly begin to wear miniskirts, or all of the men begin to wear tapered pants and shoes with pointed toes.

The elements of revolution we are concerned with here are those that seek to question and overturn the central *moral* structures upon which the life of a community is based. Thus the revolt in our inner cities seeks to overturn the notion of justice that hitherto has accepted the compression of blacks into a sector set apart from the cultural opportunities of the rest of society. The revolt on university campuses seeks to question and overthrow old assumptions about autonomy, freedom, and one's right to learn.

We are close to, but not on the same territory as, the more conventional discussion of revolution that takes *politics* to be the referent. In this conventional view of revolution, to the elements of immediacy and contagion is added the element of the overthrow of the established political order. Failure of an old government is the occasion of revolt. Establishment of a new government is the end of revolt. Apparently this classical definition takes political change to be basic and the agent and avenue of other kinds of change, whether social, economic, or cultural. Indeed, the conventional terminology and typology of revolution appear to be concerned almost entirely with political phenomena.[5]

But we must insist that the kind of revolution transforming America today cannot really be described as a *political* affair. For what seems at the root of the revolution, the real revolution now, is the ethical factor, the passion to uproot older *moral* patterns that are seen today as unjust, culturally stifling, economically stagnating, and politically repressive as well.

The black man in the South revolted not against law, but against a moral code that had captured the law and made it serve the interests of the dominant whites. The revolutionary peoples in South America are out not just to change the political regimes in their countries, although they aim to do that too; what they want more than anything else is economic justice and equal participation in cultural rights. The students in this country in rebellion against university leadership seek political power, to be sure, but to the larger end of revising the educational policies of the university, and to secure reforms that would allow greater personal and moral scope in learning. These are all fundamentally moral critiques of society, seeking political change only in order to uproot repressive moral patterns that smother human expression.

(c) *Radical Moral Upheaval*

The third element of a revolution in our world, then, is most pressingly the moral factor. The revolution seeks decisive moral upheaval. And so the three elements taken together are: the factor of immediacy—the requirement that discontinuous, drastic changes be insisted on with emphasis on the "fierce urgency of now"; the factor of contagiousness—the requirement that the uprising be infectious and widespread, traveling across the whole of one or more coherent communities or layers of community; and the moral factor—the requirement that the revolution be aimed at upturning customs, conventions, and moral codes that are felt to be not just repressive of human integrity, freedom, and growth, but mortal, lethal, fatal to the human prospect.

I have not included "violence" as such as one of the criteria, except to observe, under the element of immediacy, that the changes sought are not just any kind of change, but "violent" change. But to have violent change does not necessarily entail violence in the sense of bloodshed. On the other hand, the possibility of violence in this physical sense is already provided for in the three elements I have mentioned. If the changes sought are radical enough, discontinuous enough with the past; if they involve enough people polarized over the issues into opposed groups; and if the older moral patterns under challenge are sufficiently rigid and repressive, then there will be violence, especially in situations in which the older patterns themselves were originally imposed by force, as with colonialism.[6] We must face the question I heard put to a seminar of skeptical white journalists not long ago by a young black revolutionary from Howard University. "Must we rely on democratic means," he asked, "to undo what was done to us by authoritarian means?" As we reminded ourselves in Part One of our study, despots do not necessarily establish themselves by a vote of the people, nor are they ordinarily overthrown by a people who will not, in some fashion, "seize the day." What if the despot is not a medieval ruler, but a twentieth-century pattern of mores and customs that effectively deprives a group of its freedom to dispose of its own space?

Even so, the possibilities of violence have been much exaggerated in the popular mind where our own various revolutionary movements are in question. The primary need for the revolutionary who would dispose of his own space is to demonstrate the capacity and willingness to resist extrinsic control. Riots occurred in numerous black city neighborhoods following the assassination of Martin Luther King, Jr. But the Watts area of Los Angeles, which had earlier experienced a very serious riot, was not the scene of disturbance this time. Instead, a strange calm and order prevailed under the leadership of organized "Black Power" groups, which sponsored a memorial rally, directed traffic, and sent out block workers to set an example of coolness. Now it seems that the first riot was enough to make the point. "We have found it to be true," one of the militants commented, "that the capacity to use power often eliminates the need to use it."[7]

"I'm not for wanton violence, I'm for justice," Malcolm X declared. "The Negro's so-called 'revolt' is merely an asking to be *accepted* into the existing system!" But if this means resisting whites who would forbid the black man entry into the community, violence was among the weapons to be used. For the most part, Malcolm thought he couldn't "whip" the white man as badly with a club as with his mind. But: "If it must take violence to get the black man his human rights in this community, I'm *for* violence exactly as you know the Irish, the Poles, or Jews would be if they were flagrantly discriminated against."[8] We cannot even take up the question of revolution, in short, without taking up the question of the use of force and the possibility of violence. If one judges a revolution worth his participation, if it is really an existential matter, then he has already made the judgment that violence may in the end be justified—although this judgment does not rule out a prudential strategy that seeks to accomplish objectives first by nonviolence, then by increasingly forceful measures.

2. Can Revolutions Be Endorsed by Christians?

Now we must move to a crucial question. Our aim is not yet to judge among the various factical revolutions that are occurring in the world and in our own society today. It is rather to ask a more basic question first: What are we to make of revolution itself as a mode of reorganizing the space of the community? Can theology make a normative contribution to this dilemma of "public ethics"?

Let me proceed by laying down a drastic proposition: revolution, when it is "genuine," is just as proper an expression of the hope of shared space and reorganized community in our century as the *revival*, when it was "genuine," was in the eighteenth and nineteenth centuries. (I will come to what I mean by "genuine" presently.) To establish this proposition, I wish first to submit that the Christian faith in principle has historically called upon men and nations to engage in drastic transformations of society, just as radical as the movements we call revolutions today. In every crucial turning point of Western history, in fact, society has moved into its vision of the future by "rebounding" or "leaping ahead of itself" in a radical fashion. The Reformation was thus a re-forming of the church that was discontinuous with the past, contagiously widespread, and aimed at breaking down certain oppressive moral patterns. (It was by no means achieved without violence, we may add.) Closer to home, on the American scene, the historic form of bounding forward has been the reflexive spiritual movement toward finding new life, or of refinding life—for that is what the word "revival" means, and it is the "revival," above all, that has characterized the leaping ahead of itself that American society experienced when it first found itself a society, a new world.

"All spiritual discoveries are transforming," says Jonathan Edwards, a profound Puritan theologian and the first great critic (I am tempted to say phenomenologist) of the revival. "If there be no great and remarkable change in persons that think they have experienced a work of conversion, vain are all their imaginations and pretences, however they have been affected."[9]

The original assumption of the Puritans, moreover, was that these changes in the self would be accompanied by changes in the community at large—by a transformation of the whole society, including its political and social elements. True, the New England towns, in the historical outcome, did not change decisively enough to match the ambitious expectations of the Puritan theology, and so gradually, over the years, the revivals were taken more and more to be aimed at purely personal changes, and at purely "religious" phenomena. But it is only because we see the great revivals through the end game of the later, nineteenth-century, hard-core revivalism that we think of them as individualistic and religious. The Gospel always turns feeling and passion out upon the world, and aims at community transformation as well as at personal conversion.[10] (The same failure, we might observe here, may await our contemporary "revolution in personal morality" if too much stress is laid on personal involvement, and not enough on redeeming the hated "system" that all of the responsible selves of the day want to reject.)

Unfortunately, from the very outset it seemed that all sorts of revivals were going on in the New England communities, with all sorts of results, good and bad, just as all sorts of revolutions are going on in our society today. So the question arose: which revivals of this motley assortment were to be accepted as genuine revivals, as true works of the Gospel? Soon such thoughtful churchmen as Edwards were setting out to answer this question formally, especially by asking about the impact of the Gospel on the self and the community, and about the marks that flow from this impact.

The classical statement of the difference between a true and a false change in heart, and thus between a truly revived self and a "phony," comes from Edwards' great tract, *Religious Affections*. Edwards talks first about twelve misleading or uncertain signs that one's changed self is authentic. It proves nothing for persons to display excessive emotions, or to manifest certain bodily motions, such as jerking or twitching under the influence of a spellbinding revival sermon. It proves nothing for a person at a revival meeting to talk a lot, or to arm his rhetoric with quotations from Scripture. It proves nothing that persons may seem to be concerned about love, says Edwards, in one of his more acute observations, for there are all kinds of ways of counterfeiting love.

It proves nothing even to have religious feelings, since there are many kinds of emotions, some responsible, some irresponsible, and either may be evoked in the passions of a revival. Spending much time at meetings or other religious exercises is no certain evidence, says Edwards, nor does it establish the case when people manage to convince those around them that they are experiencing the divine.

Perhaps the most misleading sign of all among those he describes is when a presumably converted person pleases and wins the praises of the saints—as we might say, the "in" crowd. For even the saints—maybe most of all the saints—are easily fooled about religious affections.

Nevertheless Edwards concluded, speaking for most men of his day, that "true religion consists largely of religious affections."

True religion today, we are inclined to say, consists largely of *responsible actions*—not just acts of worship, but perhaps for the most part ethically responsible actions. The Gospel, that is, may be said to have its impact now through those who engage in the passionate advocacy of those acts in their community that will rescue men from outmoded, degrading, lethal moral patterns and replace these patterns with new, freeing, life-giving, being-expanding patterns. The community display of genuine religious affections in Edwards' day was called a revival. The community display of ethically responsible actions is called in our day a revolution.

The Gospel itself is revolution, it is "permanent revolution," in the phrase of H. Richard Niebuhr. The choice open to Christians is not between supporting or not supporting revolutionary approaches to the ailments of mankind. It is between versions of revolution, and it is between authentic and nonauthentic strands in given revolutions. Throughout this study, we have regarded revolution as the definitive "occasion" of republican governance, and the continuing style of time in a republican ethos. Now, we are saying, there is theological warrant for this view: to the degree that the republican experiment, founded on revolution and open to possible recurrent revolution, actually functions to awaken men and renew them in their political lives, revolution enacts a motif of the Gospel itself, a motif that found earlier religious expression in the revival.

Throughout this discussion I have examined and compared the categories of revival and revolution as a theological ethicist rather than as a historian. It may be useful to round out our remarks with a historical comparison. Alan Heimert has suggested one, working in the setting of early American history. He argues that the Great Awakening of the 1740's may have set the stage for the American Revolution. The revival was revolutionary in its potential, he adds, as was sensed by its opponents in the religious establishment of the day: "Evangelical religion embodied a radical and even democratic challenge to the standing order of colonial America." When the Revolution of 1776 did come, "it would often be concluded that what the Colonies had awakened to in 1740 was none other than independence and rebellion." In some respects, Heimert suggests, the intellectual issues that attended the Revolution were an outgrowth of the revival, even incidental to it.[11]

3. The Signs of Genuine Revolution

If revolution in our day corresponds to revival in Edwards' day, as I have just suggested, it becomes our next task to distinguish between genuine and false revolutions, just as he meant to distinguish among the revivals.

We can begin, as Edwards did, with criteria that are uncertain or misleading—criteria of nonauthenticity in a revolution.

Surely, we can say to begin with, it is not the amount of activity that guarantees genuine revolution. One can log an enormous amount of time demonstrating for this cause or that; but it is the nature of the cause that we must look to.

Nor, similarly, can we judge by the passion with which a cause is urged. We cannot judge by the amount and character of the rhetoric that accompanies one's acts. Just as Edwards warned against loud, excited talk at a revival as a misleading sign of the state of one's spirit, so we must be suspicious of the putative revolutionary who expends excessive energy in sloganizing or in seeking to hypnotize by frenzied battle cries.

One false sign is just the same from Edwards' day to ours. All talk of love, the claim to be loving, the appearance of love itself, doesn't necessarily prove anything. In fact, the obsession with love as a goal among some of the youthful revolutionaries of our day seems the best evidence that love is problematical. Love is as easy to counterfeit among twentieth-century flower children as it was among the saints at the colonial camp meetings.

To take another close parallel, just as praise of the saints for one's presumed new spirit didn't guarantee real conversion, so praise of the revolutionaries for one's newly acquired "revolutionary" stance doesn't guarantee anything: it is easy to be carried away by the crowd, whether it is a crowd of saints or a crowd of radicals.

Finally, a revolution overturns for the sake of a new start. A revolution that doesn't go anywhere, has no goal of reestablishing moral patterns, is no revolution. Christopher Lasch, in a review of the Black Power literature, discerns such falsity:[12]

> In the last few months, we have seen more and more vivid examples of the way in which Black Power has come to be associated with mindless violence—as in the recent disturbances at San Francisco State College—and with a "revolutionary" rhetoric that conceals a growing uncertainty of purpose. It becomes increasingly clear that many of the intellectuals who talk of Black Power do not understand the difference between riots and revolution, and that they have no program capable of controlling the growing violence of the ghetto.

What are the signs of a genuine revolution? Let's go back to the three elements we have set in our phenomenology of revolution—the elements of every revolution, whether it is genuine in our sense or not. These elements specify that a revolution partakes of *immediacy, contagiousness,* and *decisive moral radicality.* The question becomes: what, by our lights, is authentic immediacy? What is authentic contagion? What is an authentic moral upheaval?

At this point I can properly be asked: what are your norms? How can you appraise the authenticity of revolutions without saying more about your standards? Edwards, after all, started off his list of the authentic marks of religious affections by appealing to an extrinsic standard: that they were a supernatural work of God in us. What is our standard for appraising a revolution? Today we can no longer convincingly speak about "supernatural" standards of any kind, although as we shall see presently, something is to be said in our time, as ever, for the meaning of the transcendent in our lives. Nor can we, with a similar simplicity, quickly resort to some purely historical standard, such as what Christian tradition or biblical tradition has meant by its doctrines of man, salvation, and society. On the other hand, I am quite unwilling to proceed to the opposite extreme and simply say that historical events validate themselves. In short, we cannot solve our problem either by bringing in extrinsic norms to judge by, nor by trying to judge on the basis of the historical situation itself.

As I have already argued (in Chapter IV) against situation ethicists and other contemporary theologians who wish to make some such norm as Christian love universally operative, a better way of proceeding with the whole subject of norms is to begin with *the formal category of "Gospel"*—the good news to man, that he is promised rescue from his predicament, that he will move through lostness to wholeness. This is, admittedly, a "traditional" and "biblical" idea. But its *content* depends not on tradition so much as on contemporary situation: the way in which we are lost, and the ingredients of rescue and wholeness, are cultural and historical items definable out of our own circumstances, time, and place. Crisis reworks our view of promise, predicament, and fulfillment. The materials available to us out of the cultural resources of our own greater community shape the character of our response.

As part of the way toward finding "norms," then, it is necessary for us to describe the upheavals, the crises of our day, or, in short, the revolutionary phenomena of our day, including the "promise" and "potential" we see for human life in them. Without waiting to establish a set of norms, then, we may proceed immediately to appraise the three elements of revolution on the basis of what we may take to be the formal elements of the Gospel. In the next chapter I will go on to build on this appraisal of our situation and attempt to recover some norms for presenting the Gospel culturally and historically for our place and time.

Revolution, in the long run, is to be judged both by the formal norms we develop in this chapter, and by the concrete norms or "benchmarks" of community reorganization we will develop in the following chapter. Indeed, still a third set of judgments is on the way, for in the final chapter we will be concerned to appraise, from the viewpoint of theological ethics, the *quality* of actions that comes out of republican ethos, which is to say the quality of actions that may be found in today's revolutionary movements, if they are genuine, republican revolutions.

For the moment, however, we wish to view revolution as a form of crisis or upheaval, without entering upon the subject matter of concern or the historical and cultural aims to be sought. Simply as upheaval, as crisis, as revolution in the sense of disruption, may we enter some normative judgments on the basis of the Gospel? May we speak about acceptable and unacceptable forms of "immediacy" and "contagiousness" and "moral upheaval" just as aspects of crisis, without yet worrying about the content or goals sought in the upheaval? That is what we now wish to explore. Here we are concerned with revolution as revolution.

(a) *Genuine Immediacy*

Formally speaking, the Gospel always asks us to accept our salvation *now*. The history of Christianity echoes with cries to lost men that "now is the hour," that this night one's life may be required of him, that this is the moment of decision. Similarly, no matter what the content of wholeness may be taken to be, formally it always hinges on newness, new life, new spirit, on a decisive break with the old man, the old age, the past. Thus the immediacy that is part of the revolutionary program finds its cognate in the Christian metaphors of salvation that have always stressed the necessity of our being made new creatures.

But more is to be said. Again speaking formally, what is genuine from the viewpoint of the Gospel, is that drastic change always refers, nonetheless, to making old things new rather than to throwing them away; to making the old man new rather than shooting him in the head. The Gospel insists that creation is good, though fallen, and that the divine promise is that it will be rescued, transformed, not rejected in favor of some different creation. Thus genuine immediacy redeems the past, even finds new meaning in it, instead of dispensing with the past.

Let us take the black man's struggle. An authentic revolution in this zone does not dispense with the historic symbols that have forged our society, as inadequate as they seem in today's agony. It is true that the American "Creed," as implemented in the Constitution, was not originally intended fully to apply to black people, as Stokely Carmichael and Charles V. Hamilton point out: "Article I of the Constitution affirms that the black man is three-fifths of a person." The

American dream, they say, "was not originally intended to include" black people "and it does not include the black masses today."[13] But an authentic revolution in civil rights will not disown these instruments and symbols just because they have not, to date, delivered full freedom to the black man. On the contrary, an authentic revolution points out the new implications that today's struggle gives to these historic documents. An authentic revolution points to new meanings in our heritage that no one has seen up to now, insists that past models of man and community must be constantly under radical test from new experience. It seeks to transform our heritage into something new by revolutionary action. It says that the only true history, the only true culture, is one that is under the demand to be made new.

Equally, authentic revolution does not seize the present by simply obliterating the future. The Gospel insists that present decision, as a radical break with the past, is made precisely so the future will be opened up. Revolution is to clear out oppressive moral patterns, to make room for human scope. Revolution seeks to do away with the iniquities of the old regime in favor of a new order, of a future that will give us back our lives. Authentic revolution is not a surd, a blind spasm of fury. It is not a spontaneous lurch of emotion or a kamikaze attack on culture. It is rather the grave wager to risk a whole society's present order and even existence so as to open up the future to that society. It certainly will have elements of the absurd, despair, fury, spontaneity. But the genuine revolutions marshal these forces, turn pessimism, rage, and violence toward a goal, the goal of breaking out of bondage, seeking liberation, establishing a new moral pattern. What is promised in the act of conversion is *new* life, but also new *life*.

(b) Genuine Contagion

The wildfire spread of revolution finds its formal counterpart in the Gospel. For the Gospel itself has often been likened, in Christian tradition, to quick-spreading fire that leaps across barriers of place, race, and station to enlist men of all conditions and origins.

To say that the Gospel is meant for every man implies two things.

At one level it is to demand that its contagion be intense, that it be personally and locally real—that it become a force in *this* place, in *this* community. And at the other level its contagion is to be extensive and widespread, taking in "man" generically.

The contagion of a revolution, to be authentic, must also be real at both these levels. Let us start with the "local" or "community" level. It will help us to turn to Frantz Fanon, of the Algerian revolution, to see the point. Though the struggle against colonialism knows no compartments or boundaries, he says, yet the same struggle takes no purely general, universal form. "To take part in the African revolution," he explains, "it is not enough to write a revolutionary song; you must fashion the revolution with the people. And if you fashion it with the people, the songs will come by themselves, and of themselves."[14]

This is why we find the cry for nationalism so interwoven with the cry for justice and dignity. "A national culture," says Fanon, "is the whole body of efforts made by a people in the sphere of thought to describe, justify, and praise the action through which that people has created itself and keeps itself in existence." All of the undeveloped countries, he thinks, should identify their struggle for freedom with the evoking of a national culture. Just as a strong awareness of selfhood is part of interpersonal communication, Fanon argues, so "national consciousness . . . is the only thing that will give us an international dimension."[15] In America the same phenomenon is evident in the civil rights movement in its Black Power phase. Here the same assertion is made: the fight for dignity begins with self-identity. It is a legitimate assertion.

Genuine revolution begins in our midst, we might say, echoing the biblical notion that the Kingdom of God, if it is real, is among the disciples, not far off, not a pure idea, not somebody else's vision. It was that sense of the special challenge here among us that led to the nonviolent movement in the South over a decade ago—the local consciousness of the oppressed in Montgomery, and later in Greensboro and Nashville, that revolution, if it is real, not only begins *now,* but *here.*

There are ominous implications here. Those at home who are not direct victims of injustice are also involved. If one is not among the oppressed, but wishes to join the revolution anyway, there is scope enough both for his guilt and for his action in his own community.

> There is a definite, much-needed role whites can play. . . . One of the most disturbing things about almost all white supporters has been that they are reluctant to go into their own communities—which is where the racism exists—and work to get rid of it. . . . They should preach non-violence in the white community. . . . The white middle-class suburbs need "freedom schools" as badly as the black communities.[16]

Still, there is another level of contagion, and this level is precisely in polar tension with the "localness" of revolutionary contagion. Every struggle for human dignity is more than an isolated affair. It is a struggle for the better condition of man, and it spreads across the precincts of human misery like a crown fire through a dry forest. In fact, we can confidently say, any protest or strike or demonstration that wants to limit itself to the good of a discrete group is no revolution and doesn't deserve the name.

Genuine revolutionary contagion includes what Jonathan Edwards called "consent to being"—a sentiment that is in principle not able to be restricted to a "private system"—whether of the blacks or whites, of the young or old, of the underclass or the overprivileged. Not only must the contagion be of a sort that enlists one's "soul brothers," one's fellow disinherited; it must also be a contagion that leaps across the lines of race or class and infects others with cross-channel injustice to bear. One reason I count the nonviolent movement in the South as authentic is that its contagion, within a decade, had enlisted the sympathy of college students not just in the cause of civil rights but also in that of the political colonialism of our universities.

Just as the nowness of a revolution seeks to redeem the past and open up the future, so the contagion of a revolution seeks to restore one's community (ultimately one's society), and to open up the prospect for mankind as such.

(c) *Authentic Moral Upheaval*

Our third and most telling criterion is that a revolution, to be authentic, must be concerned with a radical, but justified, questioning of the moral structure of a community or society. What do we mean by this requirement?

The Gospel promises men who are spiritually or morally dead that they will have new life. The moral structure of a community, its moral patterns, are defensible or questionable according as whether they give life or take it away. What is "moral" or "immoral" about "moral patterns" has to do with the kind of expression of life that they permit in actions. Customs, laws, and conventions that help us to find meaningful life, wholeness, are "moral." Customs, laws, and conventions that block us off from the same values are "immoral." When moral patterns fall so far behind our pilgrimage that they become lethal to the human frame (in either the bodily or existential sense), then a revolution is in order.

The only real question is, whose definition of "life" and "death" are we to accept? On whose say-so are we to judge that life is so threatened that we are to join in a decisive, drastic questioning of the accepted patterns of conduct in a community?

My constant aim in this section is to specify the *formal* conditions of revolution, and in this case, of an authentic moral upheaval. It is not my aim to catalogue and pass in review materially all of the upheavals that are going on at this moment. But I will take one or two examples to use in making my formal point. Let us take the revolution in sexual morality. The participants in this revolution insist that nineteenth-century restrictions on mutuality, bodily propinquity and the like, have simply become intolerable, have begun to threaten the reality of fellowship and communication as we know it today, and that without this communication, meaningful existence is unthinkable. Thus a radical questioning of our social patterns of conduct in the field of sex behavior is justified. Are these revolutionaries right or wrong?

Or take the civil rights movement. The revolutionaries here insist that however successful our society was two or three generations ago in forced separation of black from white and in denying certain goods to the blacks, that pattern of conduct has become intolerable today, for it threatens life at every level, from the literal up to the symbolic. It denies the black man bread and a decent place to live, but it also denies him citizenship, justice, and dignity. Racism is so pervasive and entrenched, and the threat to life is so grave, that one is justified in radically questioning the whole moral condition of our society, and in revolting. Are these revolutionaries right or wrong?

I wish to say *formally* now what the requirements are for answering this question. Or, to put it another way, I wish to say *formally* now what the requirements of an authentic revolutionary stance are when we face the question of a decisive moral upheaval.

First, a radical questioning of society, a decisive moral upheaval, must include *self-examination,* if our analogy with the Gospel is to be continued. Second, a genuine revolution must always be subject to an "outside critique," to a *transcendent judgment* upon it.

1. *Self-examination.* Self-examination is not the first step in a revolution. Action (based on a sense of injustice) is that first step, action taken to meet the threat to meaningful life imposed by the grip of what are taken to be outworn moral patterns. Integrity, not only for revolutionaries, but for Jonathan Edwards' saints, was always to be had more readily through practice than through contemplative withdrawal. Integrity tends to validate itself in action, in aggressively dealing with crisis, in turning itself into experience, rather than in private meditation. Thus in fact a revolution has to be judged only after it is underway; one cannot simply, by introspection, decide whether to have a revolution.

At the same time, any revolution that becomes mindless and anti-intellectual loses part of its humanity; and many of the revolutionary currents about us now manifest inauthenticity for just this reason. Just as the revivals on the frontier always risked becoming blind demonstrations of blank feeling, so there is danger that the revolutions for human dignity today may deliver something less, may become mere storms of rage (civil rights), bolts of spontaneity (sex), bursts of self-righteousness (draft and war protests).

The most subtle demand on a revolutionary, however, is that he assess himself as well as the acts of the revolution, and this means taking himself (again we borrow a formal statement from the Gospel) as human in the sense of finite and fallible. That he does so does not lessen the injustices against him. It does not lessen his responsibility to act. But it does rescue one part of his own humanity, the part that is regained when one can see himself and accept himself. There is nothing particularly virtuous about being poor, or under thirty years old, or a victim of the IBM card, or classified 1-A, or black, or left-handed. One is a better revolutionary if he bases his claim not on his imagined virtues, but on the importance of a cause that has a justifiable motive, and a foreseeable, appropriate outcome.

But is it realistic, or even fair, to expect a revolutionary to stand off from his movement, to stand back and look at himself—in short, to stand still? In a sense it is neither realistic nor fair. To be a revolutionary at all requires a certain kind of recklessness. Palmer gives us a succinct description of the personality of Robespierre which we can take as a fair picture of any man who is really serious about his revolution. Robespierre displayed "class hatred," "self-righteousness," and "intolerance." But even these traits in themselves weren't enough. He also possessed "the quarrelsome habit of seeing great principles in passing incidents."[17] These are all attributes that would hardly pass muster in a course on Christian ethics; they are the signs of excellence and true virtue in a revolutionary.

Furthermore, defenders of the radical approach to truth insist, the revolutionary is fully occupied with acting on his convictions. He isn't interested in sitting down to think about his cause. He is bored by academic types who remind him of the many-sidedness of every intellectual and social issue, and of the lessons of history that he might consult before he acts. He thinks ideas are to be acted on, not thought about. "Like Thoreau, he wants firm bottom and rocks in place; he wants visions on which he can lean his whole weight; he wants history to do something more than caution against complete commitment; he wants it to help him commit himself with more precision and effect."[18]

I am willing to grant this point in the case of the revolutionary already in motion for his cause. I fully accept the argument that it is futile to ask him to stay his hand once he has plunged into the struggle.

Nevertheless, I am not willing to end the discussion at that point. To do so would be to exempt revolutionaries from the very tests of reason, justice, and integrity that they implicitly apply to their opponents and to which all men are in principle subject precisely because revolutions against extrinsic control have already succeeded in the world. The point is thus not to demand that the revolutionary submit to some list of Christian virtues—that he love everybody, become tolerant and humble and quit getting angry at passing incidents—but that he *examine* himself. And not even the plea that he is a man of action, not of reflection, can exempt him. We have agreed that he may not be required to examine himself once he is in struggle as a revolutionary. But what of the moments between battles, and of the inevitable lulls in the struggles? After all, other great revolutionaries have proved to be men of reflection as well as men of action: how otherwise could we have the writings of a Marx, of a Rousseau, of a Martin Luther King, Jr.? Conscience itself, the very stuff of revolution, is in a sense a compressed form of taking thought about injustice. To be outraged and to act can take the highly effective form of verbal proclamation—a *Declaration of Independence*, a *Declaration of the Rights of Man,* activities requiring a high order of reflection.

In a sense, however, I am still willing to leave the revolutionary himself to be a man of action, for it is really not he to whom this book is directed. But the revolutionary movements of our time are coalition activities, consisting not just of hard-core men of action but including more or less active (and less or more reflective) adherents from the Christian tradition. It is the liberal Christian who admires the revolutions and supports them who really can be required to examine himself. And this liberal should examine himself not just in respect of Christian criteria of action; perhaps his greatest responsibility is to put himself to the testing of whether he is a genuine revolutionary. In my experience, he is probably serious about neither undertaking—his calling as a Christian, his support of the revolutionary movements.

Indeed, if the liberal supporter of revolution is not exactly an enemy of revolution, he is certainly tempted to be a great misuser of the idea of revolution. Lacking the anger and intolerance of a Robespierre, he is still against what the revolutionaries are against, and for what they are for. He doesn't want to enact the cause their way, but he thinks of that as a detail. So he imagines that by going out for reform, committee work, and persuasion he can make his own place in the movement, and thus that he is after all essentially a revolutionary, too. In our day it is the liberal, bookish, conscientious Christian who debases the notion of revolution most tellingly, for he

finally thinks of any worthwhile, ameliorative change as revolutionary. Worse, he lacks the passion, commitment, and recklessness that
any decent revolutionary (or any serious Christian) must have.

At least those hardshell, fundamentalist Christians who are always
denouncing students and black militants as "revolutionists" understand what a revolution is. They did not like Stokely Carmichael,
Malcolm X, Students for a Democratic Society, and other such types
because they understood what these people were saying with a realism not always exhibited by liberals. The hardshell is right in being
horrified with revolution, for it is precisely that drastic a thing, it is
just that kind of menace to the *ancien régime*.

I hope it is now clear that I don't want to turn our revolutionaries
into thinkers, ethicists, ontologists, or pipe-smoking professors. But I
do insist that revolution, as a moral cause, is authentic only when it
includes the art of self-judgment. Militancy and mastery are ingredients of a revolution, but they are not an ethics; they require an
ethics.

2. *Transcendent judgment.* A second requirement, writ on a larger
canvas, must now be sketched. An authentic moral upheaval not only
must include self-questioning. The revolution itself must submit, in
some sense and at some point, to exterior questioning: not just the
questions that occur to its own leaders, even granted that they have
their thoughtful moments, but the questions that can be put to any
movement that claims to act on behalf of humanity. The revolution
itself must undergo judgment. It depends for its genuineness on its
ability to stand up under the tests of experience, and the world may
not necessarily be required to wait until all the evidence of history is
in before the judgments can be made. There are judgments to be
made of a revolution in its own time as well as in future times. There
are judgments to be made of a revolution by the surrounding communities. A revolution requires, in short, to be sized up by transcendent
examination.

In Jonathan Edwards' day, as we have seen, this was an easy
requirement to conceptualize in ultimate form, if a hard one to undergo. Edwards could begin by saying that a revival wasn't authentic
unless it was the work of supernatural, divine agency. Unfortunately
that extramundane modality of judgment seems lost to us today. That

style of transcendence is simply used-up transcendence in our world. Does that mean we are simply restricted to judging by our own feelings, our own immediate sense of responsibility? I think not.

Revolutions are finite programs for reorganizing the space of communities. Much like the revivals of our heritage, they come and go, flame up and die. In the nineteenth century large parts of the East were finally "burned-over districts," the fires of revival dead. In the same way every political revolution bursts into life, lives, and then turns to wood or ashes: it happened to the English Revolution of the 1640's, the French Revolution, even the American Revolution. Values remain, but revolutions come and go. If the values are to live, revolutions have to be mortal, to be replaced.

What is finite will be transcended. We may count on it that today's fast-paced revolutions will slow their gait, as time goes on, change their form, and even die away. What goes on is not the factical revolutions themselves, but something that surpasses them all, something that comes again and again to men, something that in effect is a judgment on each of the particular revolutions.

This constant factor is the perennial reality that the human condition is one of crisis, of lostness of one kind or another; but it is also the perennial hope that man can act to move through the crisis and assert himself in new and larger ways. I believe that the symbols of lostness and deliverance that come down in the Judaeo-Christian tradition are the most appropriate medium for invoking this transcendent judgment on revolutions. I recognize, however, that other symbols of crisis, hope, and redemption are also alive today, some of them quite unconnected with the historic faith that commends itself to me (the Muslim symbolism of some civil rights revolutionaries, for example, or the Eastern mysticism motifs to which some of our rebels against the Gross National Product appeal). Faith, at least as my own tradition knows it, is greater than one's subjective feelings, greater than one's estimate of the situation in a given moment of agony. Faith precedes assurance, survives its lapses, and invites man to struggle for his dignity.[19]

This will seem too "theological" a way of stating the judgment motif to some. But I am willing to make it more concrete and culturally palpable, since I expect the transcendent symbols of Judaeo-

Christian tradition to find their mark in history. Every revolution is set within a community of some kind. The revolution, on first glance, may appear to want to destroy that community, so intolerable are its moral patterns. But an authentic revolution is to be judged, in this concrete sense, by its role in its own community or society, which transcends the revolution and supplies it not only with the situation of lostness but also with standards by which to measure the lostness. "In America we judge by American standards," say Carmichael and Hamilton, "and by this yardstick we find that the black man lives in incredibly inadequate housing, shabby shelters that are dangerous to mental and physical health and to life itself."[20] A revolution, however angry, that can recognize this claim of its own society's "best self" is a revolution under saving judgment.

And beyond its own community, a revolution is to be judged by its promise toward humanity in the other communities. America has undergone two revolutions that established values and standards for judging American community. The first was the struggle for political independence, "whether we should or could run our own affairs in our own way." The second was the Civil War, in which the defeat of the slave power pointed to the mandate to open this space we had won from the British to all of the members of the American community. That was the internal meaning of reorganizing our own space. Now, even before we have succeeded in opening up access to American space to all Americans (the subject matter of most of our present revolutionary movements), we have been overtaken by a third great crisis, the *worldwide* demand for justice and full participation in society.[21] Whether our revolutions can serve the cause of the rest of the world's oppressed people becomes the greatest spatial judgment upon revolution, American style.

Revolution will continue to express the plight and promise of mankind for many years, and America will surely be involved in widening revolt:[22]

In the immediate future, the impulse to rebel will continue to grow among marginal groups like students, Negroes, migrant farm workers, intellectuals, and white-collar workers. This will happen because the generators of dissent—war, bureaucracy, guilt-producing affluence, fascism, hypocrisy, moral rot—are enduring in the fabric of American society.

The revival is a dead form of participation in the promise of the Gospel for man. The revolution is just opening up as this century's form. Discernment of the genuineness of revolution is one of our tasks as well as participation in the genuine ones.

CHAPTER VI.

BENCHMARKS

We have just inquired, in Chapter V, into the defensibility of revolutions as temporal ingredients of republican life. We arrived at a set of theological criteria for judging the urgency of occasions. Now we must turn to an entirely different set of questions. Granted that there will be revolution aimed at overthrowing extrinsic control of communal and personal space[1]—revolution, we say, that can be defended—the question arises: how is the space to be reorganized? What are the norms that we can now discern for the furthering of shared space and governance? What, in short, are the benchmarks of the new terrain? Again, we will seek to answer theologically.

1. The Meaning of Moral Norms in American Space

A few semesters ago a fellow teacher of Christian ethics and I offered, for our theological students, a seminar on the revolution in "personal morality" that seems to have swept through American life in the past five years or so. We were concerned with such subjects as civil rights, Black Power, poverty, our unhappy war in Vietnam—and, of course, sex. We were especially interested in the ways in which these topics had become matters of personal involvement and decision for many of the younger generation.

When, by and by, we got around to taking up sex as one of the salient areas of the revolution, we assigned a team of three students to introduce the subject, and it did so with an engaging bit of role-playing.

George played the role of the up-to-date reader of *Playboy*—the fellow who thinks of sex as recreation and that it shouldn't be judged by anachronistic, Puritan moral canons.

Dan played the role of the orthodox, theologically literate Protestant, defending the concept of chastity outside marriage as a requirement of the Christian faith.

Bob played the role of the situation ethicist, the advocate of "The New Morality," denouncing both the hedonism of the *Playboy* reader and the legalism of the conventional Christian, and arguing for decision-making according to the needs of love in the situation.

Aside from the fact that this performance, at the end of the session, brought spontaneous applause from the other students (a rare occurrence), two facts stood out:

1. The other members of the seminar, who were supposed in the discussion period to be critical of all three positions, heaped virtually all of their criticism on the hedonist and the legalist. This means, as a member of the seminar pointed out before the day was over, "we must all be situationists without realizing it."

2. The same students are constantly pressing themselves, each other, and their teachers for "norms" to be used in ethical reflection.

Can they really have it both ways? Can they consistently deny the authority of norms, on the one hand, as in their criticisms of the legalist, and evince a yearning for norms on the other, as in their criticisms of the hedonist, and in their general uneasiness about not having norms?

I think they are quite consistent in their attitudes, and that the apparent contradiction—rejecting norms and asking for norms at the same time—can be fairly easily explained. When such Americans as these students nowadays reject norms for morality, they are rejecting the idea that morality can be directed by authoritative canons imposed, as it were, from above. That amounts to extrinsic control of their existential space, which is the paradigmatic form of immorality in the American greater community. When they, at the same time, evince a considerable thirstiness for norms and engage in a quest for norms, they are saying they want to reorganize their space according to definite standards or principles, but that these must be developed out of the values at hand, and with the participation of the members of the community.

In other words, we are the victims of a semantic illusion. Contemporary Americans, at least those of the sort who engage in "revolutions in personal morality," have long since dispensed with conventional norms of morality—vertical norms that have authoritative force to prescribe conduct, and that are relatively permanent. They have decided not in favor of normlessness, but in favor of another concept of norms—horizontal norms that are authoritative because they are recognized by men free to dispose of their own space; norms built up pictorially with action scenes drawn from contemporary manners; norms that are connected by a feedback system to current problems and predicaments. In this kind of morality, a norm points not to what is abstractly normative (required to be done in all circumstances) but to what is "normal" (needed to be done to cope with things or restore the situation).

Unfortunately, in all of the acres of print that have been devoted to the "norms"-versus-"situation" debate in Christian ethics today, this new, operative concept of "norm" in the American ethos is scarcely recognized. Parties to the debate on both sides go on thinking of norms in the classic, Christian, European sense, as vertical directives. That is one reason there has been little forward motion in this debate. Even the situationists, I would argue, have a vertical model of norms, and not only for the norms they reject. They keep "love" as a norm, but they conceptualize it vertically, rendering the "love ethic," too, as ultimately unsatisfactory for moral reflection in the American ethos. On the other hand, if one tries to convert love into a horizontal norm, into a model of conduct illustrated out of the manners of a space-disposing community, it loses the uniqueness, the singularity, the sanitary wrapping that has to be presupposed when one is down to his last vertical norm. One immediately has to begin to ask about the form it takes in given crises, and that means one has to disassemble it into various cultural expressions—which is precisely what we are saying ought to be done.

2. The Relation of Moral Norms to Experience and Crisis

We can best proceed by laying down two propositions, one general and one specific.

Our general proposition is this:

For American theology and ethics, norms come proximately from communal experience in reorganizing space through a form of feedback rather than from authority, whether biblical or traditionary. There may be a place for biblical norms and the norms of ecclesiastical tradition, but this place is validated through a contest with experience, and ultimately through the consent of experience rather than through the ontological persistence of the original authority. The Bible is not self-evidently authoritative in American morality. Church tradition is not, either. Nor is the "American moral tradition" itself, despite our interest in evoking it as the immediate background of moral reflection in the American ethos.

Let us pursue this point by attending to the issue of the authority of Scripture for American morality. Langdon Gilkey raises it in the most general form by pointing to the problematic status of all biblical study in an age that has adopted secular canons of truth. In his view, this status was not conferred on the biblical materials by the recent "God is dead" thrust in theology, for that movement itself is only a sign or expression of something much deeper. The heart of the matter is contemporary secularism, which has become the presupposition, the atmosphere of our culture (like "Hellenism" in the patristic age). The point of reference for theology as for other disciplines has become "the fundamental mood of secularism in all of us with which neo-orthodoxy was in the end unable to cope."

What happens to the Bible in such an age? Among theologians and ethicists it surely continues to be of "immense historical, literary and linguistic interest." At the same time its direct theological authority is placed under a cloud. If, in our age, serious questions are asked about the existence of God, they also raise doubts about the status of any revelation that comes from the divine, and about documents that are supposed to mediate such a revelation. No longer, then, can the theological thinker simply take for granted the "biblical view" as an undoubted theological source or authority, "since the questions of whether there be a revelation or a revealer at all are the ones he must deal with. And it surely begs *these* questions to cite only what the Bible says about them!"[2] By analogy we could adapt the same sort of criticism to norms and truths found in ecclesiastical tradition. For the church has conventionally rested its authority upon much the same kind of warrant claimed for the biblical materials, viz., that it is a medium or vehicle of a sacred tradition that in the end stems from revelation. All of this applies equally to norms for ethics as well as to norms for theology.

In an important way, however, this rescinding of traditionary authority in theology and ethics is not just a general consequence of the secular temper of our age. There is a much more specific bias against received authority, even the authority of the Bible, in American religion itself, and it is a bias that far antedates contemporary secularism. Today, when we reflect on the American religious heritage, we like to imagine that there was a day when the Bible was a fully operative authority in the lives of Christians, tempered only to the degree that such creedal statements as the Westminster Confession of Faith, itself a biblicist symbol, were used to translate the biblical commands into apprehensible theological form. Where the Bible spoke, we imagine, our Christian forefathers spoke; where the Bible was silent, they were silent. But this is to exaggerate the role of received authority in America. Even from the first days, it is becoming clear, at least two other authoritative sources thrust themselves upon the consciousness of American Christians. One was the challenge of the new environment, which made for shifts in tradition even when the bearers of tradition thought they were reproducing it faithfully. The second was the success of a competing tradition, that of the "rights of Englishmen," which was eventually to mature into the tenets of republican governance.

That the Puritans, to take one example, read and used the Bible does not really establish the case for the authority of the Bible. For they did so in their own context of a new settlement in which both the natural and the virtuous or man-made took on revelatory significance. If the great Puritan theologian Edwards insisted that only supernatural grace could make a man loving, he could also insist that natural virtue was something real. If it was an inferior form of beauty it was still one form of *beauty*. In general, the natural world took on a heightened importance for the Puritans as the realm that furnished shadows or images of divine things. Scripture retained a powerful grip, but not so much as an authoritative source of doctrine as a source of persuasive metaphors aimed at convicting and arousing its reader. According to Heimert, it was chiefly among the "liberals" that Scripture became a stock of precedents, a kind of divinely given lawbook. "The Calvinist, on the other hand, sought to grasp the single meaning of the whole Scripture—the 'glory of the gospel'—in as aesthetic and as unitary a perception as that by which the gracious understanding apprehended the beauty of the Godhead. The Bible for Calvinists was not a chronicle of events, nor even a logical collection of doctrines, but rather a complete 'image' of the Divine nature."[3]

Moreover, as George L. Haskins has convincingly argued, the Puritans read the Bible with the implicit, hidden interpretive force of "the social, political, and legal inheritance which the Puritans shared in common with other seventeenth century Englishmen." Haskins shows how in Massachusetts the biblical laws were not bodily taken over, as might be supposed upon casual examination of the old statute books. Rather they were revised to take account of such legal conceptions as "intent" as an element of crime. They introduced such English legal presumptions as the distinctions of age, holding that a boy under fourteen is legally incapable of committing sodomy. Despite their commitments to Scripture, Haskins suggests, the Puritans were also governed by other moral norms, as is seen in "their unwillingness to follow its precepts when contrary to their own ethical and moral conceptions." Thus they were "demonstrably reluctant to prescribe death for every offense that the Bible ordered so punished." In the Massachusetts civil law the influence of the Bible is even less than in the criminal law. The Puritans added strong elements of due process and insistence that culpability be deliberate, items not cared for in the original legal models of the Bible. In general, he concludes, "the criteria applied in the colony undoubtedly owed as much to English precedent as to the Bible's texts."[4]

The displacement of traditional authority, perhaps still only an incipient movement among the Puritans, proceeded more massively in frontier religion and on other fronts. Everywhere the experience of the new environment and the increasing competition of the saving symbols from the republican tradition meant a diminution of the authority of the Bible and of churchly tradition. In America, says John J. McDermott, "there developed a highly sensitive feeling for the riches of experience as a way of reconstructing doctrine rather than as a malleable resource awaiting clarification."[5] American ethics, on this view, does not know with precision or inner certainty in advance what is good, or even, in the theological sense, what is ultimate; or how to speak of God or of ethical norms in the older vertical sense. It has "heard" the testimony of Scripture and of churchly tradition (the Scriptures continue to be quoted vastly in nineteenth-century American religion), but it does not accept this testimony as a pure directive. There is, further, a de-emphasis upon "elders" as the bearers of truth in America, a development clearly seen in the contemporary upheavals on our campuses and in other demands of the younger generation.

In America, then, so far have we moved from traditional understandings of truth, doctrine, and authority that we can now safely predict that young people of decision-making age (eighteen and up?) will now become at least as important as any other group in society in coining values, reshaping customs, manners, and norms respecting sex and a variety of other loci of personal morality. Morality, it appears, will in fact cease to be an institution administered through elders, churches, or schools by way of a process of instructing or coaching the young. The elders, with their experience, will continue to play a vital role. But morality seems certain to become more a matter of working through to horizontal norms on the basis of dialogue and conflict between equally ponderable and weighty participants, the young as well as the old. We can see this new critical function of the young already at work.

We are now ready to move from our general proposition about experience as the medium of ethical norms to a second, more specific proposition:

The most decisive ethical norms come out of a special kind of experience, the experience of crisis. We have in mind the kind of crisis that threatens meaningful life—in terms of the preceding chapter, the kind of crisis that produces moral revolution. Morality in America is not shaped alone by the competing traditions—biblical and republican—that we have just mentioned. It is not shaped by the environment alone. All of these factors are significant. But another major contribution to the formation of moral patterns is the unique pattern of national crises undergone in America.[6]

The shaping of experience into ethical norms begins with a cry for help, with the demand for relief from something unbearable, something so cruel or existentially painful that it threatens our world. In general, as we have seen, moral crisis in America has taken the form of despotism or extrinsic control of communal and personal space. And rescue has proceeded with whatever help it could get from both of the available traditions—religious and secular, or biblical and republican. That is why the words of a great leader in one of the definitive crises, Abraham Lincoln, seem both theological and political at once. They *are* both. The Second Inaugural Address calls on both traditions, biblical and republican.

When ethical norms are fully salvific, or when they are profoundly developed (as with Lincoln's resort to the ideas of the Declaration of Independence and also to the judgment of God on a perverse people), they signal not only a bare rescue from immediate crisis, but a larger vision of wholeness. If the first product of a moral upheaval is a crash program meant to handle an emergency, the long-range result is a shaped-out scenario that takes man out of fallenness into the path toward fulfillment—*Itinerarium Mentis in Deum*. Thus the proximate result of the divine-human response to crisis may be temporary survival rather than blessedness as such, and by "eternal" standards may amount to less than full salvation. The mere cry for bread or justice is not the fullness of new community or the excellence of reclaimed space—but it is a demand for an essential step toward such goals. And indeed, the arrival of temporary relief from crisis may lead to subsequent "recall" in the Platonic sense of a higher good than mere proximate survival.

All of this will be disturbing comment for those unable to think of ethics except in terms of vertical norms. Yet it does not, we believe, constitute a rejection of the role of Scripture or tradition in American ethics. Rather, we believe, it is precisely the opposite, the clarification of what these roles may be. We can argue, in fact, that the Scriptures themselves do not deal with ethics in terms of the classical view of norms. In this claim, we follow the reasoning of Josef Blank, who thinks that it is impossible and inappropriate to apply this older view of norms (which he calls "the modern concept of 'norms' ") to either Old or New Testament. The Laws of Israel have their own meaning in the community of Israel, as the expression of its covenant life with Yahweh. But neither here nor in the New Testment do we find ready-made ethical directives. Even to *ask* for such norms as deliverances of Scripture is to ask wrongly and irrelevantly "if we understand thereby a series of moral precepts which are then detached as generally valid moral principles, seen apart from the background of the faith," and then erected into a biblical ethics "with universally human implications." What we find in Scripture, let us say the New Testament, are neither legal directives nor moral indifference, but rather "ethical patterns" that are compelling presentations of the divine love and are yet flexible enough to allow and demand that we rethink the implications for our own time. The morality of the New Testament, Blank says, is thus a "signpost" rather than a "norm."[7] Or, to use our own terminology, it commends horizontal norms, models of conduct summing up that community's decisive, saving encounter with Jesus Christ.

In every case, in biblical times and in our own, crisis is the setting of the salvation episode and is the crucible out of which the moral patterns of the community are forged. Past moral patterns, including the traditionary and biblical deliverances, are tested in other communities by the new crisis itself, for the historic "authority" of these deliverances entitles them to a hearing, a testing to see if they will rescue—but no more than that. This experimental, pragmatic view of authority was well stated by Benjamin Franklin in 1740. "If what is thus published be good," he wrote in the *Pennsylvania Gazette,* defending the freedom of printers, "Mankind has the Benefit of it; If it be bad . . . the more 'tis made publick, the More its Weakness is expos'd and the greater Disgrace falls upon the author, whoever he be."[8]

3. The Accumulated "Layers" of Ethical Norms in Our Past

Crisis is recurrent in human experience. What solves one problem may unlock a whole new realm of troubles. Or a problem just won't stay solved. It keeps coming up again and again in the history of a greater community. Or what one age can live with becomes an intolerable threat to the next age. For every such crisis, we attempt to evolve responsive moral patterns.

In ethical analysis, then, we are presented with the appearance, looking backward in time at our own community, of accumulated "layers" of moral patterns, each related constructively to some crisis, or salvation episode, in the past. The ethical pattern that was forged in the Greek world gave us the familiar cluster of natural virtues that we think of as prudence, courage, temperance, and justice. In the Christian epoch these norms ceased to speak to what came to be felt as the main crisis. Faith, love, and hope were pushed to the fore as "cardinal" virtues, aimed at the new salvation crisis. The classical norms were retained—as in the systems of Augustine or Aquinas—but as a secondary layer of virtues, the natural virtues that could partially serve us but not save us. We can observe that these virtues were not only theologically secondary to medieval Christians, but that they were also historically secondary.

We could, if we liked, survey the whole history of Christendom by pursuing this way of analysis—by examining the successive efforts of Christian communities to escape what was taken, in each, to be damnation or extreme crisis.

For the first millennium and a half of the Christian era men sought escape from a cruel and burdensome nature. The crisis or predicament was seen as the misery inflicted upon them in temporal existence. The hope of salvation accordingly was seen as the promise of escaping temporal existence into impassibility—into immortality, into the changelessness of eternal life. That is why the Eucharist was thought of as the "medicine of immortality." For centuries that conception of crisis, predicament, deliverance, persisted in the Christian community and its institutions.

In time Western man discovered that he could not only live with nature, but that he could even push it back and exert control over it. By the seventeenth century, Christendom had left behind that era when man could be slaughtered in thousands and millions by the plague without protesting his fate. A new era had dawned, to be celebrated soon by the *philosophes* of the Enlightenment. Among many symbols of a new vision was the figure of Robinson Crusoe, the civilized individual who triumphs over nature. As we have seen,

Crusoe is a symbol of the new notion of salvation—that man, the resourceful individual, can win his struggle against nature and find earthly happiness.

By the end of the nineteenth century the wilderness was conquered, in the Western world, at least. It had been defeated in principle by the very emergence of Crusoe as a potent symbol, and now it was conquered in fact and in force by Americans. At this point, another grand new salvation episode begins. If nature—the wilderness, the frontier, the savagery of tooth and claw—has been taken in hand, that means that the greatest enemy left to man is man himself—the one being in nature who cannot be controlled by technical means. Savagely symbolized in World War I as the new spoiler, man himself appears in the twentieth century as his own nemesis, his own crisis.

Now the controlling salvation idea becomes that of "encounter," of restoring communication and mutality between man and man. No longer will the image of Crusoe prevailing against the elements do. No longer are we content with the image of industrial man completing his mopping-up operation against the wilderness. If Robinson Crusoe had been memorialized in a twentieth-century novel, the point of the story would not be Crusoe's victory over nature, but rather his "I-Thou" encounter with Friday. The substance of salvation is no longer immortality, it is no longer triumph over the wilderness, it is now *relationship, mutuality*.

What happens to the religious institution itself in these shifts from crisis to crisis? Simply put: the institution keeps on vending the norms that repaired the last emergency. Indeed, we can broaden this statement to include the society at large. In American society today, for example, the specific salvation assumptions of conventional religion, and the general outlook of society itself, are still tied to the industrial ethic. Even after a new moral upheaval, based on the failure of the older norms, begins in some sector, the dominant institutions will continue to refurbish and proffer the symbols and norms that worked before. But a small group of the aggrieved, aided by such types as artists (who can foresee bad existential weather before most of the rest of us), begins to clamor for a new kind of rescue. If the grievance is truly subversive of the old order, and if it portends a serious threat to life among substantial elements of the society, the stage is set for a moral revolution.

Once the revolution is underway, its prescriptions, symbols, and norms of salvation, if they are truly salvific, will begin to spread into wider channels in the society. Eventually the society will accept them, and the religious institutions will canonize them. Thus the norms of "mutuality" as a rescue from the impersonalness of the industrial ethic are by now becoming generally acceptable and even sacred. Religious institutions are hard at work converting to the new set of norms (as in the redescription of marriage as a union for mutuality, for example, replacing the old conception of marriage as aimed at stability and the production of offspring). Once the norms used to repair an old crisis become acceptable and public and sanctioned by the religious institution, we can go on to say, the crisis is over, and we might as well be prepared for moral revolution to break out in a new quarter. And yet, we never are prepared.

Now, all the signs are that the "personalness" of the recent crises, the demands for mutuality and self-identity, are becoming general societal values. This means that the revolution is losing steam. And another facet of the march toward wholeness will next be emphasized.

4. The Intersection of Gospel and Contemporary Crisis

The revolution in personal morality of our immediate past has been so obsessed with procuring love and personal response that one often gets the impression that these are the only ingredients of salvation, the only structural elements in the good news to man, the Gospel. But these needs are simply parts of the last "layer" of human realization to emerge against the settled background of assured industrial attainment. "The true novelty of the twentieth century" is personal meeting—most characteristically seen in the discovery of sex, but broadly realized in the notion of happiness, the notion that it is "right that human beings should be fulfilled, as our century strives after it. . . . For it has burst upon us, men and women of the twentieth century, that sexuality is a part of our culture, that the knowledge of the body, its mastery and development, are as essential as that of the spirit."[9]

Present crisis is the definitive one, of course, and the one that must be dealt with most seriously in any conception of our salvation. But if we are to give the notion of "Gospel" or good news its fullest scope, we must attempt to see how it moves in history to enlarge the human over a series of crises.

We are ready to undertake our final task. This is to sketch in rough (and inadequate) terms an approximation of the *several* ingredients that Gospel offers and demands for the salvation of man in our own time and place. We proceed by reading the recent existential crises that modern Americans have faced, and by stating, successively, the ethical norms that have emerged as prescriptive for each crisis. When these several crisis-and-response elements are taken together, we will have a kind of cultural approximation of what "wholeness" is for contemporary American man. There are five elements in this "synthetic" or culturally approximated Gospel: Order, Mutuality, Self-Identity, Cultural Justice, and A New Sense of Space.

(a) *Order*

Conventionally the first ingredient of blessedness is taken to be "law and order," in the phrase of those who are threatened by any disruptive change. We accept the fundamental character of order, but we propose to replace the overrigid conventional view of it with another, more salvific concept. The first ingredient of wholeness for our time and place is not the police rule demanded by the middle class, terrified at riotous summers and soaring crime rates. It is rather *relative freedom from nature* (including the baser aspects of human nature).

The first requirement of general blessedness in contemporary times is that a community acquire the bare bones of an industrial system, one that affords a modest transcendence, at least, over a hard-scrabble bondage to nature, one that lays down minimal standards of subsistence and minimal lines of governance. Making one's way in the world is a rock-bottom element of salvation for modern Western man. This means having communities with some industrial potential and with principles of supplying food, shelter, clothing. It means freedom from tribal warfare, whether the warfare be that of gangs or vigilantes.

In terms of the layers of ethical crisis that have built up our American moral patterns, we can say that the struggle to transcend nature by establishing industrial hegemony was the concern of the late nineteenth century. For in this period our nation made the transition into an industrial economy, and the lineaments of "conventional morality" that still form the received norms were here set and fixed.

The nation was indeed preparing for industrial order throughout the last century, often to the point of an obsession, and often to the point of jettisoning other moral values (which is common in the pursuit of any moral crisis). Mrs. Trollope's acidulous impressions of American life in the first half of the century give a clear picture of our obsession to conquer nature at almost any price. She visited Lockport, New York, and was astounded and dismayed at what she saw:[10]

> As fast as half a dozen trees were cut down, a *factory* was raised up; stumps still contest the ground with pillars, and porticoes are seen to struggle with rocks. It looks as if the demon of machinery, having invaded the peaceful realms of nature, had fixed on Lockport as the battleground on which they should strive for mastery. . . . Nature is fairly routed and driven from the field, and the rattling, crackling, hissing, splitting demon has taken possession of Lockport for ever.

This vector of salvation thirst is still alive in rural reaches of the country, as the plea of the small-town chamber of commerce for a "payroll" always underlines. In other, urbanized stretches, the optimal benefits of the industrial element of salvation have long since been achieved, and because of the very temptation to regard these elements as all-saving instead of partially saving, other strands of salvation (some analyzed below) are neglected. The result is that our industrial cities, raised up as cure-alls, have become demonic. But the peril of attributing complete saving power to industrial order was immediately visible at the start—to Mrs. Trollope, among others. About this nature-conquering town of Lockport, she says: "I never felt more out of humour at what the Americans call improvement; it is, in truth, as it now stands, a most hideous place, and gladly did I leave it behind me."[11]

Our received notions of time, space, community arrangement, government, and policing are largely based, even today, on the industrial ethic. It is when large sectors of the population manifest lostness and malaise not curable by the norms of this ethic that the conflict between "law and order" and "agitators" becomes obvious.

Yet an industrial order, however oppressive it becomes if it is the only sanctioned concern, is necessary for all parts of the society. And on this score some of our contemporary revolutionaries have been a bit naïve. The freedoms that we now take for granted are simply not yet available in some communities because the basic ingredient of an industrial ethic is missing. The recent civil rights ordeal in Mississippi supplies us with an excellent example. When young volunteers from the East went into one county to assist in voter registration, they were flatly and effectively squelched. Jack Newfield gives a cogent analysis of the reasons. "Amite does not have a white, business-oriented middle class," he observes, unlike, say, Greenville, in the delta, "an oasis of decency." Nor does Amite have the merchant class that at last took steps, in 1965, to curb terrorism in McComb. Newspapers in Greenville and McComb mediated a moderate view to the business people. But the only newspaper in Amite "is a racist sheet called the *Liberty Herald.*"[12]

Amite seems outside the flow of history, a backward enclave insulated from the passage of time. It has not only missed the civil-rights movement, but the Industrial Revolution as well. There are no factories, no shopping centers, no unions in the county. The longed-for educated, civilized white moderate isn't in hiding; *he doesn't exist in Amite.*

"Order," then, means first of all not riot control, but freedom from bondage to nature, and from the anarchy and terror toward which unorganized human existence tends. Order in this sense is an important ingredient of wholeness extending down even into the most personal aspects of our private lives, even in a marriage ethic based on "tenderness." Marriage, says Paul Ricoeur, offers the best context for the enjoyment of mutuality and the expression of tenderness. But marriage itself best preserves these goods because it is an institution with sacred sanctions that "can serve as discipline to Eros." A successful marriage keeps open the practice of tenderness only if it can incorporate such values from "the political sphere" as "the rule of justice, respect for others, equality in law and reciprocity of obligation."[13]

The notion of order we argue for here is part of the ethical pattern of the Hebrew Bible, with its demand that strangers in the community be cared for and fed. It is intimated in the New Testament notion that freedom is to be proclaimed not just to the poor in heart, but to the simply poor, as well. Order lays a floor of the possibility of "making it" for the whole community—by providing transcendence over nature, and access to the bare goods of living. Order, of itself, cannot save, for it assures only that nature is kept at bay. Indeed, where glaring discrepancies are found from one sector of a community to another in the availability of these minimal elements of "making it," we may say that order does not exist in the first place. The riots and violence that may follow, while not necessarily to be defended and perhaps even to be condemned, nevertheless do not themselves disrupt an order that did not exist.

(b) *Mutuality*

The industrial ethic still seems salvific in itself because the community and its norm-brokering institutions are still fixed on the last crisis—the bondage to nature that had to be overcome by providing for work, wage earning, rising standards, and leisure. In a mature industrial economy, however, the requirements for order begin to lose their sanctity as the memory of the crisis grows dim among its younger members, or as new salvation needs, not amenable to order, are signaled by a rising *avant-garde*. Thus the existentialist revolt against industrialized Europe, prophetically inaugurated with Kierkegaard and brought to overt expression in this century (e.g., in the writings of Jaspers, Heidegger, and Sartre), point to the arena of the next salvation crisis: the arena of the personal. Against the assured (and increasingly stifling) background of industrial order, a thirst arises for encounter with other human beings.

We have to conceptualize this new thirst in two ways: both as the quest for mutuality (a more personalized version of community), and as a quest for self-identity (which is hostile in some respects to mutuality, or at least separable conceptually from it). Both mutuality and self-identity are alternate ways of talking about the same sector of salvation, for each of these goods is involved in the other. And yet there is a certain progression in the historical emergence of the two emphases, an order of change that in the American society of the twentieth century first put more stress on "community" as the new overriding value, then more lately began to stress "self-identity" as a value that must be realized incident to, or even prior to, community. The transition from a mutuality-seeking civil rights program to an identity-seeking one sufficiently illustrates the progression we have in mind.

In America, then, the first great revision of the industrial ethic was in the direction of a counterethic of community, understood more and more as a drive toward mutuality or as setting the conditions for mutuality. In 1950, David Riesman described this change in *The Lonely Crowd,* contending that "above-subsistence Americans' goals were changing from the quest for power to the pursuit of resonance with relevant others."[14] The industrial ethic had its own form of personal community, centered in the nineteenth-century possibilities of small-town and family life. One was naturally in community with networks of geographical neighbors and kin, and in this respect the "impersonalness" that we associate with industrialism must at first have been softened or obscured. In our own later day of mobility and small, unreticulated family structure, new patterns of getting-with-others had to be found, and thus the problem of community in the form of quest for mutuality came to the fore.

It is this quest for mutuality, for encounter, for I-Thou relations, that still forms the primary challenge for intellectuals and liberals in our society. (They have moved beyond the industrial ethic, but only a few are far enough along in the mutuality ethic to see its incompleteness.) And yet it is an error to confuse mutuality with love, or the availability of encounter with the Gospel. The encounter ethic is only the most recent wave on the beach; the desire for mutuality is only one element of community, only one moment of the Gospel, only one aspect of love, even though a hotly pursued one in our recent experience. And it is just as demonic, when isolated and sought as a singular good, as order alone. If order pursued as the only good produces the "riot control" syndrome of our middle class, then mutuality pursued alone produces the privatism of our drop-out class. The pursuit of mutuality is best seen as a necessary countersweep to the industrial ethic, which in subduing nature produced the unintended side effect of overregulating community life and personal existence, depriving both of opportunity for encounter.

Mutuality, like order, is anticipated as an ingredient of wholeness in the biblical anthropology and in the great churchly tradition of reflection on the condition of man. The Scriptures speak from one end to the other of man's confrontation with God and with his neighbor as a confrontation in the heart, of one that demands the whole self. They speak of the mutual care that is the sign and seal of faith, and of genuine "religious affections." Just as order means that no member of the community, even the stranger, shall be suffered to starve, so mutuality means that no member of the community, even the estranged, shall be suffered to go without affection. The Gospel understands the highest form of mutuality not to be acquiring the values of encounter, but of giving these values to another self—and receiving in return.

(c) Self-identity

As seemingly simple a requirement as that a man be free to "be himself," it would seem, has not yet been guaranteed in large sectors of the American society. Much of the passion behind the revolt of college students today against bureaucracy has in view the failure of a highly organized society, and even some forms of "community," to grant autonomy and freedom to those who want it and are prepared to clamor for it, at the expense of previous conceptions of order and mutuality. Similarly, the black man seeks self-identity and self-integrity today as an ingredient he must have before he can go on to such larger goals as engagement in a loving community. It may be that the goals of the whole "mutuality" ethic have to be suspended until the goals of the identity ethic are nearer realization.

Or, alternatively, it may be that the goals of mutuality are inseparable from the goals of self-identity. "Communication is not necessarily a peaceful mode of inter-human relations," says Roger Mehl. Mutuality is possible at all only when the self breaks out of any lingering prepersonal "collective agreement," or subpersonal "tribal consensus." Insofar as outworn collective, monolithic realities "have enough power to impose themselves upon the group and to assure its unanimity, communication from self to self is neither possible, nor necessary, nor desirable."

Communication begins, then, with the emergence of the self from any prepersonal collectivity—with emergence, it may be, from what has passed for "order" or even "community." Communication may have to begin, in fact, with what Mehl characterizes as a duel or debate, for "the primary condition for communication is the acknowledgment of the other and my will of being acknowledged by him." The latest phase of the revolution in personal morality—one that has not yet enlisted the allegiance of many mutuality-oriented liberals—consciously rejects mutuality in favor of a higher-priority struggle for selfhood. Mehl's analysis of the conditions for communication surely are apt descriptions of the reasons behind some of the recent student and racial unrest in America.

Mehl goes further, however, than simply arguing for the right of the aggrieved to self-identity. He also suggests that the person who withholds someone else's personhood is lacking himself in self-identity, and that the duel should be fought out so that *both* parties can find themselves. If one man challenges another to a duel, it is certainly because he is offended. But there should be another reason, considering that the offender has behaved in an unworthy manner that has veiled his own true dignity. "By challenging him to combat, we give him a chance to rehabilitate himself, that is, to show himself as he is, beyond the inauthentic appearances. That is why it happens that at the end of the duel reconciliation may be possible, and that the two enemies may recognize each other for what they really are, that is, brothers."[15]

The struggle for identity will characterize our revolutions, personal and political, domestic and colonial, for some time to come. It is a concept that properly applies both to men and to groups. The Black

Power advocates rightly observe that to assimilate individual blacks into the dominant white society does nothing to improve the estate of the black masses left behind. Until the black people become a community, with political and cultural identity, they will remain apart from the greater society.

Self-identity is a part of the biblical pattern or picture of man, but with an added qualification that we have to notice. Selfhood is a compound of virtue and pride, excellence and selfishness, strength and frailty, quality and mediocrity. The emergence of a human being from tribal collectivity requires that he see himself not as he would like to see himself, but as he is known when he is put to the test of encountering another man—and God. Selfhood is not self-evident, in other words. One can be himself only when he can have the benefit of someone else's hardheaded judgment. The Gospel, when it confers selfhood upon man, insists that a realistic self-judgment, the mirror of divine judgment, is part of that selfhood. He will accept himself as a creature of ambivalent talents, for good or ill.

(d) *Cultural Justice*

The Gospel is never static, but sees man through his pilgrimage. Hence each increment of salvation, at the very moment it is achieved, is already in course of becoming less than enough to express the promise that still lies ahead. There is a certain recapitulation from higher ground of each older ingredient of salvation. Once the goals of bare order, community, and self-identity have been achieved, men begin to yearn for new dimensions of wholeness and they insist that their culture now begin to include them as a matter of justice. The movement, then, is next to "cultural justice."

The editor of a college newspaper interviewed in *Look* summed up this restless movement forward, so that the urgent goals of the fathers are taken for granted and newer, more culturally ambitious goals come forward instead:[16]

> Most of our parents grew up in the Depression, and they were really hurting. They are concerned with money, status, and they're very insecure. Most of us, on the contrary, grew up in the most abundant

society the world's ever seen. And to us, abundance and all the trappings isn't something to work for because you have it. You're used to it, it's nothing. So you start getting into human values because you've gone beyond the security thing.

Only when men achieve a bit of freedom from nature and from anarchy ("order") do they begin to emerge from tribal preconsciousness and begin to act as men in communication, and as selves. But once they begin to act in these ways, they become dissatisfied with the order that originally freed them. They find this old order lacking in cultural possibilities and in justice. It did suffice to pry them out of tribal suspension. But it is no longer adequate to express the secret new depths of existential awareness or the ever-refined yearning for mutuality. It does not express the renewed sense of justice that wants not only to give the barest minimum, but wants to engage the whole of humanity in the experience of civilization. In short, once the movement from order through mutuality to self-identity has been realized, there is a reflexive falling back upon order and a demand for a new order implementing the kind of cultural justice that can take account of the newly won visions.

With the new demands upon society that are emerging out of our contemporary revolutions, we are already facing the need to redesign our received concept of order. It must be taken from now on no longer primarily as a form of political arrangement and policing and industrial technology, but as a new enabler of participation in culture. Every self from now on, it will be insisted by coming revolutionaries, will be entitled not just to sustenance, not just to a policed community, but to all of the media of culture and justice—the perquisites of education, economic power, and leisure. The goal is no longer the establishing of minima—barely equal treatment of persons before the law, for example. The youth revolt, the sex upheaval, the civil rights revolution, will enter new permutations and combinations that will demand the right to dispose of space for all minorities: not just the right to attend unsegregated schools or to join white middle-class males in voting or even in governing. What will be demanded is a new humane politics; access to quality education that will equip students for higher learning, leisure, and meaningful employment; and the freedom to diverge from a mass society's norms in taste, dress, ideas, and beliefs.

At this point, we can descry a possible new *ancien régime* resisting the revolution in cultural justice. The present-day revolutionary elements, stressing such *personal* causes as mutuality and selfhood, could conceivably become the reactionaries in a new era, for the next round of cultural justice must be one based on cybernetics and automation, the kind of *communal* effort that will create leisure time, provide economic resources to all, and free us from the worst blight of our cities. "More and more," predicts Daniel Bell, "we are becoming a 'communal society' in which the public sector has a greater importance and in which the goods and services of the society—those affecting cities, education, medical care, and the environment—will increasingly have to be purchased jointly."[17] The implications for theology and ethics may be bluntly stated. In an age when the values we yearn for must come in large part from social and technical work, Richardson observes, "theology must develop new ethical principles which will enable men to live in harmony with the new impersonal mechanisms of mass society."[18]

Theologically speaking, the movement toward cultural justice must reject both the "conformist" and "self-appointment" styles of American manners that we explored in Chapter III. What is called for is not simply a new notion of society that can both act corporately and also provide for individual expression: our present society already does that, even if very imperfectly. What is called for is a new notion of ethics that sees how both person and society are dependent on technology. But even that is not enough. Once we introduce into ethics the positive effects of technology, we need for balance the opposite and equal truth that we are part of nature, a fact that technology sometimes hides from us. What is called for, in short, is a reintroduction of the biblical notion of creation into ethical thinking.

(e) *A New Sense of Space*

So far we have attempted to give a rough approximation of four benchmarks for appraising the quality of human space if the Gospel promise to man is realized. There is yet one benchmark missing.

Without it we are inevitably misled in our appraisal of the reorganizing work on space that man is called upon to perform. This missing benchmark is one that sets the other four—from order, through mutuality and selfhood, to cultural justice—into perspective. Communal space never provides fully for human wholeness if it is organized on the basis of rising expectations alone. Rather wholeness ultimately is engendered only when the space is open enough to allow for the *unexpected.*

Let us take a homely example. There are people who move quite successfully toward a more satisfactory conception of "eating out" by moving from one hamburger chain to another, finding more pleasing or nutritious hamburgers along the way. But that search, however successfully pursued, is not capable within its own structure of enabling a breakthrough to higher forms of dining than American short-order cuisine. Only the blinding transcendence of a trip to Europe, say, can introduce them to new orders of eating.

Similarly, the Gospel insists that cultural conceptions of wholeness, particularly as they are contained within the value system of a given greater community, do not finally deliver us. They may sustain life at a satisfactory level, to be sure, and even afford upward reaches. But if these values are clutched as the only values—they lose their value.

Let us take, by way of example, the enhancement of "life" that has come in the space of the American greater community, with its political stress on the person and its technological skill in caring for men. On the level of the ordinary meaning of symbols, the "pursuit of happiness" (our chief salvific myth) suggests that the goal should be to acquire as much freedom, affluence, justice, friendship, and so on as achievement holds possible. But the Christian faith, while accepting these values for the short run, poses a countervailing symbol. The pursuit of happiness, it says, is finally to be understood not as achievement or the fulfillment of aspirations. It comes by a reversal of the signs, a change, a turning upside down, a turning loose of what once we thought must be clutched with all our might. It is the overriding of expectations with the arrival of the unexpected. It is the transformation of the older sense of life with its anticipation of predictable wholeness into a new sense of life that is different from what we had first thought it would be.

We can make our point concisely in three summary statements:

1. Life is best defined as that good of the *neighbor's* that is to be fought for. The goal of revolution, finally, is not in seeing that one has advantages for himself, but in seeing that revolutionary gains accrue to the neighbor.

2. Life is best defined not as a biological span nor even as fully realized by living. The Gospel speaks of finding one's life by losing it. That is a way of speaking of the discovery of the unexpected—that the existence of man is characterized by faith rather than by literal viability.

3. Life is best defined as that system of transactions that leaves a certain kind of openness, a kind of openness that the Gospel calls forgiveness; but if that seems too personal a term, let us call it reciprocal acceptance without conditions.

The fifth benchmark then puts a new interpretation on the meaning of "space disposition." We have been arguing throughout this study in public ethics that the very heart of the human condition is the will to overthrow extrinsic control of one's space and to dispose of one's own space. We apply this description both to personal and to communal space. We have defined the very meaning of morality in the Western world as this will to dispose of one's own space. And we have insisted that however symbolic our thinking must be when we speak of salvation, the symbol of salvific space uses and builds on the ordinary meaning of space, space in the three-dimensional sense. The middle-class mother is less likely to mistreat her children, among other reasons, simply because she has more space—larger rooms, a yard—than the ghetto mother. A child has a better chance of finding himself as a person when he reaches adolescence if he has a room, or at least a bed, of his own. A community offers more prospect of humanity if the company does not own all of the houses in it. A nation offers more political blessings to its people, we believe, if the people can choose their own rulers.

The Gospel speaks to a space-disposing people not by suggesting that they cease to be what they are, but that they become *more* what they are. One has fully overthrown extrinsic control of his own space only when he has relaxed his own anxious grip on it. The salvific form of space disposal is not sequestering space for oneself, putting it under lock and key, but making it *available*. Only shared space, the Gospel teaches, is finally disposable space.

One normative undertaking yet remains. We have spoken, in the last chapter, of the temporal criteria of revolution in a republic, and in this chapter, of the spatial benchmarks of reorganized community. Now we need to turn to the theological criteria that we can bring to the task of appraising the *quality* of republican action. What are the norms for testing "willed initiative"?

CHAPTER VII

HOPES

A dozen men marched up to a piece of public property and announced their intention of staying there until they had won their point. They weren't conducting a sit-in demonstration, although it might be accurate enough to call it a "dig-in." For they had their shovels with them, and they set about preparing this land for growing crops.

These demonstrators, all landless men of England, had grown impatient with the promises they had heard. The lawmakers of the country had said they would do something about increasing freedom for the common people and improving the lot of those who had been left out of things. There had even been a revolution in the country— but, as often happens, the gains didn't spread to all the people. So these single-minded men with their spades now planned to employ direct action to "make good their natural right to use the earth and enjoy its fruits."

Some of their slogans sound familiar to us. They rejected the use of violence and arms, for "freedom is not won . . . by sword or gun." Instead, they would face their enemies and "conquer them by love." They had faith that they could, by these means, establish a new community. As we might expect, these men drew the active opposition of the power structure of the day. By turns the landed gentry, the lawyers, and the clergy all had at them. Finally the government itself took measures. There weren't any fire hoses or police dogs, but there were formidable troops of horse soldiers, and these were sent out in two waves to repel the diggers, who were subsequently hailed into court. Leading men in the country also joined in the harassment,

288

employing what we today would call "bouncers" to break up the digging demonstrations. Yet the movement went on.

The leader of this movement, Gerard Winstanely, preached his views all over the country. Though he was aware that self-satisfied religious people were his worst enemies, yet he himself based his whole program squarely on religious faith, quoted the Bible more than any other book, and drew his strength and sense of direction from what he thought he heard God telling him. Here are some of his principles:

"Work together; eat bread together; declare all this abroad."

"Whosoever labours the earth for any person or persons, that are lifted up to rule over others, and doth not look upon themselves as equal to others in the creation: the hand of the Lord shall be upon that labourer. . . ."[1] In other words, he suggests to the disadvantaged, don't go on letting people think you are happy with the way things are. Men are created by God as equals and partners. Gross inequality degrades men, gives those who must submit to it a false sense of inferiority and dejection.

Winstanely not only led demonstrations, but also called for a kind of boycott or noncooperation, although those names for such actions hadn't yet been coined. He asked workers to withdraw from their jobs in the expectation that "Christ, or the spreading power of light," will be pointed to by this action, and that "community" might be realized without resort to the sword.

Finally, he delivers himself of a dramatic and penetrating criticism of self-satisfied religion, which can only perpetuate injustice: dead religion can be, Winstanely says,[2]

> . . . a cloak of policy by the subtle elder brother to cheat his simple younger brother of the freedoms of the earth. For saith the elder brother, "The earth is mine, and not yours, brother; . . . and you must not take the fruits of it, . . . for it you should do otherwise, God will not love you, and you shall not go to heaven when you die, but the devil will have you. . . ."
>
> Well, the younger brother . . . is terrified, and lets go his hold in the earth, and submits himself to be a slave to his brother for fear of damnation in hell after death, and in hopes to get heaven thereby after he is dead; . . .

So that this . . . doctrine is a cheat; for while men are gazing up to heaven, imagining after a happiness, or fearing a hell after they are dead, their eyes are put out that they see not what is in their birthrights, and what is to be done by them here on earth. . . .

1. Ordeal of the Levellers

This nonviolent movement took place in 1649, well over three hundred years ago. It was one part of the tumultous religious and political revolution in England that eventually ushered in a new freedom of worship, and made notable gains in the direction of broader democratic rights. The Diggers, as it happened, were one of the more radical groups, with their early communism and their proposed land reforms—which didn't succeed of adoption. But the protest of the Diggers emerged out of a more general movement—that of the "Levellers"—which really did succeed in getting some new planks of freedom and democracy built into the English political system. And by the twentieth century, indeed, much of the spirit of the Diggers' program had been realized in Anglo-Saxon politics.

"What is done to anyone may be done to everyone," one of the Leveller leaders, John Lilburne, had warned. Submitting to whippings and jail, this man insisted—on grounds that he drew directly from Christian faith—on equal treatment of men before the law, on the dignity of the individual person, and on the right of conscience. Today we take it for granted that an accused in a trial may not be required to testify against himself. But this was not always a right; Lilburne had to fight for it, and we probably owe our enjoyment of this right to him. "There is good reason to believe that it is Lilburne whom we have to thank for the gradual acceptance of what our fathers have long regarded as an established English tradition." These movements—Diggers, Levellers, and others—were among the first in our tradition to raise the contagious cry for women's suffrage, extension of representative government, freedom of worship, speech, and conscience; guarantees to safeguard personal space and dignity; the right to choose one's associates and one's vocation; equality before the law.[3] These movements were thus crucial to the establishment in Western political history of those moral attributes we have been examining in this study—the refusal to accept extrinsic control, the insistence upon a shared vision of community space, and the claim, above all, that the promises of a new community could be realized only through willed initiative.

Our concern is not with these movements in themselves, however, or with the seventeenth century. We speak of them only as a way, in this final chapter, of raising critical questions about our own greater community and its manners and morals. If the modern cause of space disposition was infectiously introduced into political history by these seventeenth-century movements, what of the possibilities for a new breakthrough in our own time and space? If human promise as we have conceived of it was introduced even in a fragmentary way by political implications of the work of the Levellers and Diggers and other such groups, might it not be realized anew by the men of our own time?

We could ask this question even if we were taking only a rationalist's or social scientist's view of the work of the seventeenth-century sectarian groups, holding that "Their primary principle was a belief in the inevitable, ultimately relentless power of ideas, of man's response to reason and persuasion."[4] In this case we could go on to ask whether ideas, reason, and persuasion can become the agencies of human promise once again, in our own time and space of misused initiative and relapse into moral crisis. We choose to go on to a more theological form of the question, however, and to ask whether we may hope for political realization of the biblical promise of man's dignity and equality. For that was the form of the question as it was posed by men like Winstanely and Lilburne, who drew their visions from biblical sources, yet managed to give political substance to their theological visions. These men inserted themselves into the rough and tumble of the English politics of their day. They became thoroughly involved in the tumult of a class war in an unjust culture. Some even served in Cromwell's Army. Yet, at bottom, they spoke for one of the promises of the Gospel: that man's temporal future rests upon his overthrowing extrinsic control of his personal and communal space, and upon his sharing this space with his fellows, and upon his acting for dignity and equality.

Here is our question, then: does the human promise partially realized in the past continue to unfold in the twentieth century? We are especially aware of new obstacles to its unfolding. Much of what happens to every citizen in a technical society happens apparently without his consent or initiative. Even worse, where there is initiative, it is directed toward the mediocrities of industrial produce: we are consumed with consumption of goods. This sport and obsession seemingly takes all our energies at times, all our wills, all our passion. Besides all that, what really damages republican prospects is that deep moral problems—unjustness in realizing the benefits of space— continue to exist, and continue to be ignored. At times these disparities are not even ignored, but are advocated outright by the present possessors of existential space.

Does the human promise partly realized in the past have a chance to continue to unfold, especially when it has seemingly run aground on such factors as the barriers that continue to separate races? Does the Gospel offer the same basis of hope to the minority world today that it did to the disinherited whites of England and America three centuries ago? Who is right today, the prophet of hope who sees in the ordeal of the Levellers a basis for new hope that ought to prevail in the republic and the world today? Or the grim realist who insists that the color bar is insurmountable; that the successive entry of ethnic groups into the benefits (and, let us face it, the mediocrities) of American culture has come to an end, and that the twentieth century, as exemplified in the contemporary American greater community, offers only the prospect of racial strife and frustrated hopes?

I wish to make the case for the continued liveliness of the human hope, despite the conflict and partial failure that is involved in every realization of it, and for the theological understanding that is the most profound basis of the human promise.

Let us proceed first by subjecting willed initiative to a theological appraisal, then by considering the ambiguous role of religion in a republic.

2. A Theological Appraisal of Willed Initiative

The American moral tradition, as we have seen, is an amalgam of many strains and elements, but two of them stand out: the republican view of morality—with its revolutionary urge, bias toward political equality, and reliance on willed initiative on the part of the citizen; and the "Christian" (in fact chiefly Puritan) view of morality—with its revivalism, bias toward "cordial union" or community of the regenerate, and reliance on "consent to being," or on a will that is turned toward God and being not because of its own initiative but rather because of God's turning it.

These two currents, the republican and the Puritan, have sometimes been nearly merged, sometimes in conflict. Heimert thinks they were very closely intertwined from the Great Awakening to the Revolution and down to the beginning of the nineteenth century. In the years after 1801, he believes, the two forces of religion and politics "evolved as separate, and by no means equal, competitors for the interest and allegiance of the American mind." In terms of visible outcomes, one stream flowed toward the nineteenth-century revival, the other toward Jeffersonian and Jacksonian democracy.[5]

Our own view is that an overriding "American moral tradition" has been constituted out of these streams, employing a generalized, dechristologized theology from the Puritan tradition, and retaining many of the Christian saving symbols, but taking over the republican categories of morality. From the Puritan side there is the Christian God, even a God of three persons—Father, Son, and Spirit—but the Son has been deprived of his orthodox status as Redeemer, understood as Mediator between God and man. The reasons are twofold. First, the classical doctrine of the Trinity is intellectually unintelligible in America. Second, and far more important, this doctrine shares the fate of other European saving symbols that have sunk into impotency in America: the salvation problem is of a different order from that which Trinitarian thought served. In America the problem is not to have unworthy man evened up or pardoned as a preliminary to reacceptance by God. *Homo Americanus* is neither innocent nor perfect, but that does not mean he is unworthy. For he is more than able to even up this sort of account himself, in that his achievements in space disposition far override his mistakes and errors. The American salvation problem does not call for the ministrations of a God-man in the antique sense, then, and thus no classical doctrine of the Trinity is necessary. The American salvation problem has to do with our failure *so far* to do enough, and with our temptations to stop pushing ahead, and with our occasional perverse movement backward instead of forward as we reorganize community space. The American salvation problem is to surmount crisis and predicament in our vision of reorganizing our world, crisis and predicament that formally shows itself as extrinsic control of existential and communal space. And the remedy, as we have seen, is "willed initiative."

This means that Christ as Redeemer before God has been replaced in American public religion by the community as divine agent taking the initiative. Christology has become a communal idea, although it has not merged with the third person of the Godhead, the Holy Spirit, which is also within the community. For these two persons of the Trinity are the saving symbols that ultimately define the two foci of willed initiative: the active, initiating quality, and the inner, dispositional quality.

Thus the traditional Christian symbols, much transmuted in some respects, have entered the stream of the general American religion and of the American moral tradition. The Christian influence is more visible not so much in the form of specific symbols, however, as in the form of reinforcement of the "natural tendencies" of the ethos: Certainly the Puritan spirit of zealous, industrious response by a sort of creative, improvising readiness to do the will of God has found resonance with the secular trait of activism.

In mood and common-sense assumptions about man's responsibilities, then, the republican morality has had the upper hand over the specifically Christian view. Above all, the republican insistence on autonomy, independence, maturity, and initiative has successfully battled against the ancient Christian view, given a respectable place in doctrine by the Puritans, that human activity, to be worthwhile, must be turned about by the supervening will of God. The republican notion of willed initiative—really a strong doctrine of free will or "Arminianism," in the scornful epithet of the Puritans—has triumphed over that other view of the will, classically delineated by Jonathan Edwards, that a right heart, the ability to join in cordial union with one's fellows, and in fact all the higher forms of virtue, depend quite straightforwardly on a *determined* will.

For Edwards, the notion of the determination of the will by divine grace did not carry the draconian implications we give it (or that his opponents gave it). When he insisted that the only truly free will was one that had been determined by God's having inclined us this way instead of that, he did not mean that God coerces man against his will. Rather, Edwards was saying that human excellence is a reflection of divine excellence, and that man becomes his best self, and finds himself mostly heartily in concert with being, when his heart has been infected with the very excellence of God himself. When we do not have the sensing of God within us, we are stuck with our old selves, our worst selves: we are unfree.

Edwards was saying very much what a line of profound theologians before him had said—Augustine, Luther, Calvin, and many others. But in America, it was the kind of thing that only a genius like Edwards could get away with. For the countervailing view of the republican morality—that man is able to display excellence already without special intervention—proved irresistible. Human ability was going to be taken in America as the warrant, sign, and seal in itself of God's having entrusted man with representing him. Even Edwards' devoted followers—Hopkins and Bellamy, say—had difficulty maintaining the Edwardean insights about human ability. They repeated Edwards' formulas without always sharing his sense of the shared excellence that they promised between God and man. For Bellamy, for example, God is not so much the fountain of excellence whose qualities flow to man and are reflected in the human heart—that was Edwards' God. Bellamy's God is something of a superterrestrial monarch, in whom ontological excellence is replaced by refulgent sovereignty. As the years went on, the New Haven theologians had to tinker more and more with the Edwardean teachings on the will, and more and more they had to yield to the pressures of the American ethos. By the middle of the nineteenth century, the house of Puritanism was in wide disarray, and many of the children of New England, and their theologians, too, were abandoning the Edwardean view of man's inability in favor of the republican assumptions about man's initiative. Indeed, they had long since made this switch in their everyday world and in their common-sense assumptions about morality. Now they were doing it in their theology.

In our day, whatever the creeds of the American churches may say in writing, the older sense of man as dependent on God for a right will has to all intents and purposes been lost. The American moral tradition stresses, almost without dissent, the straight republican doctrine of willed initiative: that man in himself is capable, without decisive divine intervention, of willing and acting for the commonwealth—or rather that his willing and acting *already* represent divine intervention.

This notion of freedom is found in its most self-conscious and assertive form in the American subtradition that we loosely call "radicalism," with its roots in abolitionism and various dissent movements. It is worth our while, then, to glance at Staughton Lynd's recent summary of this tradition:[6]

> . . . The proper foundation for government is a universal law of right and wrong self-evident to the intuitive common sense of every man; . . . freedom is a power of personal self-direction which no man can delegate to another; . . . Radicalism thrust toward the conclusions that true freedom was incapable of delegation, and that what was inalienable was what could not become a commodity. At heart the controversy was between two definitions of freedom: on the one hand, freedom defined as control over the finished products of human activity; on the other hand, freedom defined as self-determining human activity itself. . . . Like the mind's quest for religious truth from which it was derived, self-determination was not a claim to ownership which might be both acquired and surrendered, but an inextricable aspect of the activity of being human.

Clearly, this view of freedom agrees in very large part with just the kind of outlook that we have been describing as "salvific" in this study. For it comes close to what we have been calling "willed initiative." And yet, as we have repeatedly seen, "free will" does not always seem to save us. All too often, as we have found, self-determining freedom itself relapses to the status of a creed—this time a republican instead of a theological creed, but just as unrealized. For Americans are in fact "determined" in much of their lives by the trivial, by the plans of the industrial system, and by other unsalvific agencies of dominion over them. Our freedom, in short, is not used to govern, to clear out the space, and rid ourselves of the new despots that reign.

Willed initiative, especially in the self-conscious, almost ferocious variant of self-determination that it takes in Lynd's formulation, cannot be a healthy doctrine *standing alone*. But here we are saying no more than we have just said, in the last two chapters, about the other attributes of republican morality. We found good reason to join up the republican idea of *revolution* with some theological criteria drawn from the American *revival* experience. Then we found it necessary to qualify the republican view of *space disposition* by setting alongside it some countering "benchmarks" from the Christian *Gospel*. The time has come to say the same thing about willed initiative. It is an inadequate notion if it stands without dialectical criticism, if it stands as a single-valued, flat assertion of the utter completeness of human self-determination.

Indeed, we find just grounds for this kind of criticism in republican theory itself. Montesquieu, let us recall, had spoken realistically of the difficulty of manifesting willed initiative. He voiced grave doubts that a people could carry it through without failing in some ways, maybe in fatal ways. Above all, he thought that one comes to consciousness of his calling as a citizen through a kind of "conversion" —a surprising parallel to Jonathan Edwards' insistence upon changed inclinations as the basis of virtue. For Montesquieu, and here let us go back to his own word and translate it literally, *la vertu* or virtue, that quality of love of country upon which the chances for a republic rest, was in effect a conversion of the self from lesser commitments to full-fledged loyalty. Not even this cautionary note about human ability, much less radical a demand than orthodox Christian views of conversion, has been retained in contemporary understandings of willed initiative: we have forgotten even how to talk, in public life, about the *quality* of public initiative, motives, and actions.

What is needed is a dialectical, countering theological symbol to say something anew to man about the nature and destiny of his freedom. In one sense he is free to do anything he pleases. In another sense he falls into straitest prison of all if he does not use his freedom to further the freedom of the spaces around him and to make these spaces, in ultimate intention, literally godlike. What is needed is a sensitive contemporary analogue of Jonathan Edwards' view of human excellence as a reflection of divine excellence. Let us not return to Edwards' specific formulation of the symbol as a "determined will." That way of uttering the symbol has long since been doomed in America, as have all other ways that speak of man as a dependent, order-taking being, virtuous only in dogged obedience to some extrinsic authority. But are those classical European ways of speaking of the divine the only ways open to us? We have already suggested that in America the older view of the Trinity was dismantled in public religion, to be replaced by the view that the community is the new locus of God's transforming work, the new community in its own transformation of space, when the latter offers men access to each other and to the wonders of being. Furthermore, this community evinces in its own passions and commitments, when these are inclined toward willing such activities, the Holy Spirit. Thus the community, when its activities and passions do tend toward reworking space for the benefit of neighbors and for the end of letting being come out into the open, can be understood as expressing the glory of God. And in that enterprise human beings become *agents,* in the fullest and most original sense of the term, rather than wards.

These are the dimensions of willed initiative that should be supplied by the countervailing potency of *religious* affirmations. There is nothing inherently wrong with the American insistence on seeing all of reality through action, achievement, and even aggressiveness if these elements are understood as divine commissions to make the world just, exciting, and excellent—and if they are criticized by such standards.

The real question before us, then, is not quite about willed initiative in itself, but about the ability of the religious forces in America to hold up their share of the joint venture of public morality, in which they are a partner along with the republican and secular component. Does religion nowadays have the stuff, the fiber, the imagination, the talent, to furnish its share of saving symbols to the common moral quest? Perry Miller reminds us that in the formative American mind, the end of perfecting the community is to be attained through two works—"the machinery of the Revival and that of the factory."[27] He notices how often the word "sublime" was thought—often justly—to be the very word to describe technological achievements in America. In the great revivals, the religious path to excellence also had its moments of truth. But what about today? Religion does not notably achieve sublimity or excellence in our time. Whatever we must say about the mediocrity of the industrial climate, too, we have to add that the new technology has reachieved excellence and even sublimity in some of its moments, as when the first Surveyor space vehicle landed on the moon and began flashing detailed photographs back to earth. A scientist who had taken part in this project tried to explain its meaning, *Newsweek* reports, while his wife, overcome with emotion, listened in tears. "In a man's life," he said, "there are so few opportunities to be in on something really great. I pity the people who never get the chance."[8] Here, on the technological side of space transformation, there can still be found ecstasy, excellence, the full equivalent of what Edwards called "the religious affections" in the technological sphere. Can religion in our day contribute its own symbols and passions in parity?

3. The Ambiguous Role of Religion in a Republic

Theology has been through a recent phase of imagining that the Gospel should or can be proclaimed without the help of religion. That, in fact, has been a tendency in a long line of recent theologians, beginning in a way with Karl Barth himself, taking on new life with Bonhoeffer and running down to the influential work by Harvey Cox, *The Secular City*.

Fortunately, a more sensible countercurrent has now set in among American theologians. Theological symbols can no more be nourished without a religious community than medicine can be practiced without medical centers, or law without courts. The problem is not religion per se, but bad religion. No one thinks we should abandon our technological enterprise—even if we could—simply because it tempts us in the direction of mediocrity. Just so, we shouldn't turn our backs on religion, even if we could, simply because it is so often shockingly prosaic and tasteless and timid.

"The scandal of the Bible," says one younger American theologian, rejecting the program of the "secular" theologians, "is that God allies himself with religion in all of its existential ambiguity."[9] He goes on to argue that the Gospel may neither be proclaimed in a nonreligious fashion, as the secular theologians wanted, nor be understood (with older liberalism and such moderns as Paul Tillich) as *essentially* religious. Rather the Gospel lives off both elements. Men must live perennially in a world that is part religious in its essence, part secular. The secular city is only the new home of *homo religiosus,* who has already filled it with rituals (celebrity worship, for example), priests (the doctor), and temples (the drugstore).

This view about religion, then, corresponds to our dialectical view of public morality, in which we have already affirmed the need for the republican symbols of revolution, community, and action to be appraised and qualified by theological symbols. Now, we go on to say, this dual source of symbols implies the permanent need for nourishing communities, and in the case of the theological symbols we must affirm the permanent relevance of American religious communities.

Doubtless our view implies a new role for religion in the country. In the first place, we are saying that religion needs to be set within the strongly dominant framework of the national or greater community. The most important horizon for thinking about theology and ethics is now the greater community, and beyond that, the international community, rather than the older communities of denominationalism. Once Christian theology could proceed in this country by taking its main thought behind the relatively confining walls represented by our diverse sectarian communions. Thus Lutherans, Baptists, and Catholics could find coherence by thinking as Lutherans, Baptists, or Catholics. Now the bonds of denominational systems are much weaker, and the awareness of national crisis calling for moral and ethical response is much greater. So the field upon which the religious symbols are to be projected has become ecumenical and national, and we are increasingly aware of the common venture between religion and republican forces in forging and realizing a broad "American moral tradition." But when all that is said and done, we still need a specifically religious sector where the religious symbols are refreshed, rethought, refitted. Religion is the sector in which men without apology still ponder the relation between the republican "pursuit of happiness" and the Puritan "glory of God." In the religious sector, men who believe in both secular commonwealth and Kingdom of God must deliberate anew all of the old questions, now with the cybernetics age in view: church versus society as locus of salvation; Christian virtues versus public spiritedness as style of living; love versus justice as norm; disposition versus act as bearer of the ethical; conflict versus identity as mode of relating church to state. Out of this reflection, let us hope, will come religious practices, images, and principles of interpretation that will help men to "respond to the divine activity in the secular."

Another need is for theologians to make closer contact with the religious forces of the country. This does not mean that prophetic-minded thinkers must endorse the implicit racism and indifference of most of the churches. There is ample opportunity in a healthy relationship for criticism. American theology, I am saying, will turn out in the end to be a much more potent force both in criticizing religion and in criticizing republican governance if its own theological views, however daring and radical, are built up out of the indigenous American religious ethos and mentality. The most recent theological movement in this country, neo-orthodoxy, failed here because its reaffirmations of tradition were reaffirmations of an *extrinsic* tradition, which made little attempt to link up with the analogous American tradition (including a wealth of possibilities in Puritanism alone, but including a number of other "Americanized" Reformation and post-Reformation strands). Neo-orthodoxy, in sociological terms, failed because its attempts to reinstate the tradition did not find confirmation in a supporting community of faith—a subsocietal sectarian affirmation of the sort that was readily available to neo-orthodox dogmaticians in Europe. That factor itself, Peter Berger suggests, had much to do with the shift to secular theology.[10] A middle ground is there for us, I say. Rather than offering an extraneous European symbol set (which some of our theologians are still valiantly attempting) and, when that fails, adopting the opposite strategy of dropping "religious" proclamation altogether in favor of secular theology, I propose that American theology cultivate the extant American religious tradition, which has a respectable past, at least, and is not wholly disgraced at present.

What is required is the recognition in principle that both republican morality and religious morality are ambiguous, and that prophecy, cleansing, and forward movement are best promised if the two entities are held together dialectically, which means taking both of them seriously.

If religious faith is then relevant to the interpretation of human destiny, as I have been maintaining, we must keep in mind that this promise is as a rule to be found ensconced within ambiguity. There is no power on earth potentially so revolutionary as belief in the divine promise for man. There is no power on earth potentially so reactionary as complacent religion. Let us recur for a moment to the Diggers, with whom we started this chapter. They based their movement on the Gospel as they saw it. The Levellers proceeded from the conviction that "so far as Christ is in us, we shall . . . honour . . . the least particle of his image in others"[11]—an early and revealing statement about the origin of the political notion of equality. Thrust as a firebrand into the stream of Western social turmoil, the Judaeo-Christian faith has time after time produced this kind of burning purpose and depth of involvement. Men of faith will affirm that it can and is doing so today. Yet the Diggers and Levellers faced, above all, the entrenched apathy and even hostility of much of organized religion, particularly on the part of the self-satisfied who already enjoyed the rights and privileges that new faces were now demanding for themselves. The same is true today.

Religion, then, can serve revolutionary justice. At the same time, we have to see that it is often a perversion of these same religious roots and ethical standards in the minds and hearts of the unconcerned that forms the chief barrier. There is no such thing as a neutral role for religion and morality in this struggle. We cannot leave them out of account. We either have to claim them for the side of the unfolding promise, or let their power go distorted to run the engines of racism, tyranny, despotism.

(a) *American Religion as Barrier to Promise*

Once when he was considerably younger, the novelist James Baldwin was an enthusiastic churchman. He was even something of a preacher, as he recounts these days of his life in *The Fire Next Time*. He knew what it was to stand before a congregation and invoke spirit and fire. By and by, though, the illusion crumbled. Young Baldwin awakened to the realities. Take all the talk of salvation in heaven as a reward for the travail and privations of this life: in America too much talk of salvation as a reward for travail only perpetuates the suffering of the black man. If God was a God of all men, and not just of the whites, then why were the blacks cast down so far and kept that way?

"When I faced a congregation," Baldwin recalls, "it began to take all the strength I had not to stammer, not to curse, not to tell them to throw away their Bibles and get off their knees and go home and organize, for example, a rent strike."[12] Religion, it turned out, was a pain-killer. Some of his friends escaped, or tried to, by entering military service, others by moving to other cities ("that is, to other ghettos"). "Some went on wine or whiskey or the needle, and are still on it. And others, like me, fled into the church."[13]

The Black Muslims cashed in on Christianity's failure. This movement naturally impressed the later, demythologized Baldwin, especially in the things it showed it could do for the black man, things that "generations of welfare workers and committees and resolutions and reports . . . have failed to do: to heal and redeem drunkards and junkies, to convert people who have come out of prison and to keep them out, to make men chaste and women virtuous, . . ."[14]

"Things are as bad as the Muslims say they are," Baldwin goes on. "In fact, they are worse." But in the end, he cannot find a final solution in Black Islam, either. Unlike Elijah Muhammad, Baldwin does not count it wicked for white and black to seek intercommunication (sometimes he doubts that it is possible, and again he says it is the only hope for any of us). What is worse, Baldwin thinks, the Muslim movement omits seeing the black man as a constitutent part of America; that is its falseness. The black man in America must learn to accept himself and his past as a part of this land and its traditions (including, we might say, the long tradition of revolution that should offer sustenance to him today). He must learn who he is, not try to lose himself in an artificial ethos, which Black Islam can well be. "I am very much concerned that American Negroes achieve their freedom here in the United States," he sums up.[15] Still, the Black Muslims' bill of complaint is mostly accurate.

Becoming part of America, however, doesn't mean for Baldwin striving for the level of the white-dominated society that has passed for America. "White people cannot, in the generality, be taken as models of how to live." What do black men want, anyway? At one level, they "simply don't wish to be beaten over the head by the whites every instant. . . ." But men, as such, want something more than that. They want to learn respect and care for each other. If white and black in America could learn that, then, America could realize her promise for this time.[16] But there are barriers, and one of them is dead and perverse religion. Baldwin's critique of such religion and his plea for countervalues remind us, in short, of the stances of Gerard Winstanely and John Lilburne.

Bad religion comes in two forms, as an opiate for the oppressed, and as a kind of artificial environment for the oppressor, justifying him and shielding him from reality. If Baldwin has helped us to see a contemporary manifestation of the first, I can point to a case of the second, for I grew up amidst it.

The South is in a sense more "religious" than other sections. By this I mean that religious faith, especially evangelical Christianity, is far more firmly rooted here than in, let us say, the urban centers of the Northeast. But religion, too, can be misused and pressed into the service of a hard and stubborn heart. When religion is used to build walls between men, then men of such religion are not near to God, as they deceive themselves into believing, but they are very far from him. The religion of the Hebrew Bible and the New Testament is not a tranquilizing kind of religion that says we never have to make any changes in our lives. God called Abraham to pull up stakes and move, God called the Israelites to make the painful effort to leave Egypt, God called the early Christians to take the agonizing step of changing their favorite religious customs and habits, God called on Peter to swallow his pride and learn to eat with strangers to his way of life.[17]

And the contemporary South is still well populated with Christians who think God would never dream of making such demands on his people.

(b) Answer: The Positive Role of Faith

If religion can encrust itself as such a barrier to the unfolding human promise, why not drop it altogether, as many of the secular-

minded have long urged? My answer is that the best rebuke (and
ultimately the only cure) for self-righteous religion is critical faith.
No one delivers more crushing blows to false piety than the Hebrew
prophets. No one offers more scathing reproaches to religious abuse
than Martin Luther, more penetrating censure of an unjust establishment than John Lilburne, more politically potent rebuffs to dead
theology than Martin Luther King, Jr. The decade of the nonviolent
movement's shaking of the South (1955-1964) already illustrates
what I want to say—that spirited religion and the moral stance drawn
from it overcome the barrier erected by pseudo-religion and begin to
make room for the human promise. "We have to start out," says the
Rev. Kelly Miller Smith, a civil rights leader in my own community,
"on the basic premise that everybody is a member of the same human
family, and that God created us all."[18] To make that promise real in
society, changes must come. Critical faith gets into the mainstream of
society and pushes for the changes.

Bur religious and ethical forces, as critical elements in the struggle
for the human promise, also have two positive roles to play.

First, the Gospel in our day reinforces among both men and nations the notions of self-respect, independence, selfhood (and "nationhood"). This thrust leads, invariably, to a "breakdown in communication" in domestic race relations and a rash of "nationalistic"
outcroppings, as in the new African and Asian countries. It is well to
view both developments as the necessary assertion of dignity or space-
claiming that must come before each self or nation can take part in a
larger community.

The Judaeo-Christian tradition tells men who they are as its first
order of business, not as something left over. In 1646 the Leveller
Richard Overton wrote a treatise from prison where Cromwell had
clapped him. It was entitled: AN ARROW AGAINST ALL TYRANTS AND
TYRANNY, SHOT FROM THE PRISON OF NEWGATE INTO THE PREROGA-
TIVE BOWELS OF THE ARBITRARY HOUSE OF LORDS AND ALL OTHER
USURPERS AND TYRANTS WHATSOEVER. What one man may not yield
up to another, Overton argues, is his "selfe propriety," his properness
to himself, his individuality. His statement is worth quoting at some
length:[19]

To every Individuall in nature is given   an individual property by nature, not to be invaded or usurped by any. . . . No man hath power
over my rights and liberties, and I over no mans; I may be but an
Individuall, enjoy my selfe, and my selfe propriety, and may write my
selfe no more then my selfe, or presume any further; if I doe, I am an
encroacher & an invader upon an other Mans Right. . . . For by
naturall birth, all men are equally and alike borne to like propriety,
liberty, and freedome, and as we are delivered of God by the hand of
nature into this world, every one with a naturall, innate freedome, and
propriety (as it were writ in the table of every mans heart, never to be
obliterated) even so are we to live, every one equally and alike to enjoy
his Birth-right and priviledge.

That same arrow stings today when James Baldwin writes that
what black men want is not acceptance and still less love from whites;
what they want is to be left to define themselves: "they, the black,
simply don't wish to be beaten over the head by the whites every
instant of our brief passage on this planet. . . . I did not intend to
allow the white people of this country to tell me who I was, . . ."[20]
That same arrow stings when youth in West Africa ask, " 'Is it
African? . . . Does it give them a status of equality with the rest of the
world?' "[21] They are asking, without always knowing it in Western-
Christian terms, of course, for one of the ingredients of the Gospel
missing from the makeup of part of mankind today: the ingredient of
self-propriety.

Second, the Gospel does not view the emergence of selfhood as a
thing in itself (which is a tendency of the contemporary radical
movement, noticeable in the views of Staughton Lynd cited above, for
example). Rather it views selfhood against the background of emergent community. The Judaeo-Christian faith, considering that man
finds himself in history and in course of a pilgrimage toward selfhood
and community, gives some hints about how to live together while we
are realizing our promise. This is where the field of Christian ethics
comes into play. In the first place, as we have seen, the critical
powers latent within a live religious faith can shatter the illusion that
we have a good and righteous community when we really don't. That
is the reason the hardheaded Roger Williams was banished from
Massachusetts. He was one of the few men who had the vision to see
that the proud Puritan society of Boston wasn't exactly the City of

God, after all. A lively faith can humble the proud who have refused
to see other men as men. It can shore up the oppressed who have not
yet realized their promise. But there is a more positive ethical role to
be played. Pending the arrival of full spatial reorganization to further
shared being, Christian ethics must consider what things are to be
done to approximate brotherhood, and that opens up the whole subject of living by justice in a community that is on its way to its promise
but is far from there as yet.

Thus we gain some view of the role of religion, ambiguous as it
must be, in republican governance.

Alternatively, we can sum it up by glimpsing the role of the church,
as institution that "bears" religion, alongside two other institutions
that have contrasting roles. The role of the *technostructure* is to
perpetuate the society—give us that fundamental transcendence over
nature that enables us to think, as men, about reorganizing the space
of our communities for greater freedom and mutuality. In fact, the
technostructure plays much more than this role. It tends to dominate
us. But one of the reasons, as we have seen, is that the value-criticiz-
ing institutions of society that should speak in dialectical terms about
technology have not spoken out. One of these critical institutions is
the *university*, which shares with the church some transcendence of
the technical system, although it is to be feared that it is losing some
of this distance. The university also should stand as a critic of religion
and the church, and should offer chairs to theologians and ethicists to
engage in that task, to lead students in careful, critical inquiry into
religion, and to offer the critical views of theology and ethics on the
technostructure. The university ought to prepare us for the kind of
willed initiative in society that builds the republic. It prepares us for
voluntary association and critical love of country by educating us and
eliciting motivation for hopefulness about our possibilities. It teaches
us to solve problems, political and technological, in accordance with
the bent toward deliverance that characterizes the line of march in the
American greater community and the world. But its main task should
not be filling the officers' corps of the technostructure. There should
perhaps be "service academies" for that comparable to West Point
and Annapolis. The university should be aimed at eliciting willed
initiative among citizens of the republic.

The church should teach that the highest motivation of all, the most qualitatively demanding action of all, is that which recognizes the quality of investing one's hopes in a divine warrant and promise. It offers a level of criticism more transcendent than that of the university. It opens to us both other possible pasts than our ontic past, and new futures, those that are not tied to the desperate optimism (so often wrong) of the middle class, or the desperate pessimism (also so often wrong) of those who know themselves to be extrinsically controlled. It qualifies the vision of the ontic, extrapolated, foreseeable future with other futures built on hope.

4. Hope as the Final Criterion of Willed Initiative

The spirit in the air at the moment is one of impatience, frustration, of a desire to get on with things, to sweep aside the dead customs and arrangements that preserve injustice. At least that is the spirit among the disinherited, those who haven't yet been able to participate in the equality revolution. And I am inclined to think it is their impatience, rather than the conservatism of the rest of us, that is going to make more difference about the quality of the American future.

Why can't we change it all, and do so now? This is the mood among the movers and shakers. Up to now, most of the blockage of progress has been reluctantly tolerated—by the black man, by the students, by the people of the Third World. Not only the nonviolent movement of the recent past showed that this patience was nearing an end; in more drastic ways so did the eruption of the Black Power movement, and the campus insurrections of more contemporary days. Now, the time has come when changes will have to be pushed through into reality whether all parties in the community are ready or not.

The American space is going to be rapped and prodded and pushed to reorganize for fuller participation in republican governance. Here, if nowhere else, among the revolutionaries, the republican spirit of willed initiative seems to be in high gear.

What I want to do is combine this spirit of willed initiative among the revolutionaries with the promise to man that we have been talking about in this chapter. That is the best way to see what this promise means—to take it up at the point of urgent demands for change. And at a time when hope fades.

The question with which we started, then, can be understood helpfully as a question of timing. It is not really enough to ask whether the promise to man comes true. We must also ask *when* it comes true. In other words, we must speak of the short-run prospects as well as the long-range ones.

There are two theological points to be made about the short-term prospects.

The first is that history does bring the really new, but never the Kingdom of God in its fullness. Part of the realization of the promise is in the struggle. Put this way, this is not a sentiment that revolutionists have usually wanted to reckon with, and I suppose I can't blame them. And yet, history will never change men so much that they aren't finite any more, so much that they aren't tempted to want more, so much that they can *really* get interested in the destinies of other men besides themselves. Is that a harsh judgment? Take four great political revolutions of the modern world—the American, English, French, and Russian. None of them brought enough change. None of them failed to bring some change, but none brought the whole vision to reality. Certainly none of them left its beneficiaries able to love each other. Perhaps it did improve the prospects of justice in each case. And each certainly kept alive the promise to man. If the American Revolution had brought all that is really promised in the Declaration of Independence, for example, surely we wouldn't now be thinking of the black man's struggle as our No. 1 unsolved domestic problem today.

My second point is that in any revolution the full-blown ideals themselves take time to emerge. As Preston Valien puts it in his essay, "The Montgomery Bus Protest as a Social Movement," while such a movement begins with a concrete incident, "it develops an ideology which progressively becomes more idealistic with the passage of time."[22] And so as late as April, 1956, Martin Luther King, Jr. was suggesting only that the black man in Montgomery sought the right, "under segregation, to seat ourselves from the rear forward on a first-come, first-served basis." But by 1963 the goals had taken on far more profound dimensions, as this later statement of King illustrates:[23]

We're through with tokenism and gradualism and see-how-far-you've-comeism. We're through with we've-done-more-for-your-people-than-anyone-elseism. We can't wait any longer. Now is the time.

These are the cautions of realism, I grant, but, I insist, of revolutionary realism. If history doesn't turn into heaven, it nevertheless is the pilgrimage on which man has realized new hopes and gains in every age. These hopes and gains, the man of critical faith believes, are a divine promise to man coming true. The hope for our age is to transcend the color barrier, and not only the promise but the prospect is that we can do it.

Significantly, there are impressive nontheological arguments in favor of the kind of outlook I have advocated here for theological reasons. Philip M. Hauser, Director of the Population Research and Training Center of the University of Chicago, is realistic enough when he concludes that " 'freedom now' makes sense," but that " 'equality now,' however, is pathetic, wishful fantasy." His outlook, however, is not that common and oversimplified one which holds that such difficulties mean there is no hope for the color barrier to be surmounted. He argues, rather, that "it is a serious mistake to assume that the 'color stigma' is different in kind or even in degree from the stigma which accompanied many of our foreign-white immigrant groups."[24]

Prejudice toward, and hatred of, the Negro by the most bigoted of our white supremacists is not unlike the attitude of the Pole who spat upon the ground when a "Christ-killer" Jew appeared upon the scene, or the attitude of the primitive fundamentalist Baptist whose hatred of "papists" similarly reached high levels of intensity, . . . There is evidence in the United States as well as in various other parts of the world, that the color difference can be bridged even as religious and other cultural differences have been bridged, through social interaction and consequent acculturation.

Even a James Baldwin, despite his destroyed illusions, despite his doubts about the white man, despite the memory of his fathers, who died believing what white men said about them, discerns some hope. And I believe he at least was tempted in his essay *The Fire Next*

Time to give it the sort of theological ingredient we have been talking about here, for he begins by quoting a hymn and ends with a biblical prophecy. More than that he talks about what it is to be saved, to be made whole. The small handful who are concerned may yet be able, at this late hour, he says, "to end the racial nightmare, and achieve our country, and change the history of the world." Here is the test to which religion and ethics are put in our time. "If the concept of God has any validity or any use," says Baldwin, "it can only be to make us larger, freer, and more loving. If God cannot do this, then it is time we got rid of Him."[25] That is also to be said of religion itself—this force that seems to be not far from the heart of every revolution but also, sadly, at the center of every resistance to the emergence of man.

Let me summarize in three closing propositions.

First, as an element of the revolutionary spirit we are witnessing today—in civil rights, on the campuses, in the yearning among new nations to dispose of their own space—we can see that the quality that we have called "willed initiative" is not dead. What is necessary for this quality to be seen in its most authentic form is simply to understand it in the context of the long and honorable struggle for human dignity of which it is a part. Whereas men are calling today, let us say, for rights denied them on account of color and race, and insisting that justice ought to transcend color, they can draw upon a heritage about them that waged the same war, although often over different issues. Style-setting protests were already made yesterday, and yesterday, directed against other inhuman grounds of discrimination and prejudice, other forms of extrinsic control. The struggle for racial justice today, then, is a continuation of a long, difficult, complex struggle for human dignity and community. It is cut from the same cloth as Magna Carta, the right of representative government, freedom of conscience, the Declaration of Independence, separation of church and state, and other milestones in this pilgrimage—most of them drawn from biblical and theological wellsprings, and all of them to be understood as implementation of the biblical promise for human dignity.

Second, such revolutionary movements as these, while they must be won by travail and by what can be called "creative disruption," and while the goals may seem elusive or impossible, can culminate in solid, tangible gains. Such concreteness is part of the biblical version of "promise." God does not constitute an imaginary Israel, but a historical one. He does not promise rescue through an idea, but through human beings in their space, in whom he now acts, as he acted definitively in the man Jesus Christ. What is promised man does not stop with the biblical events, but continues in human history. The right of an accused not to testify against himself is a solid, tangible historical accomplishment of the revolt led by John Lilburne the Leveller. The right of a person to worship as he pleases, not having to follow the dictates of bishop or magistrate, is the solid accomplishment of the creative disruption of a Roger Williams, and of the impassioned reason of a Thomas Jefferson. Today, it may indeed be premature to talk about too many solid accomplishments in our racial ordeal. Yet we see unfolding, I submit, tangible gains, summed up at this stage as the right of a person to enjoy the privileges and immunities of the public sector without reference to his color. We have a long way to go, but the revolution is underway, and it has scored gain after gain in the past.

But third, when willed initiative is set in the frame of a critical religious tradition, these gains of past and present are also joined by the claim of gains for the future. This claim—it is more than a mere expectation—is what faith calls hope. It is a hope that for the American greater community has its own concrete imagery—the refurnishing of space to serve the human prospect. The republican ethos understands hope as the belief that the space is man's, that the meaning of life is to move into the future by disposing the space to meet human needs. What faith adds is the belief that men will make of their space a place where they can be fully themselves, where being is let out in the open, and where the divine is reflected in the community.[26] In the end this kind of hope, despite the origin of the image, transcends the American greater community and speaks of man himself, all men everywhere.

NOTES

CHAPTER I. MORALITY

1. "On Seeking a Hero for the White House," *Time*, July 26, 1968, p. 23.

2. Edward C. Banfield, "Why Government Cannot Solve the Urban Problem," *Daedalus*, Fall, 1968, pp. 1239–1240.

3. R. R. Palmer, *The Age of the Democratic Revolution: A Political History of Europe and America, 1760–1800*. Vol. I, *The Challenge* (Princeton: Princeton University Press, 1959), p. 21.

4. Charles R. Dechert, "The Development of Cybernetics," in *The Social Impact of Cybernetics*, ed. Charles R. Dechert (New York: Simon & Schuster Clarion Books, 1967), p. 23.

5. David M. Potter, *People of Plenty: Economic Abundance and the American Character* (Chicago: University of Chicago Press Phoenix Books, 1954), pp. 21–25.

6. Peter Gay, *The Enlightenment: An Interpretation*. Vol. I, *The Rise of Modern Paganism*. (New York: Alfred A. Knopf, 1966), pref.

7. Margaret Mead, *And Keep Your Powder Dry: An Anthropologist Looks at America* (New York: William Morrow and Co., rev. ed., 1965), p. 18.

8. "Although English life is now (almost certainly) less aggressive than that of any other highly developed society," Gorer says, "I do not think the aggression has disappeared; it is typically held in restraint, a great part of the energy of nearly all good Englishmen being tied up in this life-long struggle. Only in a cause which is felt to be just and moral, in a righteous war or its equivalent where the enemy is patently stronger, so that 'our backs are against the wall,' can the

313

aggression be released and the restraining energy made available for other ends; and then courage, daring, and a most lethal ingenuity manifest themselves in a fashion which surprises our friends and confounds our enemies." Goeffrey Gorer, "English Character in the Twentieth Century," *Annals of the American Academy of Political and Social Science*, March, 1967, pp. 77–78. This essay was part of an issue on national character reexamined by social scientists. Hereafter referred to as *Annals*.

9. Dhirendra Narain, "Indian National Character in the Twentieth Century," *Annals*, March, 1967, pp. 124–132.

10. Potter, *People of Plenty*, p. 28.

11. Edward T. Hall, *The Hidden Dimension* (New York: Doubleday & Co., 1966), pp. 126–127.

12. Frantz Fanon, *The Wretched of the Earth*, tr. Constance Farrington. (New York: Grove Press, 1968), pp. 216, 247.

13. Ray Allen Billington, *America's Frontier Heritage* (New York: Holt, Rinehart and Winston, 1966), p. 194.

14. James C. Charlesworth, "National Character in the Perspective of Political Science," *Annals*, March, 1967, p. 29.

15. *Ibid.*

16. Geoffrey Gorer, *The American People: A Study in National Character* (New York: W. W. Norton & Co., rev. ed., 1964), p. 12.

17. Don Martindale, *Community, Character and Civilization* (New York: Free Press of Glencoe, 1963), pp. 193–194.

18. Reinhold Niebuhr, *The Structure of Nations and Empires* (New York: Charles Scribner's Sons, 1959), pp. 33, 289.

19. Seymour Martin Lipset, "Revolution and Counter-Revolution—the United States and Canada," in *The Revolutionary Theme in Contemporary America*, ed. Thomas R. Ford (Lexington: University of Kentucky Press, 1965), p. 21.

20. *Ibid.*, pp. 23, 38. In developing these contrasts, Lipset cites the work of J. M. S. Careless, *Canada: A Story of Challenge* (Cambridge: University Press, 1963).

21. *Ibid.*, pp. 38–39.

22. Michael McGiffert, Foreword to *The Character of Americans: A Book of Readings* (Homewood, Ill.: Dorsey Press, 1964), ix.

23. To anticipate our discussion of the implications of national-character study for theology in Part Two, we suggest here that the only adequate account of the "situation" in situation ethics must extend at least to the careful appraisal of the manners and morals of one's greater community. Similarly, we shall argue, the proponents of "rule morality" who wish to correct the subjectivism of situation ethics will ultimately find unsuspected resources in perusal of the moral tradition of one's greater community.

24. A more extended account of the importance of Montesquieu for our study will be found in the following section of this chapter.

25. Donald Smalley, in the introduction to Mrs. Trollope's *Domestic Manners of the Americans* (New York: Random House Vintage Books, 1949), xi.

26. Max Lerner, *America as a Civilization: Life and Thought in the United States Today* (New York: Simon and Schuster, 1957); excerpt reproduced in McGiffert, *The Character of Americans*, pp. 10–20.

27. Roger L. Shinn, *The New Humanism* (Philadelphia: Westminster Press, 1968), p. 165. ("New Directions in Theology Today," Vol. VI).

28. *New York Times*, September 3, 1967, p. 6. Quoted is Herbert Gans of the Institute of Urban Studies in New York City.

29. John Higham, "The Construction of American History," in *The Reconstruction of American History*, ed. John Higham (New York: Harper & Row Torchbooks, 1962), pp. 22–23.

30. Staughton Lynd, *Intellectual Origins of American Radicalism* (New York: Pantheon Books, 1968).

31. Mead, *And Keep Your Powder Dry*, p. 11.

32. For accounts of this influence, see Fernand Cattelain, *Étude sur l'Influence de Montesquieu dans les Constitutions Américaines* (Besançon: Imprimerie Millot Frères, 1927); and Paul Merrill Spurlin, *Montesquieu in America 1760–1801*. On the separation of powers doctrine in Montesquieu, see Louis Althusser, *Montesquieu: la Politique et l'Histoire* (Paris: Éditions Gallimard, 1961); Franz Neumann, *The Democratic and the Authoritarian State* (London: The Free Press of Glencoe, 1964), Chapter IV, an excellent introduction to the entire thought of Montesquieu which appeared earlier in *The Spirit of the Laws*, tr. Thomas Nugent (New York: Hafner Publishing Co., 1949);

Kingsley Martin, *French Liberal Thought in the Eighteenth Century* (New York: Harper & Row Torchbooks, 1962), Chapter VI.

During the American Revolution itself, Montesquieu became "a veritable oracle in the struggle for political liberty" because of his views on tyranny. Only later, during the writing of the Constitution, was his dogma of the separation of powers seized upon. Cattelain thinks that the continued memory of the despised monarchy accounts, however, for the continued influence of Montesquieu in the debates over the Constitution. His arguments against despotism not only led to the adoption of the principle of separation of federal powers, but to a much broader design for equilibrium in the Constitution: the states as counterweights to the Federal government, the House as counterweight to the Senate, and so on. (Cattelain, p. 129.)

Other critics are much less sympathetic either with Montesquieu or his doctrine of the separation of powers. The doctrine is little more than a device for neutralizing the legislature, Martin thinks, for it is made more harmless when it is divided into two parts. "It is a sober fact," he says, that "Montesquieu's interpretation of the British Constitution resulted in constant antagonisms between Senate and President: he may be said to be ultimately responsible for the non-participation of the United States in the League of Nations." (Martin, pp. 164–165.) The separation of powers doctrine is actually antidemocratic, Neumann argues. It favors the status quo, neglects the role of the administrator as a leader in social change. "Liberty is not threatened by legislative activity of the administration but by such a structure of society that makes the rise of contending political forces impossible or difficult. A pluralistic social structure and a flexible multi-party system are far more important to liberty than the monopolization of legislation by the legislature and the reduction of the administrative power into a law-enforcing agency." (Neumann, pp. 139–140, 142.)

33. The role of dissenting ideological thought is explicated in Bernard Bailyn, *The Ideological Origins of the American Revolution* (Cambridge: Belknap Press of Harvard University Press, 1967). See also Staughton Lynd, *op. cit.* Heimert's thesis is developed in *Religion and the American Mind: from the Great Awakening to the Revolution* (Cambridge: Harvard University Press, 1966).

34. Henri Barckhausen, *Montesquieu: Ses Idées et Ses Oeuvres d'après les Papiers de la Brède* (Paris: Libraire Hachette, 1907), p. 1; Émile Durkheim, *Montesquieu and Rousseau: Forerunners of Sociology*

(Ann Arbor: University of Michigan Press, 1960), p. 61; Neumann, *The Democratic and the Authoritarian State*, p. 117.

35. Werner Stark, *Montesquieu: Pioneer of the Sociology of Knowledge* (London: Routledge & Kegan Paul, 1960), p. 100; Neumann, *The Democratic and the Authoritarian State*, pp. 100–101.

36. Durkheim, *Montesquieu and Rousseau*, p. 56.

37. *The Spirit of the Laws*, XIX, 4–5. Unless otherwise specified, I have translated all citations from Montesquieu, *Oeuvres Complètes* (Paris: Éditions du Seuil, 1964). Citations from *The Spirit of the Laws* are given by Book and Section and are hereafter signified by EL. References to the *Persian Letters* and other treatises will bear page numbers of *Oeuvres Complètes*, hereafter referred to as O.C.

38. Melvin Richter, "Montesquieu," *International Encyclopedia of the Social Sciences* (New York: The Macmillan Co., 1968), X, 473.

39. EL, XIX, 4, 5, 10.

40. Stark, *Montesquieu*, p. 56.

41. Long ago the Greeks gave the name *troglodyte* to cave dwellers, a primitive, cattle-raising people who were sometimes also thought of as robbers. Montesquieu gives this name to the people of his famous story in *Persian Letters* 11–14 (O.C. 68–70) who, after reaping the misery and suffering of primitive life that consisted in injustice, were able to turn themselves around, led by two unusual men among them who "had humanity," "knew justice," and "loved virtue." It is a fable of the struggle between injustice and virtue, both options being open to men. It appears, in the telling of this story, that men are capable of virtue in spite of themselves; but the burdens of self-governance are always so heavy that men are constantly tempted to renounce them (as indeed the Troglodytes finally do, when they decide to ask an old and just member of their community to become king).

Numerous critics have seen in the story of the Troglodytes an attack on Hobbes' view of the state. How could the Troglodytes agree to give up their unhappy and unjust condition and form a just state, unless they *already* had latent within them an anticipatory sense of justice? If men can agree to a contract that sets up the structures of justice, they must have had some awareness of justice to start with. Hobbes says that before the contract with the sovereign, the words justice and injustice have no meaning. But with Montesquieu, there is an anterior appreciation of humanity that permits society to serve just ends.

Montesquieu's insistence on the rule of law as founded on the "nature of things" is a way of differing in principle from Hobbes' view that law is conventional and artificial. Man as such precedes man in the state. In pursuing this line of thought, it is not necessary to agree with Dimoff that Montesquieu, in fact, deliberately chooses to reenact a Stoic, Ciceronian mode of thinking. For Montesquieu differs from Cicero both in his view of the relativity of law, and also in his conception that the law is the instrument of human autonomy in evolving a structured community. But Dimoff is right in seeing Montesquieu as a thinker who postulates man's capacity to think morally of the mandate to justice even in his "natural" state, and in this sense Montesquieu has more affinities with Stoic thought than with that of Hobbes. See these two studies: Paul Dimoff, *Cicéron, Hobbes et Montesquieu* (Saarbrücken: Université de la Sarre, 1952; Annales Universitatis Saraviensis, I, 1); M. W. Rombout, *La Conception Stoïcienne du Bonheur chez Montesquieu et chez Quelques-uns de ses Contemporains* (Leiden: Universitaire Pers Leiden, 1958). The latter work, it should be added, is uneven and anticlimactic in its theological critique of *le bonheur*.

42. *Sur les Causes qui Peuvent Affecter les Esprits et les Caractères*, O.C., 493.

43. Alexis de Tocqueville, *L'Ancien Régime et la Révolution*, ed. J.-P. Mayer (Paris: Éditions Gallimard, 1952), p. 209; cf. Michael Lipshuetz, *Montesquieu als Geschichtsphilosoph* (Strasbourg: Les Éditions Universitaires de Strasbourg, 1927), p. 34.

44. Richter, "Montesquieu," p. 469.

45. *Ibid.*, p. 475.

46. Robert C. Good, "Reinhold Niebuhr: The Political Philosopher of Christian Realism," *Cross Currents*, Summer, 1961, p. 259; Reinhold Niebuhr, *Man's Nature and His Communities* (New York: Charles Scribner's Sons, 1965), pp. 30–31.

47. *Newsweek*, July 1, 1968, p. 61.

48. Cattelain, *Étude sur l'Influence de Montesquieu*, p. 29.

49. Neumann, *The Democratic and the Authoritarian State*, p. 7.

50. Paraphrase from Albert Sorel, *Montesquieu* (Paris: Hachette, 1889), p. 7.

51. For the contrast between Montesquieu and Voltaire that is explicated in the following paragraphs, I follow chiefly Bernard

Groethuysen, *Philosophie de la Révolution Française* (Paris: Éditions Gallimard, 1956), Chapters III-IV. Groethuysen also provides instructive contrasts of both men with Rousseau, whose advocacy of an idea essential to modern democracy—equality—is favored neither by Montesquieu in theory nor by Voltaire in practice (p. 127). Cf. the remark of Rombout: "Montesquieu restera le champion de la recherche du juste milieu. Or, cette tendance n'était pas celle de la Révolution. Au conservatisme et à la lenteur de Montesquieu on a préféré la hâte fievreuse de Jean-Jacques Rousseau." *La Conception Stoïcienne du Bonheur*, p. 11.

    52. EL, XIV, 1.

    53. Sorel, *Montesquieu*, pp. 116–117. Montesquieu, like other *philosophes*, was fairly provincial, a victim of his own European biases. This provinciality shows up plainly when Montesquieu applies the climate theory to Asia, or when he wishes to illustrate, with exaggerated cases, the evils of despotism. Kassem makes the case that Montesquieu, whenever he displays ignorance or denigration of Asia, is merely writing "in the Christian, European tradition . . . , and perhaps as well in the new spirit of imperialistic expansionism" of his time. There was a long tradition dating from the day of the Mongol incursions and of the Crusades, Kassem writes, of not accepting the East on its own terms. European Christians rather entertained, for their own reasons, a vision of Asia as a land of horrors and of monsters, as in popular stereotypes about the Tartars. "An iron curtain—which is not, alas, a creation of our own turbulent century—had already stretched itself between two continents." Thus Asia appears to Montesquieu to be a land of excesses, with its climate either dangerously cold or dangerously warm, and with its space divided into vast empires in which despotism holds absolute sway and servitude is widely accepted. Christian Europe, by contrast, is a continent of moderate climate, divided into states large and small that are governed by restrained monarchies and republics. Bayreddine Kassem, *Décadence et Absolutisme dans l'Oeuvre de Montesquieu* (Genève et Paris: E. Droz, 1960), pp. 114, 124, 126, 143.

    54. EL, XVIII, 8.

    55. Groethuysen, *Philosophie de la Révolution Française*, pp. 44, 48.

    56. *Ibid.*, p. 55.

    57. Carleton S. Coon, *The Living Races of Mankind*, with Edward E. Hunt, Jr. (New York: Alfred A. Knopf, 1965), p. 8.

58. *Ibid.*, pp. 55, 303. To take another example, William H. McNeill raises the question why the Aryan tribes in prehistoric India evolved in a different direction from the same stocks that prevailed in Europe. Allowing for the development of contrasting cultural forms of expression between the divided peoples, still another factor, the influence of climate, has also to be considered, he says: "The decisive formulations of Indian culture and attitudes toward life took place not in northwestern India, where climatic conditions generally resembled those of the Middle East, but in the Gangetic plain, where the monsoon dominated the cycle of the year. Different possibilities lay open in such a climate than in the drier and severer climate of the Mediterranean." William H. McNeill, *The Rise of the West: A History of the Human Community* (New York: New American Library, Mentor Books, 1963), p. 198.

59. Boris Mirkine-Guetzévitch, "De *l'Esprit des Lois* à la Démocratie Moderne," in *La Pensée Politique et Constitutionelle de Montesquieu* (Paris: Recueil Sirey, 1952), pp. 11–24.

60. Margaret Mead, *And Keep Your Powder Dry* (1942 ed.), p. 21.

CHAPTER II. REPUBLICS

1. *Domestic Manners of the Americans*, pp. 135, 431–432.

2. Lee Coleman, "What Is American? A Study of Alleged American Traits," *Social Forces*, XIX (May, 1941), 492–99; reprinted in McGiffert, *The Character of Americans*, pp. 21–30.

3. Cited by McGiffert, Foreword, *The Character of Americans*, viii.

4. David Brion Davis, "Some Recent Directions in American Cultural History," *American Historical Review*, LXXIII (February, 1968), 699.

5. Thomas A. Bailey, "The Mythmakers of American History," *Journal of American History*, LV (June, 1968), pp. 8, 15.

6. Jacques Maritain, *Reflections on America* (New York: Charles Scribner's Sons, 1958), p. 32.

7. David Riesman, with Reuel Denney and Nathan Glazer, *The Lonely Crowd: A Study of the Changing American Character* (New Haven: Yale University Press, 1950); George W. Pierson, "The M-Factor in American History," *American Quarterly*, XIV (Summer, 1962, Supplement), 275–89; reprinted in McGiffert, *The Character of Americans*, pp. 118–130).

Of the moral theme itself as a prism for examining the American character, George Santayana remarks: "To be an American is of itself almost a moral condition, an education, and a career. Hence a single ideal figment can cover a large part of what each American is in his character, and almost the whole of what most Americans are in their social outlook and political judgments." *Character & Opinion in the United States* (New York: Charles Scribner's Sons, 1920), p. 168.

8. Billington, *America's Frontier Heritage*, pp. 62–63.

9. *Ibid.*, p. 65.

10. *And Keep Your Powder Dry* (rev. ed., 1965), pp. 193–194.

11. Part VI of McGiffert, *The Character of Americans*, presents, among other writings, Riesman's views on the changing American character and Lipset's criticisms, plus introductory comments on both.

12. *Time*, July 26, 1968, p. 23.

13. Bailyn, *Ideological Origins of the American Revolution*, p. 142. This comment continues: "But history clearly taught that republics were delicate polities, quickly degenerating into anarchy and tyranny; it was impossible, some said, to 'recollect a single instance of a nation who supported this form of government for any length of time or with any degree of greatness.' "

14. EL, II.

15. Althusser, *Montesquieu*, p. 39.

16. EL, II, 2–3; III, 3.

17. EL, IX, 1.

18. EL, III, 1–2.

19. EL, III, 9.

20. Robert Shackleton, *Montesquieu: A Critical Biography* (London: Oxford University Press, 1961), p. 273.

21. Barckhausen, *Montesquieu*, p. 33; *Persian Letters*, 117 (O.C., p. 124).

22. In Montesquieu's republic, Stark comments, free men will prize religious freedom not as a species of religion, but as a species of freedom. "Religious freedom will be for them the first line of defense of all freedom; it will be upheld, not for its own sake, but for its importance to the constitution. In the generally democratic atmosphere of Britain the clergy will be less of a closed estate than abroad; they will tend to merge with the generality of citizens. Hence they can only assert their dignity by exemplary conduct. And they can only gain the people for religion by means of argument and persuasion." *Montesquieu*, p. 140. The same arguments apply *a fortiori* to the United States.

23. EL, IV, 5.

24. EL, III, 5.

25. Althusser, *Montesquieu*, p. 74.

26. Most notably in *The Nature of True Virtue*, written in the year of Montesquieu's death, 1755. R. R. Palmer gives us a helpful interpretation of what Montesquieu meant by honor. It was "a kind of self-assertion, a consciousness of one's rank in society, a desire for recognition and public esteem, an enjoyment of external marks of high position, a sense of obligation imposed by one's standing or the known deeds of one's ancestors, a greater readiness to accept danger than to incur disgrace, a refusal to be humiliated even by a king." Noblemen were simply too proud to succumb to the fear by which the despot ruled; by standing firm, they could then protect the liberty of lesser men. "There is doubtless more truth in this diagnosis than is palatable to popular equalitarians." *The Age of the Democratic Revolution* (Vol. I, *The Challenge*), p. 59.

27. EL, III, 4.

28. EL, III, 4; Marcel Prélot, "Montesquieu et les formes de gouvernement," in *La Pensée Politique et Constitutionelle de Montesquieu*, p. 125.

29. EL, III, 9.

30. Althusser, *Montesquieu*, p. 78.

31. *Ibid.*, p. 81.

32. Joseph Dedieu, *Montesquieu* (Paris: Hatier, 1943), p. 159; EL, II, 4.

33. Dedieu, *Montesquieu*, pp. 156–157, 161; EL, VIII, 6–8, 17.

34. Cf. Althusser, *Montesquieu*, p. 89; EL, V, 11.

35. EL, V, 12.

36. EL, VIII, 3.

37. EL, VIII, 4.

38. We have not explicated the conception of space in an aristocracy, but it is easily summarized. The nobles both dispose and dispense. Possessing original sovereignty, they share, as among themselves, the prerogative of disposing of the community space. Their participative rule is based on restraint and moderation, and is possibly analogous, as among themselves, to the restrained equality Montesquieu has described here. As to the people, they occupy the space that is dispensed to them and realize dignity but not independence, since the people, in an aristocracy, share some of the attributes of the subjects in a monarchy. But Montesquieu suggests that the "splendor that surrounds kings" plays little role in the authority of the nobility. Another important part is the respect engendered in the people for the nobles by their moderation, modesty, and simple manners. The nobles at all times should suppress excessive pride in domination. Laws should promote justice for all, and the distinction between nobility and people should not be exaggerated into "extreme inequality between those who govern and those who are governed." Thus the people, in an aristocracy, are not without influence and voice. EL, III, 7, V, 8.

39. Dedieu, *Montesquieu*, p. 61.

40. Hubert Méthivier, *L'Ancien Régime* (Paris: Presses Universitaires de France, 1964), p. 104.

41. Kassem, *Decadence et Absolutisme dans l'Oeuvre de Montesquieu*, p. 54.

42. EL, V, 9.

43. EL, VIII, 5.

44. EL, V, 9.

45. EL, XI, 19.

46. Hugh Trevor-Roper, "L'Esprit de Montesquieu," *New Statesman*, November 17, 1961, pp. 745–746.

47. Cattelain, *Étude sur l'Influence de Montesquieu*, p. 48.

48. EL, III, 9.

49. EL, XXIII, 29.

50. E.g., EL, XI, 13. "Montesquieu has a horror of disruptive revolutions and violent tumults," Dedieu comments. "It is better, he says, to submit to abuse than to correct it through such great evil. . . . The true reform is to restore the principles of the Constitution." *Montesquieu*, p. 158.

51. *Mes Pensées*, 139 (O.C., p. 869), 603 (O.C., p. 939).

52. *Ibid.*, 648 (O.C., p. 949).

53. *Ibid.*, 631 (O.C., p. 947).

54. This conclusion, of course, is my own, but I believe it is a defensible completion of Montesquieu's unfinished thought on the time of a republic.

55. Higham, *The Reconstruction of American History*, p. 24.

CHAPTER III. MANNERS

1. *The Autobiography of Malcolm X* (New York: Grove Press, 1966), Introduction by M. S. Handler, xii.

2. Cf. David Little, "Calvin and the Prospects for a Christian Theory of Natural Law," in *Norm and Context in Christian Ethics*, ed. Gene H. Outka and Paul Ramsey (New York: Charles Scribner's Sons, 1968), 187–190.

3. Samuel Johnson came to a much harsher judgment when he described Chesterfield's *Letters to His Son* as evincing "the morals of a whore, and the manners of a dancing master."

4. Arthur M. Schlesinger, *Learning How to Behave: A Historical Study of American Etiquette Books* (New York: The Macmillan Co., 1946), pp. 64–65. The very separation of etiquette from manners underlines once again the existential importance of knowing what to do in a sure and practiced way, even at the level of casual affairs. One suspects that the black man in the South today would exercise his right to vote much more massively if he had behind him in his immediately past tradition a relaxed sureness about the process of voting, a confident know-how of the sort that comes as casual second nature,

instead of novel knowledge of a sometimes painfully acquired procedure, given the hostility of the environing whites. In short, manners can be placed in the service of social change, even in their reduced status as "etiquette."

5. *Ibid.*, vii.

6. *Democracy in America*, I, 354–355.

7. *Ibid.*, p. 383.

8. Bernard Lonergan, "Metaphysics as Horizon," *Cross Currents*, Fall, 1966, p. 482. Cf. Henry David Aiken: "Certainly the contemporary state of philosophy leaves much to be desired, but its insistence upon clarity, order, and exactitude is all that has ever distinguished philosophy as a discipline from common-sense speculation concerning the organizing concepts by which we live." *Reason and Conduct: New Bearings in Moral Philosophy* (New York: Alfred A. Knopf, 1962), p. 5.

9. Looking ahead to our more specific engagement with American theology in Part Two, we can already anticipate asking again there for the study of manners as we have called for it here. But at that point our aim will be not so much to sketch a public ethics, as it is here, as to remind American Christian ethics of what its task is. In this sense, we second the plea of Paul Ramsey for the theological study of societal "rules of practices": "There can be no Christian *social ethics* (but only social pragmatics) unless there are some *rules of practices* required by *agapé*. I therefore regard an inquiry into the *meaning of practices* as of the utmost importance for the whole of Christian ethics. . . . The reader is therefore invited to attend to the *logic of practices* as a necessary part of serious reflection upon the questions of any sort of normative ethics." *Deeds and Rules in Christian Ethics* (New York: Charles Scribner's Sons, 1967), p. 8.

10. EL, III, 5, note.

11. EL, XIX, 14, 16.

12. EL, XIX, 21.

13. EL, XIX, 13, 16–18. Aiken treats this issue as a contrast between "open" and "closed" societies: "Now the rules of moral codes vary considerably in number, clarity, flexibility, and well-orderedness. In 'closed' societies they are likely to be many, specific, rigid, and well ordered. . . . In more open societies rules are usually fewer in number, highly general, capable of indefinite reinterpretation, subject to exceptions, and rather vague in order of preference." *Reason and Conduct,*

p. 72. He adds, in a comment that Montesquieu would doubtless applaud: "But in morals, unfortunately, there just is no one set of universally valid principles of deliberation to which all peoples, regardless of cultural heritage, are in conscience bound. In saying this, I am not preaching moral relativism; I am simply stating a fact. It is a fundamental *theoretical* blunder to treat the particular procedures of moral deliberation current in our own culture as paradigmatic for morality in general." *Ibid.*, p. 73.

14. EL, XIX, 27.

15. EL, V, 2.

16. In fact, the real separation is between *theology* and state, or *belief* and state, rather than church and state, since in America the churches and the state have from the beginning made common cause on a variety of moral and ethical issues. To take the most obvious example, the brief experiment with legal prohibition in America was palpably the work of a church-state coalition allied in a common moral cause.

17. Durkheim, *Montesquieu and Rousseau*, p. 43.

18. Jude Wanniski, "Lawyers Look to Social Reform, Not Law, to Cure Crime Problem," *The National Observer*, August 12, 1968, p. 4.

19. Luigi Barzini, *The Italians* (New York: Bantam Books, 1964), pp. 108–109.

20. *Ibid.*, pp. 109, 225.

21. Barbara Deming, *Prison Notes* (New York: Grossman Publishers, 1966, p. 100.

22. *Character & Opinion in the United States*, pp. 166–167.

23. Barckhausen, *Montesquieu*, p. 63; EL, VIII, 8.

24. EL, XIX, 13.

25. EL, XIX, 8.

26. Seymour Martin Lipset, "A Changing American Character?" in *The Character of Americans*, ed. McGiffert, p. 319. The excerpt is reprinted from *Culture and Social Character*, ed. Lipset and Leo Lowenthal (New York: The Free Press, 1961).

27. Douglas Gilbert Haring, "Japanese Character in the Twentieth Century," *Annals*, March, 1967, p. 136.

28. "Whether men may live without 'morals' I do not know,"
Aiken comments. "I believe, however, that moral judgments cannot long
retain their public authority as incitors when the ends which they enjoin
do not serve the permanent communal interests of men." *Reason and
Conduct*, p. 127.

29. Cf. Alexander Krappe, *The Science of Folklore* (New
York: W. W. Norton, 1964), p. 270.

30. *Democracy in America*, II, pp. 304–306. With uncanny
accuracy, Tocqueville adds: "If ever America undergoes great revolutions, they will be brought about by the presence of the black race on the
soil of the United States" (p. 307).

31. Barbara W. Tuchman, *The Proud Tower: A Portrait of
the World Before the War 1890–1914* (New York: The Macmillan Co.,
1966), xii.

32. *The American People*, p. 89.

33. *Newsweek*, November 6, 1967, p. 26; *Time*, November 3,
1967, p. 17. The perceptive reader will recognize that our aim here is
to present the conflict between the student style and the expectations of
the establishment. That is why it is appropriate to quote from the news-
magazines. Those who want to find out what happened at the Pentagon
will read Norman Mailer's remarkable *The Armies of the Night* (New
York: New American Library-Signet Books, 1968).

34. T. Walter Herbert, Jr., "The Student Protest Movement,"
Theology Today, XXIV (January, 1968), pp. 464, 468.

35. Quoted in *The Berkeley Student Revolt: Facts and Interpretations*, ed. Seymour Martin Lipset and Sheldon S. Wolin (New
York: Doubleday Anchor Books, 1965), p. 217.

36. *Saturday Evening Post*, July 13, 1968, p. 6.

37. *The Autobiography of Malcolm X*, p. 59.

38. Daniel J. Boorstin, *The Americans: The Colonial Experience* (New York: Random House, 1958), p. 41. Our warning against
withdrawing from the greater community and its history does not
mean, of course, that the "way out" of the dilemma for the black man is
to be modeled on the experience of past minority groups. The peculiar
ordeal of the black man in this country cannot be reduced to simple
parity with that of other ethnic groups; he is the oldest victim of
extrinsic control, and in many ways he is painfully furthest from
realizing the promise of the American ethos.

39. Herbert, "The Student Protest Movement," p. 467.

40. Tom Wolfe, *The Pump House Gang* (New York: Farrar, Straus & Giroux, 1968), p. 216. For the student of contemporary American manners, the entire essay, "Tom Wolfe's New Book of Etiquette," pp. 205–222, is recommended.

41. D. W. Brogan, *American Aspects* (New York: Harper & Row, 1964), p. 4.

42. Ben J. Wattenberg, in collaboration with Richard M. Scammon, *This U.S.A.: An Unexpected Family Portrait of 194,067,296 Americans Drawn from the Census* (New York: Doubleday & Co., 1965), p. 99.

43. Margaret Mead, *And Keep Your Powder Dry*, pp. 49–50, 53; Geoffrey Gorer, *The American People*, p. 71.

44. George B. Leonard, "California: A New Game with New Rules," *Look,* June 28, 1966, pp. 30, 32.

45. *Democracy in America*, II, 215.

46. Ralph Waldo Emerson, "Manners," in *Essays and English Traits* (New York: P. F. Collier & Son, 1909; *Harvard Classics*, V), p. 209.

47. *Ibid.,* pp. 214, 217, 226.

48. *Democracy in America*, I, 293.

49. Daniel J. Boorstin, *The Americans: The National Experience* (New York: Random House, 1965).

50. Reino Virtanen, "French National Character in the Twentieth Century," *Annals*, March, 1967, p. 90.

51. Cf. Tom Wolfe, "O Rotten Gotham—Sliding Down into the Behavioral Sink," *The Pump House Gang*, pp. 293–309.

52. John Hersey, *Too Far to Walk* (New York: Alfred A. Knopf, 1966), p. 21.

53. Goeffrey Gorer, *The American People*, pp. 32–33.

54. These qualities were also intermingled on the frontier, as Billington has shown. Despite strong proclivities toward individualism and the existence on the frontier of economic opportunity that encouraged them, "in the social realm the pioneer was a complete traditionalist, leaning on the community no less than his city cousins." *America's Frontier Heritage*, pp. 148–149.

55. David M. Potter, "The Quest for the National Character," *The Reconstruction of American History*, pp. 197–220.

56. *Domestic Manners of the Americans*, p. 316. Mrs. Trollope's main criticism is not that the doctrine of equality has produced bad manners and insolence. What is far worse is the fundamental untruth of the claim that "all men are born free and equal." Americans of lower station are constantly kept "in a state of irritation," she feels, by their awareness that their own lives do not manifest the equality that the American creed claims for them. They are reduced to self-delusion, boasting, and a spirit of pushiness that typifies American manners. The truth is, she concludes, that in America "the solid reality of inequality" exists "exactly as much as it does elsewhere." This "false and futile axiom," which she credits Jefferson with foisting upon the people, "is doing, and will do so much harm to this fine country." (Pp. 425, 71.)

57. Fred Hoyle, *Frontiers of Astronomy* (New York: New American Library, Mentor Books, 1957), p. 303.

58. John Updike, *Couples* (New York: Alfred A. Knopf, 1968), p. 158.

59. *Democracy in America*, I, 304–305.

60. John Kenneth Galbraith, *The New Industrial State* (Boston: Houghton Mifflin Co., 1967), pp. 37–38.

61. *Time*, July 12, 1968, p. 55.

62. Gorer, *The American People*, pp. 153–155.

63. Hannah Arendt, *On Revolution* (New York: The Viking Press, 1965), p. 174.

64. Daniel Bell, "The Year 2000—The Trajectory of an Idea," *Daedalus*, Summer, 1967, p. 645.

65. D. W. Brogan, *American Aspects*, p. 1.

66. Clinton Rossiter, *The American Presidency* (New York: New American Library, Mentor Books, 2nd ed., 1960), p. 37.

67. *L'Ancien Régime et La Révolution*, pp. 165, 1964.

68. *Ibid.*, p. 194.

69. *Democracy in America*, I, 221, II, 128.

70. *American Aspects*, p. 110; John Kobler, *Luce: His Time, Life, and Fortune* (New York: Doubleday & Co., 1968), p. 80.

71. *Democracy in America*, II, 283.

72. Clinton Rossiter, *Conservatism in America: the Thankless Persuasion* (New York: Alfred A. Knopf, 1962), pp. 134–135.

73. *The New Industrial State*, p. 111.

74. *Ibid.*, p. 393.

75. *Ibid.*, p. 154.

76. *Democracy in America*, I, 292.

77. Billington, *America's Frontier Heritage*, p. 167.

78. Tocqueville, *Democracy in America*, II, 203, 268; Wesley Pruden, Jr., in *The National Observer*, July 8, 1968, p. 9.

79. *Character & Opinion in the United States*, p. 172.

80. *Domestic Manners of the Americans*, p. 306.

81. This view is developed most notably in *The Nature of True Virtue*.

82. Arthur M. Schlesinger, Jr., *A Thousand Days: John F. Kennedy in the White House* (Boston: Houghton Mifflin Co., 1965), p. 910.

83. *Domestic Manners of the Americans*, pp. 86–87, 170–174.

84. This lack of taste is pervasive, limited to no single class or group in American society. If lower-middle-class tourists are more likely to buy the JFK dinner plates, suburbanites with salaries in five figures were aimed at in promotion from a boutique in a new shoppng center near Nashville. Offered were Eisenhower, FDR, and JFK decanters at prices from $5 to $12.95. The Ike decanter "pays tribute to Dwight David Eisenhower, 34th President. . . . On the face of the decanter, 'Ike' is depicted in the statesman-like manner most associated with him. And, on the back is engraved his promise to the Allied peoples during World War II: '. . . Peace with Justice.' . . . In patriotic red/ white/ blue gift box."

85. EL, VIII, 16.

86. Brogan, *American Aspects*, p. 159.

87. *Ibid.*, p. 163.

88. Edmund Stillman and William Pfaff, *Power and Impotence: The Failure of America's Foreign Policy* (New York: Random House, 1966), p. 23.

89. Dwight Macdonald, *Against the American Grain* (New York: Random House, 1962), p. 61.

90. *Ideological Origins of the American Revolution*, p. 19.

91. EL, XIX, 27.

92. Althusser, *Montesquieu*, pp. 60–61.

93. *Time* (Atlantic edition), March 18, 1966, p. 18.

94. EL, V, 18.

95. Arnold J. Toynbee, *America and the World Revolution* (New York: Oxford University Press, 1962), p. 35.

96. Quoted in *The National Observer*, July 8, 1968, p. 18.

CHAPTER IV. TOOLS

1. To see how the same arguments are repeated and reprinted, one might examine, back to back, John C. Bennett *et al., Storm Over Ethics* (Philadelphia: United Church Press, 1967) and *The Situation Ethics Debate*, ed. Harvey Cox (Philadelphia: The Westminster Press, 1968). For an example of the tendencies toward scholasticism in this debate, see the essays in Part I of *Norm and Context in Christian Ethics*, ed. Gene H. Outka and Paul Ramsey (New York: Charles Scribner's Sons, 1968). Nevertheless, as we show below, American Christian ethics appears to be moving in some ways toward the proper study of its ethos.

As to my own position, the reader is directed to my *Theological Ethics* (New York: The Macmillan Co., 1966), in which the theological assumptions underlying my theory of public ethics are more fully laid out then seems possible or necessary here.

2. I have adapted this section from my review of Herbert W. Richardson, *Toward an American Theology* (New York: Harper & Row, 1967), published in the *Journal of the American Academy of Religion*, XXXVI (June 1968), 146–150.

3. Julian N. Hartt, *A Christian Critique of American Culture* (New York: Harper & Row, 1967), pp. 14, 88.

4. Ian G. Barbour, "Five Ways of Reading Teilhard," *Soundings*, LI (Summer, 1968), 135.

5. Paul Tillich, *Theology of Culture*, ed. Robert C. Kimball (New York: Oxford University Press, 1959), p. 38.

6. The landing of Americans on the moon is perhaps more comparable to the discovery of the North and South poles than to the discovery of the Western hemisphere, C. P. Snow suggests, and it thus points to a probable dead end in space exploration rather than to the opening up of any new worlds. Scientists have long known, he argues, that the solar system is a disappointingly empty sector of space, mostly (except for earth) "barren lumps of inorganic matter." After we explore it, "Then we come to the end. . . . There is nowhere else in the entire universe where man can ever land, for so long as the human species lasts." "The Moon Landing," *Look*, August 26, 1969, p. 72.

7. *Toward an American Theology*, p. 44, xi, p. 27.

8. *Ibid.*, p. 111.

9. *Ibid.*, pp. 112, 162.

10. *Ibid.*, p. 137.

11. *Ibid.*, p. 119.

12. *Ibid.*, pp. 111, 126–127, 151.

13. *Ibid.*, p. 106. Richardson amplified his position in extemporaneous remarks at a colloquium for graduate students at Vanderbilt Divinity School in October, 1968. Here he laid much stress on a theology of the "holy spirit" that he believes to be supplied in the American experience, and in such a way that the other persons of the Trinity seem subordinated. In short, he appeared to be less trinitarian, more "spiritistic" than he does in his book. But I may be mistaken in this impression.

14. I have adapted this section from my article, "Mr. Ramsey and the New Morality," *Religion in Life*, Summer, 1968, pp. 282–291. Used by permission; copyright © 1968 by Abingdon Press.

15. Paul Ramsey, *Basic Christian Ethics* (New York: Charles Scribner's Sons, 1950), pp. 57, 59, 78.

16. Paul Ramsey, *Deeds and Rules in Christian Ethics* (New York: Charles Scribner's Sons, 1967).

17. *Deeds and Rules,* pp. 131, 107. He also argues the converse, not only that his new book allows for acts-morality within the context of a rules-morality, but that long ago, in *Basic Christian Ethics*, he provided a place (admittedly secondary) for rules as media of agape

(*Deeds and Rules*, p. 122). But this gets us into another issue, *viz.*, whether any theologian who enthrones agape to the degree that neo-orthodoxy (Ramsey included) did in 1950, or that situation ethics does now, can ever provide an adequate place for rules, principles, and laws. We return to this issue below.

18. John A. T. Robinson, *Christian Morals Today* (Philadelphia: The Westminster Press, 1964).

19. *Deeds and Rules*, p. 35.

20. Paul Lehmann, *Ethics in a Christian Context* (New York: Harper & Row, 1963).

21. *Deeds and Rules*, pp. 58, 94–96, italics supplied.

22. *Ethics in a Christian Context*, p. 131, italics omitted.

23. Joseph Fletcher, *Situation Ethics: The New Morality* (Philadelphia: The Westminster Press, 1966).

24. *Deeds and Rules*, pp. 187, 180, 190, 194.

25. *Ibid.*, p. 217.

26. Ramsey follows the philosophical ethicist William K. Frankena in dividing agape-derived Christian ethics into *act*-agapism, and three forms of *rule*-agapism: (1) that which allows only of working rules (as with Bishop Robinson)—*summary-rule* agapism; (2) that which allows only of general, binding rules (Ramsey gives no exemplars) —*pure-rule* agapism; and (3) "*combinations* of act-agapism and rule-agapism" based on the notion that sometimes it's the act and sometimes it's the rule that better expresses love. Ramsey seems to include himself here: "It would seem, in fact, that if a Christian ethicist is going to be a pure agapist he would find this . . . possibility to be the most fruitful one, and most in accord with the freedom of *agapé* both to act through the firmest principles and to act, if need be, without them." (*Deeds and Rules*, pp. 106–107.)

Ramsey himself contributes to the refinement of the notion of rules by distinguishing two concepts of general rules in Christian ethics—(1) those applying to the *person*, concerned with his own needs and fulfillment; and (2) those applying to society generally as a *practice*. Thus one may ask two questions: "What ought I to do generally?" and "What generally ought to be done in a community?" (pp. 7–8).

27. *Deeds and Rules*, p. 79. This analysis also delivers the *coup de grâce* to the obsolescent rationale of "middle axioms" once *au courant* in American Christian ethics.

28. An illustration: in *Basic Christian Ethics*, Jesus' "strenuous views on marriage and divorce," i.e., the ethic of steadfastness to one's mate, is viewed as a case of *abrogation of a rule*, the traditional Jewish law, and as "another manifestation of unclaiming love transcending enactment into statute" (p. 71). This ideal of marital steadfastness is commended once again in *Deeds and Rules*, but this time *as a rule*, "the rulelike practice of marriage" (p. 141). Indeed the covenant of marriage may be both a general rule of personal obligation and a societal rule of practice as well (p. 7). One observes here a loss of inwardness that is characteristic of the latest phase of this debate on both sides.

29. *Deeds and Rules*, p. 201; *Basic Christian Ethics*, p. 5.

30. *Deeds and Rules*, p. 122.

31. *Ibid.*, pp. 135, 137.

32. I have tried to show elsewhere that Ramsey's refusal of a teleological ethics involves him in a contradiction. See my review of *Deeds and Rules* in *Theology Today*, XXIV (January, 1968), 512–513.

33. *Democracy in America*, II, 282.

34. Rudolf Bultmann, "The Meaning of the Christian Faith in Creation," in *Existence and Faith*, tr. Schubert M. Ogden (New York: Meridian Living Age Books, 1960), p. 214.

35. *Deeds and Rules*, pp. 176–177. Part of this paragraph is adapted from the review mentioned in note 32 above.

36. *Democracy in America*, II, 295; Marcus Cunliffe, "American Watersheds," *American Quarterly*, XIII (Winter, 1961), 480–494.

37. Cf. Gibson Winter, commenting on the social thought of George Herbert Mead: "I become a social self through the community, or the community creates man in its own image—the community as expression of the evolutionary process becomes the 'deity' or creator. Man is thus the reflection of the society through which he is created—the internal expression of the process of communication within the society. The 'me' is the social process in its internal expression as the social self. The 'me' is the product of the mores of the community, albeit shaped through internal relations rather than through an adaptive process of external relations." *Elements for a Social Ethic* (New York: The Macmillan Co., 1966), p. 24.

38. Alexander H. Krappe, *The Science of Folklore* (New York: W. W. Norton, 1960), pp. 39–40.

39. *Democracy in America*, II, 89.

40. Leo Marx, *The Machine in the Garden: Technology and the Pastoral Ideal in America* (New York: Oxford University Press, 1964), p. 226.

41. Palmer, *The Age of the Democratic Revolution* (Vol. I, *The Challenge*), pp. 214–215, 228.

42. *On Revolution*, pp. 195–196.

43. *Democracy in America*, II, 268; Martindale, *Community, Character and Civilization*, pp. 357–358.

44. *On Revolution*, pp. 195–196.

45. Richard M. Dorson, *American Folklore* (Chicago: University of Chicago Press, 1959), p. 39.

46. *Democracy in America*, II, 86–92.

47. Samuel Eliot Morison, *The Oxford History of the American People* (New York: Oxford University Press, 1965), p. 290.

48. R. W. B. Lewis, *The American Adam: Innocence, Tragedy and Tradition in the Nineteenth Century* (Chicago: University of Chicago Press, 1955), p. 117.

49. *The Americans: The Colonial Experience*, p. 314.

50. *American Folklore*, p. 5.

51. Michael Novak, "Christianity: Renewed or Slowly Abandoned?" *Daedalus*, Winter, 1967, p. 250.

52. Dorson, *American Folklore*, p. 89.

53. *Ibid.*, p. 253.

54. Marshall McLuhan, *Understanding Media: the Extensions of Man* (New York: New American Library, Signet Books, 2nd ed., 1966), p. 21.

55. See, for example, the first two issues of *Journal for Theology and the Church* (published simultaneously in 1965 as Harper & Row Torchbooks), a scholarly periodical launched, in part, "to cultivate an indigenous English language theological conversation no less than to foster an international dialogue" (2, xi). These issues consist almost entirely of translations into English of articles from *Zeitschrift für Theologie und Kirche*, a German theological journal upon which the American periodical was consciously modeled.

56. *The Americans: The National Experience*, pp. 338–339.

57. *The Autobiography of Malcolm X*, pp. 241–242.

58. *Ibid.*, p. 403.

59. Dan Wakefield quotes Ron Karenga, Black Power leader in the Watts district of Los Angeles: "We marry our own people, and we are developing our own holidays. 'Uhuru' is the anniversary of the revolt (the one in Watts), and on May nineteenth we celebrate Kuzaliwa, which is the birthday of Malcolm X. We had the children stay away from school this year on Kuzaliwa, and in one school here almost one hundred percent of the children didn't go that day, and the principal had to dismiss classes. Here at the Center we have classes in Swahili, and in Afro-American culture, trying to give the black people a powerful self-image. Of course, we are free from the self-deprecating concept that results from having to worship a white God." *Supernation at Peace and War* (Boston: Little, Brown & Co., 1968), p. 86.

60. Staughton Lynd, "A Radical Speaks in Defense of S.N.C.C.," *New York Times Magazine*, September 10, 1967, p. 155.

61. *The Enlightenment*, xi, 280.

62. "The words and acts of the founding fathers, especially the first few presidents," says Bellah, "shaped the form and tone of the civil religion as it has been maintained ever since. Though much is selectively derived from Christianity, this religion is clearly not itself Christianity. For one thing, neither Washington nor Adams nor Jefferson mentions Christ in his inaugural address; nor do any of the subsequent presidents, although not one of them fails to mention God. The God of the civil religion is not only rather 'unitarian,' he is also on the austere side, much more related to order, law, and right than to salvation and love. Even though he is somewhat deist in cast, he is by no means simply a watchmaker God. He is actively interested and involved in history, with a special concern for America." Robert N. Bellah, "Civil Religion in America," *Daedalus*, Winter, 1967, p. 7.

63. Harold Chestnut, *Systems Engineering Tools* (New York: John Wiley & Sons, 1965), p. 1.

64. *The National Observer*, March 13, 1967, p. 10.

65. For a full treatment of this subject, see Yves M.-J. Congar, O.P., *Tradition and Traditions: An Historical and a Theological Essay* (New York: The Macmillan Co., 1966).

66. In a sense the theologian serves tradition in somewhat the same way that the grammarian serves grammar so far as it is his task to identify current "normative" examples of tradition in practice. Cf. Theodore M. Bernstein, *The Careful Writer* (New York: Atheneum, 1965), viii-ix.

67. *The Oxford History of the American People*, p. 1073.

68. Justus George Lawler, "Theology and the Uses of History," in *New Theology No. 4*, ed. Martin E. Marty and Dean Peerman (New York: The Macmillan Co., 1967, pp. 147–161.

CHAPTER V. REVOLUTIONS

1. Richard Yates, *Revolutionary Road* (New York: Bantam Books, 1962), pp. 21–22, 237.

2. *Ibid.*, p. 44.

3. *Ibid.*, p. 97.

4. *The Wretched of the Earth*, p. 70.

5. See George Pettee, "Revolution—Typology and Process," in *Revolution*, ed. Carl J. Friedrich (New York: Atherton, 1967; *Nomos*, VIII, Yearbook of the American Society for Political and Legal Philosophy), pp. 15–18.

6. "The violence of the colonial regime and the counter-violence of the native balance each other and respond to each other in an extraordinary reciprocal homogeneity. This reign of violence will be the more terrible in proportion to the size of the implantation from the mother country." Fanon, *The Wretched of the Earth*, p. 88.

7. Ron Karenga, quoted in *Newsweek*, April 22, 1968, p. 26.

8. *The Autobiography of Malcolm X*, pp. 77, 366–367.

9. Jonathan Edwards, *Treatise Concerning Religious Affections* (London: Banner of Truth Trust, 1961; *Select Works*, III), p. 267.

10. The revivals had in view to "save the country," Perry Miller comments. They were not just a religious phenomenon, nor, as another school of thought long insisted, little more than useful devices that figured in the economic growth of the country. If the revival aimed

at transforming the whole community, it had effects in both realms—religion and economics—and in other domains of life as well. "Hence, when we ask to what the Revival really aspired, we are obliged to recognize that in the early nineteenth century it was accepted as a uniquely *American* ritual, and that its aims were molded accordingly." *The Life of the Mind in America* (New York: Harcourt, Brace & World, 1965), p. 13.

11. *Religion and the American Mind: From the Great Awakening to the Revolution* (Cambridge: Harvard University Press, 1966), pp. 1, 12.

12. Christopher Lasch, "The Trouble with Black Power," *New York Review of Books*, February 29, 1968, p. 10.

13. Stokely Carmichael and Charles V. Hamilton, *Black Power: the Politics of Liberation in America* (New York: Random House, Vintage Books, 1967), pp. 77, 141.

14. *The Wretched of the Earth*, p. 206.

15. *Ibid.*, pp. 233, 247.

16. Carmichael and Hamilton, *Black Power*, pp. 81–82.

17. *The Age of the Democratic Revolution* (Vol. I, *The Challenge*), p. 472.

18. Lynd, *Intellectual Origins of American Radicalism*, p. 162.

Nevertheless, some present-day revolutionaries accept the task of reflection. The same radical who writes that "white America . . . is working overtime qualifying for the right to be annihilated" adds: "One of the most difficult responsibilities of the revolutionary is to be self-critical. To be self-critical means to ask yourself if you are wrong and, if so, to admit the fact and correct it." Julius Lester, *Revolutionary Notes* (New York: Richard W. Baron, 1969), pp. 67, 200.

19. Cf. Conrad Cherry, *The Theology of Jonathan Edwards: A Reappraisal* (New York: Doubleday & Co., Anchor Books, 1966), p. 151. See also Peter Berger's suggestive reinterpretation of "signals of transcendence" in *A Rumor of Angels: Modern Society and the Rediscovery of the Supernatural* (New York: Doubleday & Co., 1969).

20. *Black Power*, p. 155.

21. Robert N. Bellah, "The Civil Religion in America," *Daedalus*, Winter, 1967, p. 16.

22. Jack Newfield, *A Prophetic Minority* (New York: New American Library, Signet Books, 1967), pp. 154–155.

CHAPTER VI. BENCHMARKS

1. "The social protest of the nineteen-sixties has to do with *inequality*, with the pervasive inequities remaining in American life. So far the demand for greater equality has come largely from the young and the black, but I wish to suggest that in the years to come, America will face a demand for more equality in various aspects of life from many other types of citizens—a demand so pervasive that it might well be described as the 'equality revolution.'—Herbert J. Gans, "The 'Equality' Revolution," *The New York Times Magazine*, November 3, 1968, p. 36.

2. Langdon Gilkey, "Secularism's Impact on Contemporary Theology," *Christianity and Crisis*, April 5, 1965, p. 66.

3. *Religion and the American Mind*, pp. 197, 225.

4. George L. Haskins, "The Sources of Law in Massachusetts," in *Puritanism in Seventeenth-Century Massachusetts*, ed. David D. Hall (New York: Holt, Rinehart & Winston, 1968), pp. 61–70. Reprinted from George L. Haskins, *Law and Authority in Early Massachusetts* (New York: The Macmillan Co., 1960).

5. John J. McDermott, *The American Angle of Vision* (Nyack, N.J.: Cross Currents, 1966), p. 454.

6. Martindale, *Community, Character & Civilization*, p. 340.

7. Josef Blank, "Does the New Testament Provide Principles for Modern Moral Theology?" in *Understanding the Signs of the Times*, ed. Franz Boeckle (New York: Paulist Press, 1967; *Concilium— Theology in the Age of Renewal*, 25), pp. 12, 22.

8. Quoted in Daniel J. Boorstin, *The Americans: the Colonial Experience*, p. 154.

9. Menie Grégoire, "A Final Word About Love," in *Sexuality and the Modern World: A Symposium* (special 1964 issue of *Cross Currents*), p. 269.

10. *Domestic Manners of the Americans*, p. 378.

11. *Ibid.*

12. Newfield, *A Prophetic Minority*, pp. 49–50.

13. Paul Ricoeur, "Wonder, Eroticism, and Enigma," in *Sexuality and the Modern World*, p. 137.

14. David Riesman, "Some Questions about the Study of American Character in the Twentieth Century," *Annals*, March, 1967, p. 36.

15. Roger Mehl, *La Rencontre d'Autrui: Remarques sur le Problème de la Communication* (Neuchâtel: Delachaux & Niestlé, 1955), pp. 5, 11–14.

16. Ernest Dunbar, "Campus Mood, Spring, '68," *Look*, April 2, 1968, p. 27.

17. Daniel Bell, "The Year 2000—The Trajectory of an Idea," *Daedalus*, Summer, 1967, pp. 644–645.

18. Richardson, *Toward an American Theology*, p. 25.

CHAPTER VII. HOPES

1. H. N. Brailsford, *The Levellers and the English Revolution*, ed. Christopher Hill (London: Cresset Press, 1961), p. 660.

2. From *The Law of Freedom*, quoted in Brailsford, *The Levellers*, p. 668.

3. *The Leveller Tracts 1647–53*, ed. William Haller and Godfrey Davies (New York: Columbia University Press, 1944), p. 455; Brailsford, *The Levellers*, pp. 75, 83; Joseph Frank, *The Levellers* (Cambridge: Harvard University Press, 1955), pp. 243–252. Let me emphasize that it is not my point here to suggest a genetic connection between these movements and the origins of the revolutionary ideology in America. I speak rather of the persistent ontological connection between biblical faith and political criticism as exemplified here by the Levellers. As for the specific origins of the American ideology, I am inclined to follow the arguments of Bernard Bailyn in his *Ideological Origins of the American Revolution*, whom I have cited frequently in this study.

4. Don M. Wolfe, *Leveller Manifestoes of the Puritan Revolution* (New York: Nelson, 1944), Introduction, p. 108.

5. Heimert, *Religion and the American Mind*, pp. 492, 541.

6. Lynd, *Intellectual Origins of American Radicalism*, vi, pp. 46, 120.

7. Miller, *Life of the Mind in America*, pp. 300–301.

8. *Newsweek*, June 13, 1966, p. 34.

9. David Baily Harned, *The Ambiguity of Religion* (Philadelphia: The Westminster Press, 1968), p. 111.

10. Peter Berger, "A Sociological View of the Secularization of Theology," *Journal for the Scientific Study of Religion*, Spring, 1967, p. 13.

11. Brailsford, *The Levellers*, p. 86.

12. James Baldwin, *The Fire Next Time* (New York: The Dial Press, 1963), p. 53.

13. *Ibid.*, p. 34.

14. *Ibid.*, pp. 64–65.

15. *Ibid.*, p. 97.

16. *Ibid.*, pp. 110, 35.

17. Cf. my *The South and Christian Ethics* (New York: Association Press, 1962), pp. 33–67.

18. *Nashville Tennessean*, June 2, 1963.

19. Frank, *The Levellers*, pp. 95–96.

20. Baldwin, *The Fire Next Time*, pp. 35–38.

21. Paul Abrecht, *The Churches and Rapid Social Change* (New York: Doubleday & Co., 1961), p. 14.

22. Preston Valien, "The Montgomery Bus Protest as a Social Movement," p. 116 in *Race Relations: Problems and Theory*, ed. Jitsuichi Matsuoka and Preston Valien (Chapel Hill: University of North Carolina Press, 1961), p. 116.

23. *Time*, June 21, 1963, p. 14.

24. Philip M. Hauser, "Demographic Factors in the Integration of the Negro," *Daedalus*, Fall, 1965, pp. 874–875.

25. Baldwin, *The Fire Next Time*, pp. 119, 61.

26. Cf. George Steiner in *The New Yorker*, November 16, 1968, p. 237, where the interrelation among hope, the future, and the West is briefly discussed. It strikes me that the recent "theology of hope" movement associated with Jurgen Moltmann is not likely to make any more headway as a live option for American theology than any other of the post-neo-orthodox German theologies, and for the same reason. Though one would think that hope is a theological nexus that might be appealing in America, Moltmann takes it up entirely as a theme to be developed within the context of eschatology understood as a constructive theological category. American theologians who think Moltmann's thought is worth a hearing in America might try to get a hearing for it by developing a point of contact out of the American materials, historical, theological, and even technological, that amount to a veritable tradition of hope, or at least to a tradition of hope turning into the human quality of hopefulness. Cf. Lewis, *The American Adam*, p. 175. Moltmann's book is *Theology of Hope: On the Ground and the Implications of a Christian Eschatology*, tr. James W. Leitch (New York: Harper & Row, 1967).

INDEX OF NAMES

INDEX OF SUBJECTS

70 71 72 73 10 9 8 7 6 5 4 3 2 1